LEADING THE SMALL POLICE DEPARTMENT

ABOUT THE AUTHOR

Gerald W. Garner is chief of police for the city of Corinth, Texas. A veteran of 53 years in law enforcement, he has served as chief executive officer for police departments serving 9,000 people, 26,000 citizens, and over 100,000 residents. Prior to retiring he served for 30 years with the nationally renowned Lakewood, Colorado Police Department where he worked in virtually every leadership rank and assignment available in a municipal law enforcement agency. Chief Garner holds a master's degree in Administration of Justice. He has instructed for the FBI National Academy at Quantico and the International Association of Chiefs of Police in addition to numerous police academies, university classes, and law enforcement leadership institutes. He has authored 13 books and over 200 magazine and journal articles, all on various aspects of law enforcement leadership and officer safety.

LEADING THE SMALL POLICE DEPARTMENT

By

GERALD W. GARNER

Chief of Police
Corinth Police Department
Corinth, Texas

CHARLES C THOMAS • PUBLISHER • LTD.
Springfield • Illinois • U.S.A.

Published and Distributed Throughout the World by

CHARLES C THOMAS • PUBLISHER, LTD.
2600 South First Street
Springfield, Illinois 62704

ISBN 978-0-398-09404-1 (paper)
ISBN 978-0-398-09405-8 (ebook)

Library of Congress Catalog Card Number: 2022057119 (print)
2022057120 (ebook)

With THOMAS BOOKS *careful attention is given to all details of manufacturing and design. It is the Publisher's desire to present books that are satisfactory as to their physical qualities and artistic possibilities and appropriate for their particular use.* THOMAS BOOKS *will be true to those laws of quality that assure a good name and good will.*

Printed in the United States of America
MX-S-2

Library of Congress Cataloging-in-Publication Data

Names: Garner, Gerald W., author.
Title: Leading the small police department / by Gerald W. Garner, Chief of Police, Corinth Police Department, Corinth, Texas.
Description: Springfield, Illinois : Charles C Thomas, Publisher, Ltd. [2023] | Includes index.
Identifiers: LCCN 2022057119 (print) | LCCN 2022057120 (ebook) | ISBN 9780398094041 (paperback) | ISBN 9780398094058 (ebook)
Subjects: LCSH: Police administration. | Police--Supervision of.
Classification: LCC HV7935 .G37 2023 (print) I LCC HV7935 (ebook) | DDC 363.2068--dc23/eng/20221206
LC record available at https://lccn.loc.gov/2022057119
LC ebook record available at https://lccn.loc.gov/2022057120

To: Kathy, Sandi, and Samantha

PREFACE

Almost ninety percent of the police departments in the United States employ 25 officers or fewer. Many are staffed by fewer than 10 peacekeepers. The leaders of these small departments face some of the same challenges as do the bosses of the larger departments, but they encounter many additional problems, as well, and they labor in a somewhat different environment.

A lot has been written to assist the CEO of the larger department. Much less effort has been devoted to aiding the smaller agency chief in navigating the operational, personnel, and political landscape to be found in the smaller agency, to name but some of the challenges. This book is intended to fill that knowledge gap.

The author is a 53-year veteran of law enforcement who has served as a successful police chief in cities of 9,000, 26,000, and over 100,000 citizens. The book is a compilation of real-world experience and lessons learned, bolstered by the observations of many other police chiefs. Its goal is to assist the small agency chief in building and maintaining an exceptional police department. It is additionally designed to help the leader enjoy a successful and rewarding career for as long as he or she chooses to serve as police chief.

This is not a book about the theory of leadership or management. Rather, it is a handbook focused upon providing practical, time-proven advice for handling the small department chief's daily fare of challenges and opportunities. It will prove equally useful to the leader of a larger police department or the chief wannabe, but the focus will remain on the small agency boss.

Let the journey begin.

INTRODUCTION

There can be little doubt that today's American police chief has a tough job. That job can become even tougher if the chief is responsible for leading a small police agency.

This book will provide the small department chief with practical advice for mastering the special challenges of his or her difficult job. It will be very helpful to a chief serving in any size law enforcement agency, but its greatest focus will be on the department with fewer than 25 officers. The chief leading 10 officers or fewer may find it even more useful.

The volume's 18 chapters address a number of critical situations and conditions facing the small department leader. If you are coming to the agency from the outside, Chapter 1 provides a comprehensive checklist of things to examine and, if necessary, handle early on. If you are a long-term insider with the department, the chapter will help you in determining if there are still areas needing to be freshly examined by the new leader. Chapter 2 delves into some special challenges facing the small department leader and offers advice on how to address them successfully. Chapter 3 examines your vital role as a leader and offers you assistance in rising to the challenge. Meanwhile, Chapter 4 furnishes you guidance for the always critical decision-making process.

There is no more important task for you as a chief than serving as an exceptional role model for your employees and your community. Chapter 5 will help you fill that role well. Chapter 6 provides guidance for establishing an effective working relationship with your command staff and the rest of your employees, while Chapter 7 offers sound advice for working well with one of the most important people in your work life: your boss.

As chief you will occupy a major leadership role in your community, and Chapter 8 will help you to handle it well. Discipline of your employees also will be a responsibility of the chief, and Chapter 9 furnishes the guidelines for applying it both fairly and effectively. Chapter 10 recognizes that you have a host of responsibilities involving the different elements of your department and presents some proven guidelines for carrying them out effectively. Then, Chapter 11 explores each of your extremely vital obligations in taking care of your most precious asset: your people.

The news media can have a lot to do with your success (or lack of same) as a law enforcement CEO, and Chapter 12 gives time-proven advice for establishing a mutually beneficial relationship with the minions of the press. Chapter 13 will help guide you through troubled waters when the news is bad. It also will help you take care of your own people when bad things happen. Next, Chapter 14 shares skills for communicating within your own organization and beyond, whether what you have to say pertains to "routine" matters or something quite beyond the ordinary. Then, Chapter 15 presents some practical guidelines for evaluating the job performance of your employees and providing them with some direction for their future endeavors. The critical incidents you must handle well as a leader are discussed in Chapter 16, with solid advice provided for effectively handling each.

The book's final two chapters will help you deal with the complex political challenges that accompany your role. The very last chapter features some life- and career-saving advice for the small department leader intent on surviving the job and eventually leaving it while still in good health. That leader, of course, should be you.

Not merely surviving but prospering in your role as a small department chief is absolutely within your abilities as an intelligent and courageous leader. Here is how it is done.

CONTENTS

LEADING THE SMALL POLICE DEPARTMENT

Chapter 1

THE NEW CHIEF

Chief of Police. There is no other job in the world exactly like it. With the title comes joys, successes, failures, and disappointments. Fortunately for those holding or aspiring to hold the position, the good days far outnumber the bad.

Regardless of the size of their department or the location where they serve, police chiefs face many of the same challenges. Recruitment, selection, retention, and many other "people issues" make up the agenda for the average police leader's day. But when the top cop is responsible for leading a smaller law enforcement agency, say, one employing 25 officers or fewer, new challenges can and do arise. Some of those also faced by the larger department leader can be magnified for the small agency head.

Challenges as well as opportunities exist beyond the reach of the small department chief. If you happen to be a mid- or upper-management leader working beneath the chief executive at one of these small agencies, you will share the CEO's challenges. You will be expected to help address them. That is not a bad thing, as it will help you prepare to take on the role of head of the agency or another one at some point in the future. Even if you are not Number One today, what is contained in these pages will aid in equipping you with the knowledge, skills, and abilities you will need to succeed as a police chief. If being the chief one day is definitely not in your plans, the information to be gleaned here will help make you a better leader in your current or another position of authority. It will help you excel.

For present purposes, assume that you *are* preparing to be chief or have just been appointed to the position. Mentally place yourself in the role as if it were happening tomorrow, if it has not happened already.

What follows will aid you in succeeding as a leader of any rank at a small department.

DO YOUR HOMEWORK

Whether you are an outsider or someone who has moved up through the ranks in the organization, you will need to know as much as possible in advance about the agency you now lead. A lot can be learned from public sources such as newspaper stories, editorials, and letters to the editor. Social media also can tell you a great deal. Here you can learn what your citizen-customers have had to say about your people–pro and con–on your own agency's social media platforms. Be sure to mine all of these sources for what they can tell you.

Now that you have been anointed as the new chief you will have access to many human sources of information that will help you discover what you are getting into. The list of sources can be practically endless and range from the janitor to the mayor, but the known, local "movers and shakers" are among those you need to sit down with, one on one, to get their views on how the department is doing and what they would like to see more or less of. Your city or town manager as well as your own staff should be able to tell you who these people are. Seek them out. Most of them will be honored to have a sit down with the chief. For you, this is a time to listen, not make promises or pronouncements. If your boss has no objections, connecting with each member of your city council or town board should be especially informative to you. These officials are important to you as, along with your town manager, they will control your department's budget. Listen for any issues they bring up that may be hot buttons for them. Be especially conscious of any issues that are repeatedly mentioned. These topics certainly require your attention and, possibly, your action once you learn more.

Do not overlook your own employees while doing your homework to determine what is going on in the department and the community. They probably can provide you with opinions and insight that you cannot get anywhere else. Listen carefully but do not be tempted to respond instantly to concerns and complaints. A bit more information may reveal some of them to be unfounded. Always listen more than you talk during these interactions. You will learn a lot more that way.

It is important to get the opinions of your top leadership staff members about how things are going and where they see the need for change. You may or may not agree with their observations. Again, avoid making any major pronouncements until you know more. You can push your information-gathering even farther if you ask your leadership staff to put their observations in writing. Doing so may make them think a little more deeply about what they have to say. It also will give you an early opportunity to evaluate their written communication skills.

Other city or town employees, such as your fellow department heads, also should be good sources for information. Try to sit down individually with them over coffee or a meal. If you do not already know them well, this is a good time to meet with other area law enforcement agency officials, such as the sheriff and district attorney. You are seeking their read on your agency and its reputation. Keep in mind that they will be sizing you up as you are doing the same with them. Be sure that your connections with these people are as strong as possible. You are likely to need them down the road.

Finally, take advantage of the police department's own documents for what they have to teach you, assuming you have not done this while you were still in the chief application process. These information sources can include General Orders, Policies and Procedures, and other directives. You will be learning much more about the department while scanning for areas that may need shored up. Make notes if you need to aid your memory.

Doing your homework and taking in the big picture now can save you time, effort, and unnecessary headaches in the future. It will help you in making informed, solid decisions as you commence to mold your new organization. That will mean making it better.

DETERMINE WHY YOU WERE CHOSEN

It is vital to learn as early as possible in your tenure *why* you were selected as the new chief instead of someone else. If you were already part of the organization and have been paying attention, you already may have some idea as to why. If not, reviewing any recent news stories about the organization or its leader may prove highly informative. Past press should tell you if there have been concerns about corruption, malfeasance, excessive use of force, or unlawful or unethical behavior by any member of the department, most especially the chief. Your meetings with your rank and file as well as your top staffers, as soon as you can arrange them, should assist you in determining if you are the new chief because someone else fouled up badly. If that turns out to be the case, you will need to know exactly what went awry. That's because you will be responsible for repairing the damage and rebuilding trust within the department and community. Naturally, your new boss also can fill you in on what went wrong and what you are expected to do about it.

It's your new boss, of course, who will be your best source of figuring out why you are the new chief. He or she may tell you at your very first post-hiring meeting why you are the new leader. It's great if you are now in the chief's chair because the old boss decided to retire or otherwise move on under clear and sunny skies. But often that is not the case. If your boss does not offer to tell you why you were chosen, *ask*. Knowing that will help you figure out what you are expected to do. It may help you determine what needs fixed and what seems to be working just fine. Use your good judgment in sitting down with the last chief, assuming he or she is willing and available. You can learn a great deal but remain mindful that what you hear will be colored by the former top leader's opinions. At the same time, you may learn of some mine fields to avoid. Per usual, listen more than you talk.

If all (or at least most) of what is going on in the department is peachy, your boss, your community, and your people may be looking for a *status quo* chief, or one who will not overturn the apple cart too much by changing things that really don't need changed. On the other hand, if general unhappiness or dysfunction reigns within either the community or the department, you will be expected to be a *change agent,* or one who stirs things up for improvement's sake. On occasion, a new chief will find himself somewhere in between the two roles. His early information-gathering and listening sessions should help him determine what truly needs repaired and what can be left alone, at least for now.

Ask plenty of questions when you are the new chief, especially of your boss. Watch, listen, and investigate thoroughly before you expend a lot of time and energy addressing things that really did not need addressed. Save your efforts for the truly important stuff that demands your attention. More about that later....

ASSESS THE ORGANIZATION

In the unlikely event that you did not already know, there is not a flawless organization on the face of the earth. Your new organization, no matter how good it may be, is not perfect, either. There are virtually always things that could be done better. That may be why you were selected for the position you now hold. By now you should have talked with quite a few people both inside and outside the police organization. That has probably given you at least an early picture of your agency's perceived strengths and challenges. You can learn even more by applying your experience and eye for what works to what you have observed to date. Consider keeping a checklist of tasks you need to accomplish. In addition to providing you with direction it also will give you a needed sense of accomplishment as you are able to check items off the list.

Hopefully you have discovered that you have inherited a pretty good organization, perhaps even an excellent one. There will be strong points already in place for you to build upon. But there may be things that need your attention, too. The issues could include just about anything. Perhaps officer safety practices are dangerously lacking. Maybe policies, procedures, and general orders have not been updated in a very long time or vehicles and other equipment may be in bad shape due to a lack of funds for maintenance and replacement. Those are just the "things." If your people have been neglected and have become jaundiced through lack of supervision and discipline, you and your agency could be headed for serious difficulties unless you act promptly and decisively.

None of this means that Armageddon is knocking at your door. Not every issue you discover will require instant, Herculean effort on your part. Make notes. Keep lists. Set timelines and deadlines for yourself. Check tasks off as you accomplish them. Keep asking yet more questions as you thoughtfully prioritize the things that need to get done. Celebrate the early victories but remain in motion, ready to take on the next challenge.

Your early days as the new chief will be busy ones as you assess your new department and initiate the actions needed to meet your new priorities. The good news is that you will not have to do it alone. That's where your good people come in.

MEET YOUR PEOPLE

If you have been part of the organization for a while, you likely already have at least a partial picture of who's who and the strengths, weaknesses, and peculiarities of the people there. The smaller the agency, the more likely it is you know something about most or all of the players.

If you are coming in from outside you will have a bit more work to do, but your task is nonetheless quite do-able. Getting to know your people and their abilities should start with your top staff. You probably already have some opinions about them from tidbits you have picked up from talking with others around the community. Take that information in for consideration, but realize it may be heavily colored based upon the speaker's personal experiences with a particular staff member.

Your best information, of course, will come from your one-on-one conversations with your top staffers and the discourse that ensues at your command staff meetings. Ask questions about your staffers' personal lives and let them know that you are interested in them beyond their workday roles. Get their views on what they would do to make the department better. Take care not to make any major pronouncements just now, as you may not have all of the relevant facts yet. Let your staff know early on where you are planning to take the department. You will need their help to get there. Share your vision with them. Let them know that you will count on (and expect) their assistance in realizing that vision. Do not forget to acknowledge their past good work (surely there has been some!) that has brought the agency to where it is today. Share with your staff your goal of building atop the good work that has already been done in order to make the department that belongs to all of you even better. Also let your people know that you are not a "drive by" chief already thinking about your next job. Let them know you plan to be around quite a while to see your goals attained.

You expect your command staff to be totally honest and open with you, so do the same for them. They cannot read your mind. If you already have detected something in a top staffer's work or behavior that you want changed, let that individual know in a private conversation. One new chief found that his Patrol commander virtually never wore his uniform. The troops noticed, and so did the chief. A quiet word about his expectation for change was all the chief needed to do to address a behavior that the commander apparently never realized might be problematical. Problem solved.

It is just as important that you get to know your other employees as quickly as possible. They are curious as to who and what you are, and how the change in chiefs is likely to affect them. This will be especially true if you are an outsider essentially unknown to them. (Know, however, that they likely have researched you well in advance of your arrival.) It is important that you get to know your new team well. The smaller the department, the easier it should be to accomplish this vital task.

You can begin your mutual get-to-know-you effort with one or two all-employee meetings. Do not overlook your civilian employees. It is vital that you do not put off meeting them until later, as they might interpret this as a sign that they are not as important to you as your sworn employees. As you probably know by now, a police agency's non-sworn people have a big role to play in determining whether the agency functions smoothly–or not. Listen to what they have to say.

Following your all-hands meetings, make it clear that you are anxious to meet privately with every employee who is willing to talk with you. These are great opportunities for your people to see that you do not have horns or a tail and are actually a pretty good person. Hopefully, you will be able to discern the same about them. Take in everything your people have to say without becoming obviously judgmental. This is the time to gather information, not make judgments and pontificate. You also must avoid criticizing the department that now belongs to all of you. Listen much more than you talk.

Even if you know or suspect that the department has some significant problems that will need to be addressed, this is not the moment to dwell on them. Your new subordinates need to hear you say that this is a good place with good people and you are glad to be part of it all. Give them an idea of what is important to you. Making this a better place to live and work. Helping people. Putting righteous crooks in jail. And enjoying work every day or night. It is also alright to acknowledge that there are things that you will all have to work on to make the department an even better place to be. Just don't tear the previous administration down in the process. You may be speaking with some of the prior chief's good friends.

Never introduce yourself to your people by stating or inferring that the organization they are a part of is a hot mess that you have been hired to clean up, even if that is the case. This is a cardinal rule. Instead, commend your people for who they are and what they do. Let them know that you are still a cop and you like cops a lot. Let them know that you are glad to now be a part of their family.

MAKE THE IMPORTANT CONTACTS

While you were doing your pre-hiring homework you probably learned who some of the movers and shakers of the community happen to be. You likely can identify other community leaders, both formal and informal, by asking your boss and your fellow city or town government department heads to point out these individuals. Go out of your way to meet these people, whether it is at a community function or over coffee or a meal that you have arranged. Very few will turn down an invitation to meet with the new top cop.

Your purpose here is to let these leaders see that you are a normal, likeable human being (you are, aren't you?) This really is not the time to ask for things or grant favors. You simply want to meet these folks and gauge them for character, just as they are measuring you. These informal conversations also may give you another opportunity to learn early on of any hot buttons or special concerns these people may have. It is perfectly alright to query these individuals concerning their observations and opinions on the police department that you have just taken responsibility for. How you eventually respond to their legitimate concerns can go a long way towards determining their opinion of you and what you are doing. Beware of making any promises other than revealing that you are gathering information and ultimately will act appropriately on what you have learned.

Your contact with these community influencers should not be a "one and done" thing that you can cross off your "to do" list established at the start of your new job. Assuming that you have determined that a particular local leader is an honest and ethical one, seek to nurture and continue that relationship throughout your tenure. It would not be unusual if some of these early contacts turn into long-lasting friendships.

CONNECT WITH YOUR BOSS

No one will have as much influence on whether or not you succeed and prosper as the new chief as will your boss. It is critical that you spend time with your supervisor in the early days of your new job. With your boss's schedule and your own it may feel hard to do. Figure a way to make the time, whether it's over coffee or in the boss's office. Early, crystal-clear communication between the two of you is that critical. Take every opportunity to visit with him or her.

In your boss interactions try to do more listening than talking. Listen for your new supervisor's opinions and comments on the community, the city or town organization, and your department and the people in it. Remain alert for hints of your boss's ideas about what the cops and their leader (that's you!) should and should not be doing. Ask clarifying questions, if needed.

By listening carefully you may be able to identify what the boss's big issues happen to be. One new chief found out that his new boss abhorred cursing and would not tolerate it among his department heads. Thus alerted, the chief was able to watch his own language and make it clear to his people that he expected the same of them. Your supervisor almost certainly has some eccentricities or at least things he or she feels very strongly about. Knowing what they are can make your boss relations a lot smoother.

By spending some time with your boss you can learn just how much he or she knows about policing. More than a few city and town managers will admit that they don't know a whole lot about your profession. They are counting on you to handle law enforcement issues and make their police-related problems go away so that they can spend their time and energy on other things.

If you find out via your conversations with your supervisor that he or she holds views on the role of the police and the police chief that are very different from your own, you have some work ahead of you. Keep an open mind. The boss may even be correct in some of his or her views. You might need to adjust your thinking a bit. If not, you will need to gently educate your boss about some things he or she may not have had time to assimilate. Frequent contact with your supervisor should make him or her more comfortable with you, assuming you do not come across as a nag or an arrogant, self-appointed "expert." This kind of gentle interaction should help you in your long-term relationship with your supervisor. It also will help you know what he or she is thinking, perhaps before those thoughts or plans are voiced.

Understanding where the person you work for is coming from at any given time is important to you. So is having an open, mutually supportive relationship with your supervisor. More about that later....

CHECK OUT THE CRITICAL AREAS

There is no doubt that you are going to be very busy in your first days as the new chief. You are going to be pulled in a lot of different directions. Nonetheless, for the sake of yourself and the organization you now lead there are potential "problem pits" that demand your immediate attention. These areas need to be examined by the new boss to ensure that he or she is not inheriting a ticking time bomb from the previous administration. If you detect a problem, it does not necessarily mean that your predecessor was guilty of malpractice of some sort. Sometimes in the crush of day-to-day business some seemingly obvious things get missed. Or some practice has been in use for so long that no one has noticed its potential to cause big trouble. Promise yourself right now that you will never be guilty of looking but not seeing. Or becoming apathetic as your tenure grows. Either practice could bring your leadership career to a screeching halt.

Many agencies have really handsome binders containing well-written, detailed policies, procedures, rules, and general orders. If you have not examined them earlier, you probably are right now. But here is the catch: are these comprehensive, impressive-sounding directives and guidelines actually being followed in the daily operations of the department? By asking questions and observing the actions of your officers you should be able to answer that query. More than a few new chiefs have discovered to their dismay that their agency has a great-looking set of official guidelines that are largely unknown or ignored by the front-line personnel of the department. If that happens to be the case where you are, trouble has either already occurred or is just around the corner. You will need to act promptly before bad things happen. Your employees deserve to know what they are expected to do and how they are expected to do it.

But just what are these "high risk" areas? They can vary somewhat from place to place, agency to agency. Some of the most commonly encountered ones demanding your immediate attention include the following:

Use of lethal and less-lethal force. Do the stated directives satisfy your state's legal mandates? How about the rules of an accreditation or Best Practices body that your department may belong to? More important still, do your people actually comprehend and follow these guidelines? This area requires emergency repairs if you find guidelines or actual practices lacking.

Property and evidence handling. Are the department's policies, procedures, and actual practices all in synch here? Has a recent inventory of what is in your property room or locker versus what is *supposed* to be there been done, preferably by an outside agency? If not, self-preservation requires that you get one done promptly. Once again, you do not want to be penalized through intentional or unintentional malpractice under the previous chief's administration. The areas most deserving of careful audit include money, drugs, weapons, and other high-dollar items, such as jewelry and electronics. Promptly let your boss know if discrepancies are discovered. Also let the boss know what you plan to do about it.

Vehicle pursuits. Today's increasingly litigation-minded world mandates that when and what your officers are permitted to pursue must be tightly restricted by guidelines that are uniformly enforced by engaged first-line supervisors. Officer safety and litigation survival demand that the rules intended to protect both cops and innocent citizens are obeyed. You as agency head will need to see careful documentation of why and how anytime a pursuit takes place. Careful officer and supervisor training in your agency's pursuit policy is also a must.

Off-duty employment. Where are your off-duty cops allowed to work in an enforcement capacity? You need to keep close tabs on this. For example, officers should not, for a number of very good reasons, be permitted to work as bouncers or security guards in bars. How many hours of off-duty work should an officer take on during a given period and still be sufficiently rested and alert to do his primary job of police officer? If your department does not pay well, it is understandable that officers may need the money brought in by extra work. But limits must be enforced. You will need to get a handle on off-duty work practices if, over time, they have crept out of the department's control. Don't forget that you are ultimately accountable for what they do with that badge each of your officers has been given.

Cash-handling. Ideally, your officers should not be handling citizens' money at all unless it is being booked in as found property or evidence. They certainly should not be handling it in connection with tickets and fines. Your civilian support personnel also should handle cash as little as possible. If animal tags, alarm permits, solicitor licenses, and the like require some currency handling, you should have a careful accounting system in place to track the money. More than one chief has "retired without cake" because a department flower fund, donation account, or similar slush fund came up short. Certainly you want your people to know that you trust them, but a periodic fund accounting process handled by, say, the city's or town's finance department can help protect everyone, the chief included.

Depending upon where you work, there can be other potential problem spots you will need to investigate. Your careful homework, personal observations, and conversations with others, especially your own employees, can help you identify them. Stay alert and do not hesitate to inquire for fear of rocking the boat or hurting someone's feelings. After all, it is *you* who will face the consequences for problems that you could have discovered and dealt with but did not.

DEAL QUICKLY WITH SERIOUS ISSUES

If you have taken the helm at a law enforcement agency lacking anything at all that needs to be dealt with right away, consider yourself extremely fortunate. Even if you are coming in behind a highly competent leader, there likely will be *something* that your good sense tells you needs handled right away. If you are arriving following a chief who departed under less than favorable circumstances, you may discover even more that needs fixed immediately. The same could hold true if you are assuming command at a department that has been without an actual chief of police for quite a while. In other words, your common sense and need for self-preservation should tell you that there may be areas requiring immediate corrective action. Start scanning for them right away.

Serious problems requiring prompt attention can come in a wide variety of forms and degrees of severity. They can involve unethical or even unlawful acts by police employees, such as sexual harassment or racial profiling. These misdeeds may be intentional or the result of a lack of training or supervision. Whatever the case, it is now on *you* to see that problems are solved and the ship set on an even keel. And you must do it *now* rather than sometime later. Whether intended or not, any hesitation on your part to address serious issues may be viewed as your being complicit in the wrongdoing. That is not the jacket you want to wear as the new CEO.

Again: Major problems, such as unlawful or unsafe practices, demand your immediate attention. Sometimes a change in policies, procedures, or rules that is promptly disseminated to all hands can help address the issue successfully. In other cases, an executive order or directive issued by the chief can be utilized to fix a problem that cannot wait for a Department Manual revision. Whatever the case, you will then be responsible for assuring that the mandated change actually occurs, and occurs in the manner you intended. This will require the support of your command staff and first-line supervisors. If either of these sources of command and control fail to carry out your directions immediately and as intended, you will have another problem that you must address immediately.

In addition to actual criminal acts, new chiefs have encountered an almost endless list of bad practices. One rookie chief of a small department discovered that his new agency's unarmed, civilian community service officers were routinely transporting prisoners to a jail a half-hour distant. Another found that the acting chief had given the departing chief a brand new, grant-purchased department shotgun as a going away gift. (The new chief had to go retrieve it.) Another new boss found that his officers sometimes put juvenile offenders in the same cell with adult prisoners. Yet another found that the town denied overtime pay to officers despite the existence of labor laws prohibiting such practices. In each case, and in countless others, a new chief had to act quickly and decisively to right a real wrong. You must do the same as the new boss. In many instances, you are both ethically and legally required to do so. In every case, it is the *right* thing to do.

SEEK SOME EARLY VICTORIES

You do not have to win the Super Bowl the first year of your employment in order to be considered a successful coach. By applying "little" changes that are legitimately desired by your cops and/or your community you can gather the support needed to take on some bigger issues later on. The changes do not have to be expensive or disruptive to the department or the community.

One new chief granted his officers' requests to wear baseball caps with the department's logo affixed when out on the street. While his command staff was not excited about this "concession" to the troops, the chief reasoned that the command staff members were not out standing on the hot pavement at the peak of summer. Another new boss granted his sergeants' request to have a "supervisor" decal placed on the side of their marked units. For very little cost the chief acknowledged and pleased his first-line supervisors. Yet another new chief did away with an archaic rule that required an officer to don his or her uniform cap when outside the car on a traffic stop. For zero cost the new guy won some affection from his officers.

Listen carefully to your employees. You will learn a lot and in the process identify some early "wins" that could benefit both you and your people. But realize that you do not have to fix everything that anyone complains about. Some things do not need fixed because they are not broken. If you are both observant and thoughtful you should be able to come up with some early victories without being lured into doing things that you will regret later.

SUMMARY

After you pin on your badge as the new chief, continue the research into your new department and community that aided you while you were still a candidate for the position. Meet your top staff as well as your officers and civilian employees and learn what is on their minds. Meanwhile, you will start gaining some knowledge of your employees' character, skills, and abilities. Spend some time with your new boss and learn what he or she is all about. Determine if you were hired to be a change agent, a status quo chief, or a little of both. Meet the leading lights of the community and learn the "who's who" of your locale. Examine the potential problem spots in your organization and determine if any emergency repairs are necessary. If so, make them promptly. Seek some early wins if you identify things that can be quickly "fixed" for the betterment of the organization and its members. All of this is simply what a smart, new chief does. That chief is you.

Chapter 2

SPECIAL CHALLENGES FOR THE SMALL DEPARTMENT CHIEF

- Attracting and retaining outstanding employees.
- Finding adequate revenue to operate the department.
- Obtaining quality training for employees.
- Navigating local politics.
- Avoiding "suitcase" cops.
- Dealing effectively with inaccurate public perceptions of policing.

All American police chiefs deal with these issues, and many more. For the small department chief, however, the challenges can be more acutely felt. They can be more difficult to overcome. They can be more detrimental to effective and efficient law enforcement operations. They can result in more sleep-troubled nights for the small department chief who must deal with them.

Every police chief, no matter how large or how small his or her agency, must respond to demands emanating from any number of sources. There are the community's needs to be addressed. There are the incessant demands of the news media in addition to those of local government officials. The often-voiced demands of special interest groups and underrepresented minority communities also must be answered. The sincerely felt concerns of the police employees and their unions or associations also require the chief's attention. Once more, these very real pressures may be felt more intensely by the small agency chief for the simple reason that in a small jurisdiction he or she is often closer to all the voices of concern. And he or she must be an excellent listener.

ATTRACTING AND RETAINING EXCEPTIONAL EMPLOYEES

You have heard it your whole professional life: the employees determine the success or failure of any organization. Or: the people make the difference. Or: the employees are your most precious asset. All of these things are true, even if omitted is one equally important element upon which the ultimate fate of the organization will depend: the leader. That's you. More about that later.

As a law enforcement leader, you are in competition with every other law enforcement leader in your region or state. Unless he is foolish, every other law enforcement CEO is seeking the same applicants you are: the cream of the crop, not those who have been passed over (or passed along) by other police agencies.

That is the correct position to take, even in an era when quality police applicants are becoming harder and harder to find. You cannot afford having your small department get a reputation for being the soft landing place for every failed cop who has been fired or been the recipient of "outplacement counselling." Some of these folks are called "suitcase cops," because they hop between departments so frequently that they don't have the time to unpack their clothes. The potential safety and liability risks associated with accepting questionable goods are simply too great. You and your employer cannot afford it.

It is said that a leopard cannot change his spots. But occasionally it may happen, at least where police employees are concerned. Maybe that has occurred in this individual's case. The truth remains, however, that what any individual has done in the past is a pretty reliable indicator of what he or she will do in the future. At the same time, try not to confuse a cop with clear, problematical behavior in his or her past with the often-young officer who is idealistically searching for the perfect department and has changed employment, perhaps more than once, in a quest to find it. (You may even have been such an officer early in your career.) As this officer matures, he or she likely will find that virtually every police agency has issues of some kind, and of varying degrees of severity. If upon interview you can convince this young man or woman that the absolutely perfect employer does not exist and the one he has now applied with is a very good one, you may find that he or she is worth a shot. It's your call.

Believe it or not, a few leaders of employee-strapped small agencies only do very cursory checks of applicants' backgrounds and work history, for the reason that they do not *want* to find something that would preclude their giving the individual a badge and gun. Following such a flawed practice is irresponsible, unethical, and possibly career-ending for the chief foolish enough to pursue it. Perhaps good fortune will shine and the suitcase cop will conclude a whole career without a serious, new misstep. But disaster could happen the day after he or she is hired. Do you really want to take that chance? Once again, it's your call.

On occasion you nonetheless may find an exception to this "take no chances" hiring rule. While it is quite common for a terminated or "forced resignation" officer to claim he lost his job for "political reasons," most often there was a legitimate reason for his departure. If, after a very careful inquiry on your part, you find that the officer did, in fact, receive a raw deal at his old department, he may be worth bringing aboard. Do your backgrounding work in depth. Then, if what you have learned tells you this is really an individual worth another chance, go for it. All the while, remain mindful of the rule in baseball: a tie goes to the runner. In this case you, the potential employer, are the runner. If doubt remains, take a pass on this one.

You already know that your ability to draw good applicants to your department is negatively impacted by the fact that your pay does not compare favorably with many of the larger police agencies in your neighborhood. That is simply a fact of life. Obviously, you are going to press your boss to upgrade the salaries for your police personnel, at least to the limit that he or she will tolerate your nagging. But reality dictates that your agency probably never will be able to pay what the Big Boys do. For that reason, you will need to look at other factors in your effort to attract the best and the brightest.

Most likely the police work in your jurisdiction will be less intense than would be found in a major city. This can be a big recruiting benefit to point out to experienced officers who may be looking to slow down a bit as their career (and age) progresses. The key for you, of course, is to check these people out thoroughly in your effort to ensure that you are not hiring someone who wants to "retire on duty." Another group you may want to seek out are the newly-minted cops who have just graduated from a basic training academy and are looking to gain some experience before perhaps moving on to a larger, better paying agency. If you aggressively seek to recruit these police officer candidates you will have to accept the reality that your agency will almost always be in the training mode with well-intentioned youngsters who are going to make some rookie mistakes. You also should realize that you have a good chance of losing them in a couple of years or so after they have a little experience under their belt. You and your employer will have to decide if it is worth the investment to keep many of them only for a while. Your hope, of course, is that some of these officers will like their first police "home" enough to stay there. It does happen, perhaps more often than you would think.

Today the social media is the most fertile recruiting ground for attracting new cops. Be certain that your social media sites are up to date, active, and creative. You probably have someone on staff who is quite comfortable performing in this arena. He or she should be your social media recruiter. Still, for a number of good reasons you will want to remain alert to what is being posted there. In today's world, your agency's recruiting posts should emphasize that you are seeking officers who truly want to help people and make the world a better place. The era of seeking males (only) who want to drive fast, run and gun, and blow things up has passed. As you already know, you are fishing in a very different applicant pool today. That is not necessarily a bad thing. You must adapt to the new reality.

Your officers are your best recruiters. Arm them with adequate information about the benefits of working where they are and task them with finding good people they would want to work with and rely on to watch their back. They should have as big a stake as you do in hiring good officers. They also will have more opportunities at recruiting than you do as they interact with cops from other places at court, training, and on the street. Be sure what they have to say about your agency is positive: We have great equipment. We get to work with skilled, likeable fellow law enforcers. We are treated fairly by our bosses. The last one is vital. As you know by now, money is almost never the sole reason that cops engage in department-hopping. They routinely cite "the administration" and what they see as unfair treatment as either the primary or contributing reason for leaving. Often their perception of their department's leadership is incorrect. Nonetheless, you must ensure that your people never have just cause to accuse you or your subordinate supervisors of creating anything that even faintly resembles a hostile or even unpleasant work environment. That is more than a means for keeping good people on board. It is also the right thing to do.

When you get right down to it, fair and legitimate practices by leadership are among the most reliable means of attracting and retaining exceptional police employees. Treat your people justly. Let them know that they are valued and appreciated. Give them ample cause to want to stay with you. Some of them will.

SHORTAGE OF RESOURCES

One veteran law enforcement leader relates his eye-opening experience of moving from a large police agency to a small one as its new chief. "I was accustomed to being the guy who loaned resources to the smaller agencies in the area. I had SWAT, K-9, a bomb squad, and a gang unit. Now, I am the little guy who needs to go hat in hand asking for help. The chiefs in my neighborhood have been super helpful, but my ego and I are still having to get used to it."

The good news is that law enforcement leaders are almost universally supportive of one another when the need arises. If you have spent your earlier career at a larger department, you will need to swallow your ego just a little and *ask* when you need assistance. Rare would be the police leader who would not supply it if he or she possibly could.

There is a way to make it a lot more likely that the ready help is there when you need it. Making contact with the leaders of the surrounding law enforcement agencies is mandatory when you are the new chief. Invitations to coffee or lunch will work just fine. Just like your employees, the other law enforcement leaders in the area need to see you up close in order to determine that you are a pretty good person. The idea is to get them to *want* to help you. In turn, you will assist them in any way you can. The last thing you want to have happen is to be required to make a cold call for help after the stuff has already hit the fan.

Another key resource you may find yourself short of is money. Smaller department, smaller budget. No matter how supportive your boss and your elected officials may be, and hopefully they are *very* supportive as a result of your earnest efforts, they cannot give you funds that they do not have. Like every one of your cops, they have a budget to "live" on, too. There are other governmental functions that they have to finance besides police. Young cops often have a hard time grasping that reality.

You must keep your boss apprised of your budgetary needs. That means *honestly* apprised. Your credibility with your supervisor is, in the final analysis, more important than obtaining an additional, perhaps short-term benefit by stretching the truth or nailing any of your important body parts to the wall in order to win a "victory." Case in point: A small city police chief who was very popular with his troops had the habit of doubling whatever he thought he really needed when going to his city manager with budget requests. The manager got wise to the charade, stating: "If his troops ask for four bazookas, he asks me for eight. I get what he's trying to pull for his own popularity, and I don't appreciate it." So much for employee-boss relations. You do not want to be that employee.

Keeping your boss in the know regarding your legitimate needs is obviously very important. In realization of the fact that your city or town only has so much to give, you will be smart to explore some other possibilities for financial support. Internet research should be one of your first tasks. The U.S. Department of Justice and Community Oriented Policing Services (COPS) websites will lead you to a whole host of financial grant possibilities from the federal government. There can be a lot of potential help to be found there, but read carefully the grant requirements (sometimes called the fine print) before signing up. Some grants have some pretty detailed application and reporting requirements. Others may require a monetary match from you. Yet others may require you to keep doing something beyond the actual grant time period, such as assume the whole salary for a grant-hired employee. Grants can be helpful, just know what you are getting into before you jump in.

There are also private sector funding sources available to first responders. Some time spent exploring the Internet for these sources of financial help could pay off. Big corporations sometimes provide funding for public safety projects, especially if they are focused on crime prevention or police-community relations. Walmart has been a big contributor in the past, as has Motorola. Don't be shy about asking for needed financial help.

As you get to know your community you also may identify local sources of financial aid for worthy community projects. One small department found that a local civic club was willing to purchase a patrol dog for the agency. Another discovered a civic group that was anxious to help replace outdated body armor. Take care not to go to the well too often in reaching out to individuals and groups to ask for help. When a person or organization does help you, be sure to express your appreciation in as public a fashion as possible. Some people like to provide help anonymously. If that is the case, respect their wishes. More often people and organizations want some publicity for their good deeds. Be sure you know which is which and respond accordingly.

Paying for what you truly need can be a difficult task for the small department chief. But you might be surprised at the amount of help that is out there if you look hard enough.

OBTAINING NEEDED TRAINING

You would be an unusual and fortunate chief indeed if you have ready access to all of the high-quality training you could ever want for your people. If you do, by all means take full advantage of it. It may be more likely, however, that you will need to look beyond your own organization for at least some of the training you require. That is where the need to cultivate positive relations with your larger department neighbors comes into play. Unless those neighbors are very unusual, they almost certainly will be willing to include your people in some of their training classes. Also, do not overlook some of the training opportunities that may be provided by state and regional training sources, such as councils of government. Remain always on the lookout for on-line training opportunities, too.

For the smaller agency, backfilling officer positions while these people are sent to training can be problematical. Filling them with officers on overtime can prove difficult to a department with a tight budget. It is important that your boss understands the necessity of adequate training both for officer safety and risk management purposes. Be sure he or she knows that untrained or poorly trained officers pose a serious risk to the financial well-being of the town or city employing them. Lawsuits brought on by a lack of training can be extremely expensive. Mentioning that reality may help win you some monetary support for officer training efforts. That support may need to include a boosted overtime budget.

Your boss and your elected officials also must understand that training for emergency responders needs to be the last thing–not the first thing–cut when budget trimming needs to be done. Too often some city and town officials tend to look at employee training as "fluff" that can be slashed when the budget is tight. Once more, it will be your job to ensure that your officials realize that budget trimming should avoid training dollars.

In meeting your officers' training requirements do not overlook the so-called "soft skills" that cops need more than ever today. Firearms and arrest control training is important. But so are classes in de-escalation, defusing mental health crises, and working with special populations, such as the autistic community. Leadership training for your first-line supervisors and mid-level leaders is also extremely important. These are the people who will control the day-to-day operations of the department. They will translate your directives into action–or not. Take care of them and they very likely will take care of you. You can help care for them by equipping them with the knowledge and skills they will need to do their difficult jobs well.

The takeaway for you in all of this? Make sure that training for your officers is always near the top of your "to get done" list. Never short change your people in what they must have to stay safe and well-prepared for the challenges of their jobs. Get creative in meeting their training needs. The results should be evidenced in safer, more competent police officers.

"SMALL TOWN POLITICS"

Every city or town, no matter how large or how small, has its politics. So does every city or town government. As the old saying goes, all politics are local. In reality, local government represents the last level of officialdom that citizens actually can reach out and touch. Community members can get these people on the telephone relatively easily and give them an earful at city council or town board meetings. Often as not, much of the community knows where their hometown leaders reside. Politics can be up close and personal in the smaller town or city. That can impact you when a citizen shows up on your front porch waving a ticket he just received or seeking advice for handling his disobedient teenager. One chief recalls being accosted by a naked man with a beef in the locker room of the local rec center while the chief was trying to towel off from his post-workout shower. Yes, small town issues can feel personal and, sometimes, downright invasive to the police boss.

Good advice for you is to keep a thumb on the pulse of the local politics without becoming actively involved yourself. You always can respond to requests to participate by noting that your agency's ethical guidelines bar you from taking part. You need to know who the players are and which issues are important to each. You also need to get a feel for the level of integrity displayed by each player. Your top staffers as well as your boss should be able to supplement your own observations as to who's who and the baggage, if any, of each player.

Do your very best to stay out of the political plots and campaigns. Don't spout off with your negative opinions of a local politician. You practically can be assured that your comments will get back to him or her, perhaps amplified and supplemented in the process. Politely make it clear that as an appointed official you cannot take part in personal electoral campaigns. You can explain to Mayor Joe that you like him and will vote for him, but your professional ethics will not let you put his electioneering sign in your yard or his Pro-Joe bumper sticker on your vehicle.

At one time or another virtually every town or city has its plots and intrigues among its elected and appointed officials. Your career is more likely to be extended if you courteously decline to participate. First, that's the right thing to do. Second, there is often a winning side and a losing side in these affairs. While those on the wrong side are no longer drawn and quartered, those on the losing team not infrequently find negative things happening to them. A loss of employment can sometimes be one of those negative things. Avoid the anguish. Just do your job as an ethical leader of police personnel. Know where the games are and who the players happen to be. Just stay above the fray. You are apt to have a happier life and almost certainly a longer leadership career.

INACCURATE PERCEPTIONS

Your town or city is not Mayberry. You are certainly not Andy or, by any stretch, Barney. But you cannot escape the fact that some people, including some law enforcement practitioners who should know better, may regard you and your small agency as, well, somehow substandard.

You and your people are not bumpkins. You didn't just fall off the turnip wagon. Thanks to what you are doing, your department is now or will soon be a place where compassionate, competent professionals work. There are good people with integrity here. You are very proud of them. You say so publicly every chance you get.

The best way to shut down the naysayers is to prove them wrong. You do this by striving for excellence in everything you and your people do. You never fail to serve as an exceptional role model for both your employees and the community to see. You insist on the same behavior from your troops. You maintain personal and departmental transparency and accountability. When you or your employees mess up, you admit it and seek to fix it right away. You acknowledge the mistakes as well as the victories. You act like the ethical leader that you are.

Reputations are built over time and through examples. That holds true for both bad precedent and good. Your work will be a bit harder if the department was lacking in competency or even woefully troubled before you took over. But if that was the case, the contrast that is visible under your leadership will be even easier for all to see. Before long your citizens and your officers alike will feel pride in what has been and will be accomplished. Barney does not work there.

SUMMARY

Being a small department leader is unique. It brings both rewards and challenges. Among the challenges is the ability to attract and keep excellent employees–not the suitcase cop variety that is, on occasion, attracted to the small agency. There is the ever-present need to pay your employees a competitive wage and obtain for them the training and equipment they need on a too-often very limited budget. There is the requirement that you make plenty of friends but remain aloof from local, bare-knuckles politics that have laid low more than a few police chiefs. Finally, you will find yourself working to overcome the false images of small departments that exist in some uninformed minds.

You will be able to overcome all of these challenges by doing what good law enforcement leaders do, regardless of the size of their agency. Be a positive role model. Get innovative in meeting your agency's financial and training needs. Be exceptionally careful of who you permit to wear your department's badge. Don't get involved in political games. Be proud of your people and say so in public. A lot.

You are good at what you do. Meeting special challenges is what a special leader does well. You *are* that special leader.

Chapter 3

YOUR ROLE AS A LEADER

You probably have been in law enforcement for quite a while. In that time you have seen more than a few leaders in your profession. Some of them you likely have admired and deemed to be successful. You might even have determined to emulate their behavior. On the other hand, you almost certainly remember one or more that you felt were failed leaders, for one reason or another. You may have promised yourself never to mimic their less-than-stellar performance.

What makes one leader a success and another a failure? Certainly a lot of things can be involved. Many of those things that help make a specific individual a true leader worthy of the name are identifiable. Following those guideposts can help *you* succeed as a leader in a small law enforcement agency, or one of virtually any size. But exactly what are those "things," those traits and character and actions of a successful leader? Read on.

SHOW PRIDE IN YOUR PEOPLE AND YOUR ORGANIZATION

As the leader of your organization, you will have responsibilities to meet and tasks to accomplish. A lot of each. In everything you do you will be expected to provide a great example for your employees and the world at large to see. In getting all of this done successfully you will find your multiple jobs and obligations easier to accomplish if you follow some basic, common sense guidelines.

You have heard this before, but it is so vital to your success that it merits repetition: Whether you are addressing your employees or members of the public, *your people and your organization are the best.* You are proud of your department and the individuals who give it life and purpose. Yes, it is always possible to get better. Things are not perfect. They can improve and they will. But this is a great place to be and these are great people to work with.

This is not just a rule, it is a *cardinal* rule for a leader. It is one that you must obey at all times if you want to succeed in leadership. Publicly denounce your people or your organization and you have dug yourself a hole it may prove impossible to get out of.

Let your employees know that you are proud of them by what you communicate to them, both publicly and in private. You can do this via texts, e-mails, and personal notes. Even better, you can let people know through one-on-one personal contact. You can do it when you are walking around your facility or meeting an officer on the street. (Don't overlook your civilian employees, either.) One highly regarded police leader set himself the personal goal of praising someone for something every single workday. That's not a bad practice for you to emulate. But beware of uttering false or meaningless praise. Cops are pretty good at sensing phoniness. Be sure that what you intend to commend really merits the good words. After all, you *expect* Officer Bob to put on his pants before he comes to work.

It is indeed important to single out individuals for deserved praise, but it is also vital to let people both inside and outside the department know that this is an exceptional police agency staffed by some very good people. Even if you know that there is a lot of work to be done to shape the organization into what you believe it ultimately can be, this is not the time or place to broadcast that fact to the world. This is a police department that you and everybody else can be proud of. Get in the habit of saying that a lot.

None of this means that you must ignore the things in your agency that need fixed. In order to address them, you will need the support of your command staff. Be open with them in what needs repaired and the roles they are to play in getting it done. At some point your first-line supervisors will have to be made aware (if they aren't already) of what needs changed and their part in accomplishing the needed revisions. Your boss also will need to know what you are doing and why. But all of this can be accomplished without broad, public statements about what's wrong and how you are going to fix it. Just get on with the task without public pronouncements.

ESTABLISH YOUR GOALS AND COMMUNICATE THEM

Your on-the-job experience probably has taught you that police people are remarkably good at what they are supposed to be doing. That is, of course, if they *know* what it is they are supposed to be doing. That is where your skills as a decision-maker, planner, and communicator come in. You need for your employees and the community, including its elected officials and your boss, to know what it is that the police organization is trying to accomplish. But before you announce where it is you are intending to go, you first need to know where you are presently. Take an in-depth look at your organization and the community it serves. What's being done *now*? What perhaps needs done differently? What is working well and what is not? Trust your own observations, but also get the opinions of your people, especially your command staff, to the extent that they want to have input. One new chief gathered his whole supervisory staff and asked them what they felt the organization's goals should be. Crickets. He asked again. More crickets. Finally, one grizzled sergeant spoke: "We kind of thought that was to be your job, Chief." Okay. So, the chief set the goals himself and was relieved to see that his leadership team supported them in practice. Get participation in setting the goals you feel are appropriate, assuming you can. If not, call upon your own observations and experience to establish them yourself. Get it done, regardless. It is vital that your employees have that necessary guidance, and without unnecessary delay.

Keep your goals concise, succinct, reasonable, and do-able. "Wipe out crime in Whoville" is an admirable goal, but it may be a tad on the idealistic side. Obviously, there are causative factors of crime that you and your officers, no matter how well-intentioned, are unable to control. Also, be cautious about how many goals you set. It has been said with some truth that when there are too many targets none of them gets hit. Again: Keep it realistic.

One chief of a small agency established the following goals for his people:

- Work safely.
- Deliver exceptional customer service ("Find a Way to Help").
- Do the right thing, on-duty and off-duty.

He and his subordinate leaders could then flesh out the details and serve as positive role models in seeking the attainment of each goal. The department's guideposts were clear, direct, concise, and easy to comprehend, for police employee and community member alike. They established an easily readable road map as to where the leader wanted and expected his people to go. As directions they were highly effective.

Once the goals are set, your next task is to ensure that everyone–most especially your employees–knows what they are. Disseminate them widely. Put them on your agency's web home page and plaster them on your social media sites. Put them on display in the Patrol briefing room. Consider emblazoning them on your department letterhead. Just get them out there. Repetition works well as reinforcement. It is your job to get your goals and expectations placed in front of your people. It is their job to know them and work towards their accomplishment.

REALIZE MAJOR CHANGE TAKES TIME

You have things that you want to get done. You have things that you *need* to get done in order to make your police department the best. If you are like many good leaders, you are in a hurry to get these things accomplished. You want very much to see and feel positive change and you want others to be able to see it and feel it, too. Change needs to happen *now.*

You are quite correct to desire immediate results from your considerable efforts. Some change you can and will see and feel almost immediately. Your personal drive and energy can make that possible even if early on you are laboring with little help. The positive outlook and demeanor of the new leader should be something the whole organization notices and begins to emulate because it is contagious. That's good. But more wide-ranging, department-altering change most often takes longer. It has to be gently massaged into place as opposed to being delivered with hammer blows. It will be up to you based on your knowledge of your organization and its people to determine just how rapidly to implement major change. What will be termed "major change" often will vary widely from one organization to the next. How promotions are handled could serve as an example of a major change at one department. What color to paint the patrol cars could be a big deal at another.

It is important to remember that change—even very positive change—can prove very stressful to those it is imposed upon. Change of any kind can seem even more stressful when those it most directly affects had no role in devising it. Keep that in mind when implementing change and then demanding that it be supported and executed. While it may not be possible every time, that's why it is good to have employee participation in the change process whenever feasible.

All of this results in another cardinal rule for the new chief: *Implement change only at the pace your people can tolerate it.* Sometimes moving too quickly, changing too many things at the same time, can result in opposition that would not have arisen had the reason for the change been clearly explained in advance. It also might have worked better if everyone had sufficient time to think about and discuss significant change before it became practice. It might be a good idea to bring out the second major change next month rather than piggybacking it with the first big one just revealed today.

If you sense that you are experiencing more resistance than you expected in implementing significant change, consider slowing down a little. Give your people a clear view of what is you are all trying to accomplish. Respond to any lingering questions and seek opinions. You may even decide to modify the planned change just a little based on what you have just learned. Then, nudge the change into place. Even now, be willing to revise the change if the results clearly indicate that you should. Remain patient as you observe the results. It will not be unusual if you note a bit of griping before change is accepted by all hands. After all, you're dealing with cops!

As frontier warrior and homespun philosopher David Crockett allegedly said, "First be sure you're right. Then, go ahead." It's not bad advice for you.

SHARE THE INFORMATION AND PRAISE

From the places you go, the people you talk with, and the electronic and printed media you access, you are going to gain information not routinely available to your employees. Some of it they likely would not be interested in. But that is not the case with everything that you learn and know. It is up to you to share the map of where the department and jurisdiction are going in order to help your people stay informed about relevant plans, objectives, and happenings that will impact them, to one degree or another, sooner or later. Err on the side of telling them too much as opposed to too little.

Go to any law enforcement organization–perhaps any organization at all–and when questioned at least a portion of the employees will claim that they really don't know what's going on in their own outfit. True or not, that will be their perception. It's often called the old "keep me in the dark and feed me manure" syndrome. If true, that would be a proven means for growing mushrooms but not reasonably content employees. You do not want to be accurately accused of raising mushrooms. Over-inform, if need be.

Your personal goal is to lead a well-informed workforce. Where reliable information is absent, too often rumor finds fertile ground to grow. And that is a new problem that you don't need.

Share the kudos, too. As you go about the community you are going to hear from a diverse group of people about the work your officers are doing. Most of these comments are going to be positive in nature. Promptly share those commendations with the people who earned them. Anytime specific employees are named, be sure that they and their immediate supervisor get the good words, perhaps with an added message from you attached. Whether they will admit it or not, most of your people enjoy hearing those things.

Praise feels good. You know that you enjoy receiving it. Ensure that your people have a chance to do the same.

ENSURE THAT EVERYONE KNOWS THE MISSION

You already have let your employees know what the goals of the department are. You hopefully have laid out for them your priorities, the things that are especially important to you, their leader. If you have not done so already, now you need to share the overarching purpose–the primary mission–of the entire police organization. It is the basic "why we are here" message.

Your best advice for preparing a Mission Statement that your people and your community can understand and get behind? Keep it simple. You undoubtedly have seen mission statements that ramble on through numerous, perhaps lengthy sentences and maybe even multiple paragraphs. The result? Virtually no one knows what's in it, let alone what he or she is supposed to do to fulfill it. These statements may be chock-full of currently popular pop-management words and phrases. But your employees can be forgiven if they do not understand precisely what it is they are supposed to do when they encounter such pronouncements.

Keeping it simple means trying really hard to keep it to a sentence or two, and not overly lengthy ones at that. For example: *Our mission is to help preserve the excellent quality of life in our community.* It's simple. It's clear. It gets to the point quickly. People do not have an excellent quality of life if they are fearful of being a victim of crime or being run over by out-of-control traffic violators. In reading this your cops can grasp that they have a big role to play in providing their community with a safe environment. Your citizens also can comprehend what it is your department, with help from the community, is trying to accomplish.

Check out the web sites of some other law enforcement organizations if you are looking for ideas. Many will have their mission statement posted. Seek some input from your staff. You can even ask your troops to contribute, if they are willing. Once you have identified your mission, get it out there by every means possible. Put it on your web homepage and broadcast it via social media. Hang it in the lobby of the police station and post it in the briefing room. Advertise your mission. Then, lead your people in a unified effort to carry it out.

SEEK OUT GOOD IDEAS

There are a lot of them out there. Your first-line people have some of them if you just ask. You have said it yourself: the people actually doing the work generally have the best ideas for getting the job done well. You won't get those ideas unless you make it clear to your people that you are accessible and want to hear their suggestions.

Getting and adopting good ideas is another good reason to network with others in your profession. Attending regional or county-wide gatherings with your colleagues will expose you to good ideas from elsewhere. You may discover one or more that you want to adopt as is or modify somewhat for application in your agency. When you can afford to attend the national police professional conferences you can harvest even more ideas. Meanwhile, stay current with the publications and Web sites specific to your profession. What is happening in other parts of the country may give you some more good ideas of things to try in your own neighborhood. Do not hesitate to share your own good ideas and initiatives with your peers. Your profession gets better through the sharing of knowledge among its leaders. You are one of those leaders.

BE SEEN AND HEARD WHEN APPROPRIATE

This is an era when the cop-haters and self-appointed police "experts" are not hesitant to loudly express their heavily biased views about police officers and policing. This is not the time for police leaders to remain silent when their livelihood and their people are under attack. Beyond responding, when necessary, to the hateful rhetoric, there are things pertaining to your own department and your chosen profession that your community and your employees need to hear from you.

Your preferred approach to life may be as an introvert. You may want to avoid people and attention as much as possible. You cannot project that style at work, however. On the job you must function as an extrovert who is comfortable meeting people and representing his or her officers and department on virtually every topic of public interest where law enforcement is even remotely concerned. You must, in a few words, be able to "perform" in front of an audience of five or 500. You must be able to address a briefing room full of cops or a city council meeting populated by agitated citizens. You must look and sound like the leader you are.

It is vital that you remain visible when controversy erupts involving your profession, your department, and (especially) your people. This is not the time to shove someone else out front to speak for your department. Both your officers and your citizens want to see the chief out front, talking about what happened and answering the tough questions, if necessary. It is moments like this that will help define you as a leader. Your reputation for good or ill will be built from how you respond when difficult, and, oftentimes, emotion-generating events are the focus of all the attention.

You do not have to be a polished, professional public speaker to acquit yourself well in front of an audience, even a less-than-agreeable one. Just be yourself. Tell the truth. Make eye contact with those you are addressing. Keep your emotions under control. Never show fear or uncertainty.

You get better at speaking to an audience by speaking to an audience. You get better at answering tough questions by answering tough questions. You get good at standing out front by standing out front. People will like seeing you do it. You will like seeing the results in increased trust and respect for you and your organization.

DON'T CRITICIZE PUBLICLY

There are going to be times when people, including your own, seriously disappoint you. There are going to be occasions when they make you downright angry. You are very familiar with the old but accurate rule that requires praising in public and criticizing in private. That is yet another of those cardinal rules that apply to you as a police chief–a leader. It harks back to one of those other cardinal rules: in public your people and your organization are always the best.

The mandate against public criticism extends beyond your own turf. You also must refrain from carrying out public feuds with neighboring police departments, the sheriff, the District Attorney's Office, or any other element of the criminal justice system. The news media thrive on conflict and controversy, and any negative comments you make in public are highly likely to make the news. At the very least, they will make their way onto the local grapevine or gossip network. The omnipresent social media will take it from there. Whomever you are criticizing probably will feel the need to respond in an equally public manner, and the destructive feud is on. It is a contest that will, in the end, benefit no one. Seldom is there a clear winner as the mud flies and bad feelings accumulate that may smolder for years. None of this will make you look like an admirable leader.

Certainly you must speak up for yourself and your people, if any of you has been wronged. But try to do it calmly and quietly without emotional outbursts. Look and sound like the mature and exceptional leader you are. Strive to remain above the fray and out of the mud. Come across as the positive role model that you are. And that merits further discission....

NEVER FORGET YOU ARE A ROLE MODEL

The biggest compliment your people can pay you is to want to be like you one day. This is the goal you are seeking to reach, even if you are doing so without consciously thinking about it. The role should come to you naturally if you are truly the leader you ascribe to be. This pertains to both your on-duty and off-duty behavior. It flows from who you are as a person with compassion, empathy, deeply felt ethics, and a clear vision of both who you are and who you desire to be. Being a positive role model means doing the right thing even when no one will ever know what you did, one way or another. It means doing what you believe to be the correct thing, the ethical thing, even when it might not be crystal-clear to others what the right thing is. It means doing the right thing even when it will not be popular.

Being an exceptional role model can encompass a great many things. It includes the way you wear your uniform and maintain your personal grooming. It applies to your manner of speaking and how you respond to an individual who has sorely tried your patience. It certainly includes how you treat others in your professional and personal life. And it absolutely involves how well you follow the rules of your own organization as well as the laws of the land.

Being a positive role model does not allow you much room for inappropriate behavior of any kind, on the job or off. All of this may sound tough, but it is what you signed up for when you applied to be the Top Cop in the agency you now lead. You can still make a mistake. Everyone does. You can even experience a temporary lapse in judgment in how you comport yourself. If the lapse occurs in spite of your best efforts, as a positive role model you are obliged to apply the universal antidote for responding to personal mistakes:

- Admit it and apologize.
- Fix it, if you can.
- Do not repeat it.
- Learn from it.

It's what a positive role model does.

No doubt you have talked with your subordinate supervisors about being positive role models for their team members. If you have not, do so without delay. You owe them a demonstration of what a good role model is. You obviously cannot hold them accountable for failing as role models if you are falling short yourself. As chief you are always "on," regardless of your duty status or where you happen to be. Whether you realize it at the time or not, oftentimes a lot of eyes are watching, and any number of ears are listening. Not every single one of their owners may wish you well. You deny them the ammunition to harm you if you never fail to serve as a positive role model. That includes admitting it when you are wrong.

YOU ARE NOT ALONE

It has been said that the chief's job is the loneliest in law enforcement. That may feel true at times, but it does not have to be that way. You actually have a lot of friends out there, colleagues who will help you if you ask. A chief in a neighboring jurisdiction may have encountered and ably handled a situation identical or similar to the one you are facing now. Learning what that leader did and how well it worked may be only a phone call away. That is another reason for keeping up your contacts through association meetings, conferences, and one-on-one contacts. You will make acquaintances who may have advice that will help you through a crisis one day. But you won't be able to access any of that assistance if your ego keeps you from asking for needed help. In turn, you will make known to your peers that you are available to them with advice or a second opinion. It's just the neighborly thing to do.

You may find help within your own organization. A veteran staffer may have faced a situation like the one you are confronting. Once again, do not let ego keep you from seeking assistance when you need it. Your subordinate likely will be honored that you are seeking his or her input. Someone in the private sector also may be a good source of help. Hopefully you have met some of these leaders through your personal outreach efforts. One new chief found he could rely on the local hospital CEO for some solid advice on personnel matters. Keep an eye out for where you might reach for reliable advice when you need it. Naturally, department heads within your own town or city government could be great sources of help, too. All these non-police people may be good sounding boards for tentative decisions you have made. Do not hesitate to call on them.

You are not really alone in your leadership position. Help is at hand if you will reach out for it. Then, remember to return the favor when needed. It is what solid leaders do.

SUMMARY

Your life experience has taught you that the work world includes both successful and failed leaders. What makes the difference? The answer can be found in some of the things you are and will be as a successful leader of law enforcement officers. You are a self-confident but never arrogant person who shows pride in his or her people and organization, neither of which you ever criticize in public. You help your employees and your police department succeed by establishing a clear mission and goals and communicating them to your people and the community you all serve. As you accomplish these things you display patience and never forget that real change takes time. Along the way you share needed information and earned praise with your people for the progress accomplished. You also both borrow and share good ideas and ask your peers for help when you need it. You speak up for your people and your profession when necessary. You never fail to serve as a positive role model for your officers.

It is well-known that the followers of an admired and trusted leader almost always display high morale and a desire to do the right thing. By serving as an exceptional role model and competent leader you benefit your people, your organization, and your community. These things you are capable of today and will only get better at as your knowledge and experience grow.

Chapter 4

DECISION-MAKING: DOING IT RIGHT EVEN WHEN IT'S HARD

As a living being you make countless decisions every day. What do I want for breakfast? Do I choose the red tie or the blue one? What do we want to do this weekend? As a law enforcement leader, you also have a lot of work-related decisions to make. Some of them can feel much more far-reaching and critical that the ones you make in your personal life. What is the appropriate discipline for Officer Smith's transgression? Do I push harder on my boss for that raise I want for my people? Do I order a forced entry or do we wait? Indeed, decision-making can be a very critical task for you, the leader of a small law enforcement agency.

One of the reasons you were selected to be the police chief was because somebody or several somebodies felt you were capable of making good decisions. Now you will be expected to live up to that trust. Your employees also will expect that you will be able to make sound decisions when the situation warrants. It is unlikely that they all will agree with every call you make, but they will expect you to make it, anyhow. None of your audiences, above or below you, will be favorably impressed by unnecessary delay or indecisiveness on your part. They won't applaud a clearly "bad" decision, either. So, how can you meet all of these elevated expectations?

By avoiding some decision-making killers and employing some experience-proven guidelines for making good decisions as an effective leader you can meet and master those challenges. It starts with knowing what *not* to do.

ENEMIES OF SOUND DECISION-MAKING

In addition to the numerous, "routine" ones you make every day that you are at work, not infrequently you have to make decisions that may be potentially life-altering ones, for one of your employees or someone else. It is especially important that these calls are the right ones. Unfortunately, one or more miscues can intervene and derail your decision-making. Some of the most common offenders include the following:

Procrastination. Putting something off because it is unpleasant or could have an uncomfortable outcome for you or someone else is a natural human tendency. But it is unlikely to make the final result feel any better. A decision delayed without a very good reason can even cause real harm. Having sufficient information to make a good decision is vital, but putting off deciding until you have every scrap of data you could ever desire is neither realistic nor helpful. A decision still has to be made. Postponing it unnecessarily will benefit neither you nor those who will be directly impacted by your call. (In a tactical example, picture the on-scene commander who cannot make a decision on forced entry while shots are still being heard inside the school building.)

Rushing Unnecessarily. It's the polar opposite of procrastinating. Emergency situations that literally may involve life or death scenarios often will require a very quick decision that, if delayed, could result in some very bad consequences. Fortunately, however, you will not be faced with such decisions on a daily basis. Much more often, you will have time to gather pertinent facts, take some deep breaths, and analyze the information that you have been able to assemble within a reasonable amount of time. Decisions regarding personnel matters often will fall into this category of decision-making. While unjustified delay is still not called for, you nonetheless will have much more time to consider your decision and its potential consequences before making the call. During that pause you can do research and obtain advice, if need be. Having the luxury of time to think is a good thing. Do not throw that gift away by acting rashly.

Noise. This detractor of good decision-making can be mental or physical. "Noise" can consist of mental or emotional distractions that can weaken your decision-making abilities. Here might be found the example of a disciplinary decision you must make regarding an employee who, truth told, you have really disliked for quite some time.

To make a good and fair decision you will have to do your best to put behind you any biases and personal feelings you may harbor. Actual, physical noise such as might be found at the scene of a critical incident also can hamper your decision-making abilities. If at all possible, you must remove yourself from the proximity of the worst of it if you are to allow your decision-making machinery to function reliably. Some slow, deep breaths may help, too.

Personal Bias. This one is a cousin of the mental version of "noise." Be careful that your decision-making is not contaminated by personal beliefs or prejudices. If you have already decided upon your course of action prior to having sufficient information to make a good call, it is doubtful that your decision will be as solid as it otherwise might be. Virtually everyone harbors biases of one kind or another. Just be aware of yours and work to keep them at arm's length from your decision-making efforts.

Reluctance to Decide on Change. At times it requires considerable personal courage to do something differently than has been done before, something that is at least a little out of the proverbial box, something that might make someone uneasy. You already know not to change things just for the sake of change. But sometimes deciding to do something differently is the correct answer. Don't be afraid to try it.

Failure to Consider All the Evidence. On occasion decision-makers are guilty of seriously considering only the facts or factors that back up a decision that they have already made, perhaps prematurely. Work at widening your field of vision a bit. Try to remain impartial as you examine *all* of the information that is available. Be willing to look for it.

Trying Too Hard to Please Everyone. Life has taught you that your decision that pleases Officer Jones may gravely disappoint Officer Schmuck; your call that motivates Sgt. White may send Sgt. Burns into a funk. Life and decision-making are like that sometimes. Your decisions, no matter how carefully crafted, will not always please everyone. Sometimes people will dislike you, at least for the moment. You cannot be paralyzed by that reality when it comes to decision-making. Do your best to be fair and proceed to make the call. The really tough decisions are the ones you are entrusted to make. And they will not always please everybody.

Failing to Learn from Experience. Maybe the situation you are facing or one very similar has been met before by you or someone in your agency. If you do not use that experience, you are denying yourself a valuable tool. History and precedent often can tell you what has worked–and what has not. Knowing that could aid you immeasurably in making a sound decision today. Never overlook experience as a helpful guidepost in making the decision you are facing now.

Unnecessarily Flying Solo. Some decisions will have to be made so quickly that you, of necessity, will have to go it alone. But more often you will have the opportunity to get input from others before you make the call. There is nothing shameful about picking the brains of your colleagues when there is a tough call to be made. To the contrary, it would be foolhardy not to take advantage of available assistance

MAKING A GOOD DECISION

When it comes decision-making time in a personnel matter, there are both benefits and negatives in being the leader of a small police agency. On the positive side of the ledger, with fewer employees it is likely that you know your people pretty well. That should help you to make a sound decision when it comes to something that will affect an employee's job and, perhaps, future. The negative side may surface when you are having to discipline someone who may be a friend, perhaps one whose family and personal situation you know well. Decision-making can then be difficult if not actually painful. You realize that you have to get it done, all the same.

There are several things that will aid you in making a sound decision, whether that call involves a personnel issue, tactical situation, or something else. These things include the following:

Information. To make a good decision you need to have as much *reliable* data as possible prior to making the call. Who and what is involved? What are the time constraints, if any? Are there other limitations placed on your decision-making ability? Assuming there is time, is it possible to obtain help to aid you in your decision-making? Indeed, is there potential assistance available? While you may never have every single piece of information you would *like* to have in hand before you must decide, gather all you reasonably can in the time you have available.

Your Experience, Education, and Training. There is a good chance that you have handled something at least similar previously.

What did you learn from that experience? If the situation you are facing is entirely new, your education and training hopefully have at least provided you with some ideas for addressing the challenge. That is yet another good reason for being a life-long learner. Try to apply what you *do* know to the decision you must make now. Chances are your capabilities in decision-making are more robust than you may think. As always, personal courage and self-confidence, appropriately applied, can help you through.

Judgment. Your brain has a record of the decisions you have made in the past and the outcome of those decisions. All of those have helped you formulate sound judgment practices. Call on the depths of your proven good judgment when you have a new decision to make. It should not let you down if it is based on logic and sound decisions from your past efforts.

Common Sense. It is probably a combination of your life experience, education, training, and intuition. Every decision you make should pass the common sense test. If that little voice in the back of your head is telling you that the decision you are about to make is the wrong one, use whatever time you have available to at least reconsider your pending call. You might have missed something important. You may decide to proceed anyhow, or perhaps alter your decision in some way. But if you can, at least pause before going ahead when the little voice speaks. Listen and think.

Courage. Your decisions will not always result in unbridled joy for everyone involved or impacted. On occasion a decision you make will result in tears or outright anger. You must have the courage to make the call, anyway. Sometimes that is the emotional fallout that has to be experienced by the decision-maker. You do not have to enjoy making a decision that results in unhappiness or outright opposition. Hopefully, your ability to sense and understand the feelings of others would keep that from happening. But you do have to fulfill your role as a courageous decision-maker all the same. Your boss and your subordinates will expect that you will be able to reach a decision regardless of the consequences. It is one more of your position's important responsibilities.

Empathy and Compassion. Making a decision that you know may negatively impact others does not require that you be heartless. Just the opposite is the case. You cannot be a just and ethical decision-maker if you have no comprehension at all of the impact your actions will have on the lives of those involved. All good decision-makers display an ample supply of both sincere empathy and compassion. But neither of those will keep them from making a needed decision. You must be able to do the same.

Willingness to Accept Input. Your actions are not dictated by ego. You know well that you are not the only smart person in the room. You also realize that oftentimes the most valuable information available to a decision-maker comes from those closest to the work: your first-line employees. Someone in your organization may have some great ideas that will help you make the right call. But you won't know if you don't ask. Never let your ego preclude you from getting help when you need it.

Timeliness. The best potential decision in the world will not help you or anyone else if it is not made in time to influence the outcome. Of one indecisive chief his people said "if he puts one more decision on the back burner, we're going to have to buy a bigger stove." The man had a great deal of trouble making decisions and his failed response was to delay making them. You do not want your people saying that about you. Granted, most of your decisions will not require a call to be made within seconds or minutes in order to forestall disaster. You will have some time to consider what you are dealing with and examine your options. But do not delay unnecessarily, either. You must master the art of thinking on your feet in the time you have available.

Grasp of Consequences. Before you finalize your decision, give some thought to what the results are likely to be. Who will be affected and how? How radical a change in practices, policies, or procedures will be required? What will be the response from both your employees and the community? By thinking your decision through thoroughly you are seeking to prevent negative consequences that had not been anticipated. Remain alert to the possibilities.

Willingness to Revise a Decision. Those unanticipated consequences may provide a very good reason to make changes to your initial decision. Or the situation requiring a decision may have changed since you made it. Whatever the case, do not hesitate to alter a decision that is not having the desired result. Again, do not let your ego get in the way. It does not mean that your original decision was the wrong one. It may simply mean that the picture has changed as new information has become available or the initial situation has now gone in a new direction. Never allow pride to keep you from adjusting your decision when solid evidence tells you that you should.

Clear Communication. The best decision ever made is of no value if the people it will affect do not know of it. Everyone whom your decision will touch must know what the leader—that's you—has decided. Use any and all means at your disposal to disseminate your decision to those who need to know. It may be transmitted in both oral and written formats. The decision must be clearly stated so that anyone hearing or reading it knows exactly what it is. Be willing to respond to questions. Be equally willing to provide clarification, if needed. Realize, too, that very often repetition is needed to ensure that everyone gets the word.

You make numerous decisions every day. Many of them are not super-critical ones, but all need made well, just the same. The tough ones will require more mental energy and effort from you, the decision-maker. You can ably handle those decision-making challenges. That is what good leaders do.

WHEN THERE DOESN'T SEEM TO BE AN ANSWER

You regularly rely upon your experience, education, and training to help you determine what to do when a decision must be made. All serve you well. But no matter how much of each you possess, on occasion you are going to encounter a decision-making situation for which you may initially feel your past has not adequately prepared you. Fear not. New and unique decision-making challenges are still things you are well-equipped to handle with the aid of a few, common sense guidelines. Guidelines such as:

If Feasible, Slow Things Down. Yes, a pending life-or-death decision may leave you with little or no time to ponder the situation. But those instances will not occur with great frequency. Anytime you can, slow the decision-making down just a little to allow for information-gathering, input, and contemplation. The added time to think and plan just might allow you to come up with a novel solution to a novel problem.

Know That There Are Few Absolutes. Okay, law enforcement has a few of them. You don't provide a weapon as part of negotiations with a barricaded offender, for example. Experience probably has taught you, however, that there are fewer absolutes than your early training may have led you to believe. Thinking "out of the box" does not call for being reckless with your decision-making. But it does give you permission to stray from the well-trodden path if your common sense (there's that phrase again!) tells you that something different just might work. Don't be afraid to try.

Realize That There Are Few "Perfect" Decisions. Few things in this world are totally flawless. Decisions do not represent an exception to the rule. If the call you make results in an overall positive outcome, you most likely have done a good job, especially if the decision you had to make was an unprecedented one. Take comfort in that fact and move on.

Keep Things in Perspective. Certainly you could be called upon to make a life-altering decision at any time. You signed up for that and you are willing to do it. But most of your decisions will not determine the fate of the planet. Try to keep that in mind, especially if your call does not turn out to be a perfect one. It is a fact of life that a lot of things that seem to pose a picture of disaster and mayhem on Monday are largely forgotten by Friday.

Get Help. And do not wait too long to ask for it. If time permits, see if trusted colleagues and/or members of your own staff have ideas that may help address your dilemma. Kick the situation around in some free-flowing discussion. Propose some ideas and get others' reaction to them. Listen critically to their ideas. You really *are* allowed to ask for help on the tough calls. Ask for that aid when you are facing a challenging, novel situation. You may be surprised to find assistance coming from an unexpected quarter. Then, be willing to return the favor when needed.

Get It Done and Go Ahead. It is possible and quite human to agonize over a decision you have made, particularly if it didn't have the results you had hoped for. That holds especially true for decisions made in response to unique circumstances. It is human alright, but not really helpful. You did your best with what you were given to work with. Be content with that and move on to the next decision-making challenge. It's out there, perhaps just over the horizon. Utilize what you have just learned in order to master it. You can do it well.

LEARNING FROM EXPERIENCE

Personal experience may be the most effective mode of learning that exists. Human beings get better at handling future decision-making by recalling what happened from their efforts at decision-making in the past. Those humans include small police department leaders.

How do *you* think you did with your most recent decision-making exercise? Hint: it is likely that you did much better than you think. Do not dwell on it, but do give it some honest consideration. What might you do next time a similar situation arises that could make the outcome even better? It is alright to ask some respected colleagues for their opinions. As you figured out long ago, the world of good ideas does not reside exclusively with the man or woman at the top of the chain of command. There are a lot of smart and innovative thinkers out there. Almost certainly some of them work for you.

Sometimes people seek to quickly forget their decisions that disappointed them. They should not. Some very successful leaders report that they learned more from decisions that did not go as planned than from those that did. Many of these same leaders confess to learning just as much from the less-than-stellar calls by others as they did from their own. Of course, these episodes do not occur only in law enforcement circles. By simply keeping a sharp eye on current events you can learn a lot about decision-making that went awry in other lines of work. Unfortunately, there is no shortage of examples today.

Learning from your own decision-making experiences, good and not-so-good, can be very helpful. Learning from the admirable and questionable decisions of others can be equally beneficial (and a lot less painful) than those of your own.

SUMMARY

You get better at making decisions by making them. You have made important decisions throughout your life and your law enforcement career. Now that you are in charge of the entire organization some of those calls will be made at a little higher level and potentially affect more people—because you are the boss.

You now are aware of some of the enemies of effective decision-making: procrastination, rushing when unnecessary, distractions (noise), personal bias, failure to consider all the evidence, trying too hard to please everyone. You also know what works in the creation of a good decision-maker. Things like the application of common sense, personal courage, timeliness, willingness to accept input, empathy, compassion, clear communication of the decision, and a ready willingness to revise a decision if the evidence indicates that you should. You also know that there are few absolutely perfect decisions and that it is often beneficial to think outside the box when facing a totally unanticipated challenge. Finally, you are conscious of the great value of experience in decision-making.

Your employer and your employees count on you to make the hard decisions. Doing so is one of your most important responsibilities as a leader. At times you will have to make those decisions under very tough conditions and with critical time constraints. You will make them all the same. You are the leader of a small police agency. That's what you do.

Chapter 5

YOU AS A GREAT ROLE MODEL

It is a fact that intelligent employees the world over expect their boss to set the example for the attitude and behavior expected of them. That reality is especially true in the law enforcement profession, where the employees already expect a lot from those who would profess to lead them. That expectation directly impacts you, their boss, in your role as leader of the agency that employs them. Cops being cops, they are unlikely to cut you any slack if they see evidence that you are falling short of meeting those expectations.

Doubtlessly you have high expectations of yourself as the leader of your police department. (And it truly is *yours*, for better or worse.) You want your people to see and hear what you do and how you do it, perhaps in hopes of being like you one day. In that role you are virtually always "on" and under close scrutiny by others, your employees included.

So, how do you go about serving as that exceptional role model who will be both admired and emulated? You can do it and do it well. What follows are some tips for accomplishing that noble and mandatory goal.

WHAT IS A ROLE MODEL?

You may have admired and followed someone in your past whom you saw as a really positive role model. That person may even have been a factor in why you decided to be a police leader one day. Very likely you learned from some of the examples your role model set in order to be where you are today.

A role model engages in behaviors and displays an attitude and demeanor that he or she hopes others will copy. That is especially true when those "others" happen to be his or her employees. In your line of work, serving as a poor role model could have truly dire consequences. Someone could be injured, or worse. You want your people to mimic your actions, not studiously avoid copying them. You never want to disappoint or mislead your people by providing a poor example. You have become who you are at least partially from observing the actions, good and bad, of diverse others. You have learned much from taking in their observed strengths and weaknesses. You want your people—your future leaders—to be able to do the same. And you want what they see in you to be heavily weighted towards strengths.

Positive role models are not flawless, nor do they claim to be. They are fallible human beings who are always striving to do better. They continuously seek to know and understand more. They work to expand their job knowledge and hone their skills. They labor to coach and mentor their employees while setting positive examples in both their on-duty and off-duty behavior. All of these things you can and must do.

None of this is beyond your abilities as a good leader. You are most assuredly capable of serving as an exceptional role model for your community and your department. In doing so you will need to identify the characteristics that you want others to admire and copy.

WHAT TRAITS DO YOU WANT YOUR PEOPLE TO DISPLAY?

As a great role model, you will earmark those traits, attitudes, and behaviors that you want others, especially your employees, to copy. These are the things that you want others to see because they constitute what you, a positive role model, happen to be. Your personal list of traits to be emulated probably will differ somewhat from a listing established by another exceptional leader. That's not a problem. But many of those characteristics will appear on any positive role model's list. They almost certainly will include the following:

Credibility. Once fractured, a reputation for truthfulness is almost impossible to reconstruct fully. Half-truths and lying by omission are still lying. Your subordinates must know from experience that what you tell them is the whole truth.

Loyalty. That means unwavering loyalty to your organization, your subordinates, and your profession. As a loyal leader you will not betray or otherwise fail in any of these. You cannot expect loyalty from your followers unless you first demonstrate what loyalty looks and feels like.

Competence. You may not be a street cop anymore. Or at least most of the time you are not. Nonetheless, your people will expect you to have a street cop's sense and be able to comprehend what they are doing and why. They will expect you to be competent in a police officer's skills and be able to function in a first-line law enforcement officer's job, if required.

Courage. A chief who purports to be a positive role model has the fortitude to enter a darkened building in search of a bad guy. Your people will demand that of you. They also will expect that you have the intestinal fortitude to make the tough calls even when you know your decision will be unpopular or controversial. As you know, there is more than one kind of courage.

Sound decision-making. You look for it in your subordinates; they rightly expect the same of you. They require that your good judgment and decision-making skills will help keep them safe and out of trouble. Exceptional role models are exceptional decision-makers, too.

Honest and ethical. No one, especially a police leader, can serve as a positive role model without a rock-solid, proven reputation for integrity. You want your subordinates to see that your reputation for ethical and honest behavior prevails without exception whether you are on or off the job. As chief, you are never really off the job, anyway.

Empathetic and compassionate. A great role model displays both empathy and compassion in all of his or her interactions with others. This does not mean that he or she is a pushover. It simply means the leader possessing these traits can appreciate and respond appropriately to what someone else is feeling.

Fair. Your subordinates need to see that you are unbiased and fair in all of your actions, just as you expect the same of them. Impartiality in all of his or her dealings with others is a hallmark of a positive role model and a solid leader.

Forgiving. A positive role model and an exceptional leader is willing to let go of past errors and grievances as opposed to incessantly stewing over them or plotting revenge. Neither of the latter actions will result in good physical or mental health for the individual practicing them. It is possible to forgive without necessarily forgetting. That's what a good leader does.

Physical, mental, and emotional fitness. You want your officers to follow your lead in demonstrating for the public what their peacekeepers look, sound, and act like. You cannot expect your people to be excellent role models of all-around wellness if you fall short of that professional image yourself. You cannot afford to let yourself go in any of those areas.

Humble. Exceptional leaders are modest. They realize that the sun does not rise and set based upon what they do. They also realize that whatever success they may enjoy is based upon a team effort. They know that much of the organization's reputation for professionalism and effectiveness depends upon their employees. They have an expression in Texas that fits the situation here: "Never get too big for your britches." That applies to police chiefs, too!

Sense of humor. That may sound like an odd one, but it goes along nicely with remaining humble. You know that too many cops take themselves way too seriously, often to the detriment of their relations with others. You must reserve the right to laugh at yourself. As a positive role model, you have pledged never to become officious or badge heavy. You can and should expect the same of your people. After all, *appropriate* humor oftentimes can take the edge off a tense situation. Positive role models never lose the ability to laugh, particularly at themselves.

The list of traits you want to see in the people who are following you, their positive role model, could be practically endless. But the preceding list gets to the core of what an exceptional role model and leader is and does. It is the job of a leader to make more leaders. In serving as a positive role model, you are doing that. By adopting and nurturing the traits, skills, and abilities you model as an exceptional leader your followers can get there.

YOU ARE NEVER INVISIBLE

It can be tough being an "always on" role model. Hopefully you thought about that before you accepted the leadership position you now hold. But you can do this. As a positive role model, you must. Getting it done successfully depends upon remaining alert to both your actions and your environment at all times.

Whether you are engaged in a loud conversation with officers in the hallways of your police station or having an off-duty drink–or three–with a social companion in a local restaurant, as chief you are highly visible to everyone around you. Often you are being observed even when you are completely unaware of it. This informal "surveillance" even can extend a long way from the city limits of your own municipality. One small town chief, meeting with another police chief in a nearby, larger city learned that from the greetings he received from a whole restaurant full of citizens from his own town. His experience was not an unusual one.

You may have talked with your young officers about the need for always passing the "video test", on-duty or off-duty. The same test applies to you. If your behavior was being recorded for the world (and your people) to see, would you be proud of what the camera captured? As you well know, virtually every individual carries an audio and video recording device on his or her person these days. Your being always "on" has more than one meaning.

If you want to retain your moral authority to require always-appropriate conduct from your people, you must never fail to set a good example yourself. There are common sense things you can do to ensure that you are never placed in an untenable situation. It starts with your not being in a place you should not be in the first place. A bar where disturbances routinely break out offers a prime example. A cop party where somebody is likely to get a snootful and pick a fight—maybe with you—provides another one. Exercise your good judgment and common sense. If you are not someplace you shouldn't be doing something you shouldn't be doing, you will never have to worry about who might be observing (and recording) you.

More than one or two police leaders have lost their reputations and their jobs through off-duty stupidity. Your employer and your employees will show you very little forgiveness for obvious misbehavior, on-duty or off-duty. That's fair. You are, after all, expected to be a positive role model for your people and your community.

Over the years you have learned to practice good street survival skills, whether you are on or off the clock. You must also practice excellent *career* survival skills regardless of your duty status at the moment. By doing so you also will be serving as an excellent role model for your always-learning people.

NEVER CHEAT ON THE RULES

As a law enforcement officer you have a strong sense of justice. When you detect the presence of "double standards," you probably get irritated. It is a reasonable assumption that your people do, too. Like you, they expect fairness and a level playing field. As a consequence, you as the leader of your agency cannot do with impunity things you would punish your officers for doing. For you, there can be no bending of the rules. Not ever.

One ill-advised police chief routinely disciplined any officer who failed to attend mandatory training. Yet he almost never attended the training himself. His officers knew this and granted him little respect due to his duplicitous behavior. The chief had unwisely surrendered the moral high ground that an ethical leader must occupy at all times.

First: you cannot cheat on the rules–any rules–because doing so would be an unethical, dishonest thing to do. Second: the nature of your job as police chief practically guarantees that there will always be someone out there who wishes you ill. He or she would like nothing better than to hurt you by spreading the word about your alleged bad conduct. When you decline to cheat or otherwise behave badly you deny these individuals the ammunition they would love to use to harm you.

Simply put: Obey the law. Follow the rules. Pay your taxes on time. Don't kick the dog. Turn down the gift or favor that your agency's ethics rules do not permit you to accept. Don't cavort with people you know you should not be cavorting with. All these rules (and plenty more) a positive role model obeys. You are that positive role model.

DON'T FORGET HOW TO WORK THE STREET

If you are a working chief at a really small department, you probably won't have any problem working the street because you do it every day. If that is not your situation, it would be a very good idea for you to invest some time and energy in staying competent enough to meet the challenges of frontline police work.

Your officers will not expect you to be the best cop on the street, but they *will* expect you to have a cop's sense. They will expect that, when necessary, you can direct traffic, help control a resistive drunk, assist in securing a crime scene, or carry out the other basic duties normally performed by a Patrol officer or investigator. Many of your citizens will expect the same of you. The members of your community will not care if it's the greenest rookie or the police chief who happens by when they need help. They will desire that help to be competently and courteously delivered. They will expect more than a wave as you drive by.

To serve as a real cop when necessity calls you need to look and act like one. In one department the chief never wore a sidearm. His cops joked that he had probably forgotten where he left it. In another small agency the chief never wore a uniform unless he was attending a police funeral. Neither of these police bosses had cops that regarded them as positive role models. You do not want that to be the way you are viewed by your people.

As in the other aspects of your job, your intent must always be to set a good example for your people. Wear your sidearm. Wear the same uniform your Patrol officers wear, at least some of the time. Be sure that it, your other personal equipment, and your footwear look good. Ensure that your personal grooming meets the standards you set for your officers. Always display excellent officer safety practices. Set a positive example in your customer relations and courtesy towards others. You cannot expect your officers to treat those they encounter with compassion and professionalism unless you first set the example for doing it the right way. When you show up on a call or contact, ask your officers what you can do to help. Do not take over the call unless it is being very badly handled, however. Word will get around that the Boss is willing to help.

Never forget how to be a cop. Your officers will appreciate it, whether they ever tell you so or not. You will feel better about yourself as a bonus.

ADMIT IT WHEN YOU KNOW YOU ARE WRONG

Doing that is sometimes very hard to do, especially for a police chief who has something of an ego. On occasion it can feel even harder to apologize for a personal error. It is absolutely OK to do both. Even if you expect it of yourself, no one else expects you to be perfect. Be able to forgive yourself. Let those who are observing you see that you are intelligent enough to realize that you have erred and courageous enough to admit it. An honest apology is a part of the time-proven formula you should rely on to address a mistake:

- Admit it; apologize.
- Fix it, if possible.
- Learn from it.
- Don't repeat it.

The same good advice holds true if your actions or those of your department clearly have harmed a citizen. Americans are not accustomed to hearing sincere apologies from government officials. An apology from the chief may be all that is required to calm an agitated citizen. It can make that individual a lot easier to deal with. Be sure that an apology is truly merited before you go that route. Then, swallow your ego just a little and do the right thing.

LOOK AND SOUND LIKE WHAT YOU WANT YOUR PEOPLE TO COPY

Although some may be hesitant to admit it, most of your employees want to be proud of their department and their boss. It can happen that a chief does such a poor job of leadership that his or her people are literally embarrassed to admit that they work for that individual. That amounts to a disastrous state of affairs that you never want to be the cause of. Your officers want to see you as their strong, in-charge leader. They want to believe that you will lead them through when things get tough. They want to know that you are highly regarded in both the community and the profession. In short, they want to be able to brag that you are their chief.

If you want your people to think highly of you (and you should), you must be consistent in showing them what a compassionate, competent, courageous leader looks, sounds, and acts like. Pledge to yourself never to fall short of that goal. If you stumble on occasion, be quick to admit it and offer an apology if one is appropriate. When you are honestly content with who and what you are as a leader, chances are that your small department subordinates will be equally satisfied.

SUMMARY

As the formal, appointed leader of your police department you have no greater obligation than to serve as an exceptional role model for those you would lead. You must set the example for what you would have your subordinates be and do. You expect a lot of yourself, and your people expect it of you, too. You cannot afford to let them down.

As a positive role model, you will say and do what you want your employees to copy. You will want them to follow the example you set for credibility, courage, competence, loyalty, compassion, and ethical behavior. You will expect them to follow your example of working safely while treating others with respect. Even as you recognize their differences and individual personalities you will hope that those observing you will want to be at least a bit like you. There is nothing wrong with that.

As a positive role model, you will never forget that you and your behavior are always on display. As a result, you will endeavor to pass the "video test" and follow the pertinent laws and rules at all times. You will never forget how to be a real cop and offer hands-on assistance to your officers, when required. You always will strive to do things right and never hesitate to admit your mistakes when you fall short. You will not do anything that you would punish your employees for doing.

In short, you always will perform as the exceptional leader you are. By that act alone you will serve as a very positive role model for those most important to you: your officers and the members of your community.

Chapter 6

BUILDING A POSITIVE RELATIONSHIP WITH YOUR PEOPLE

It is certainly true that your working relationship with your boss will have a lot to with whether or not you succeed as a leader. But there is a special group of people that also will have a major impact on your effectiveness as the leader of a small law enforcement agency. That group is made up of your employees—the people who work for you.

Those who make up your top leadership—your command staff—have everything to do with translating your directions into actions. Without their active assistance you can jump up and down until your face turns purple and nothing much will happen. Equally important, however, are those who actually will carry out your directives: the first-line employees. These are the people who will do the police work upon which the effectiveness and reputation of your organization will depend.

People being people, it is doubtful that you ever will have the affection and active support of every single one of your employees. Very few police chiefs ever achieve that distinction. It will have to suffice that the vast majority of your people respect you and are willing to help you take the department where it is you want it to go. But first you will need to let them know where it is you are all headed. That's to be found in the mission and goals you establish for the organization. Your troops have to know exactly what these guidelines are. All of this will be part of what you must provide in building a positive relationship with your people at all levels of the organization.

YOUR LEADERSHIP TEAM IS KEY

No matter how great your abilities, you will need some help in moving the department in the direction you want it to go. You will require the assistance of your top managers who will share your vision of where you are all headed, as well as what is acceptable job performance and what is not. These people will be the members of your command staff, your top leadership team.

If you have come up from inside the department, you probably already know much about the character and abilities of each of these individuals. If you are coming from the outside, you will need to learn these things as quickly as possible.

Meet with your leadership staff as a group. See who contributes to the discussion and has good points to make. Meet with them individually, run your ideas and plans by them and get their reactions. You are not just looking for "yes" people. You are seeking intelligent individuals who can engage you in an intelligent fashion.

Unless you are saddled with one or more staffers who are clearly involved in unethical or even unlawful behavior, you would be unwise to start chopping off heads as soon as you take office. Take some time to assess your people. Listen to what they have to say. Observe how they interact with others, especially their subordinates. What do others have to say about them? (Warning: As you know by now, not everything you hear will turn out to be the unbiased truth.) Observe carefully and thoughtfully.

It is possible that you will inherit one or more top command personnel who wanted the job you now hold. Keep your feelers out for any lingering resentments or even open hostilities. If you do encounter a member of your top leadership team who obviously has it in for you for whatever reason, this is someone who well may fail to support your leadership or even seek to sabotage your efforts. This is a problem that oftentimes is unlikely to get better. You should have determined in conversation with your boss very early on how much authority he or she is willing to grant you in dealing with personnel issues. If you have ultimate authority utilize it now in a frank conversation with your recalcitrant staffer. If he or she cannot go with you or the program, that individual will have to go, preferably via a face-saving resignation or retirement. But go he or she must.

In a very large department, the chief may have the option of reassigning a non-performing upper management staff member to count airplanes at the airport. As a small department leader, you need to have all hands working at 100% all of the time. Check with your employer's Human Resources office and legal departments to be sure you do everything the right way. Then, seek to unburden yourself and your agency of an individual who cannot or will not lead in a constructive manner. Do it by the numbers and you are much less likely to be handed back a problem you thought you had shed.

If you do have to make changes in the makeup of your command staff, it is often a good idea to do it within the early months of your tenure, once you have sized up your staffers and the work they are producing. This is the period when people both inside and outside the department will anticipate change. Particularly if you have someone who cannot or will not support your agenda it is important to make the appropriate alterations in the starting lineup before your plans can be hampered or derailed by a bomb-thrower.

As you make changes in assignments now or later, remain mindful that most often you will need your strongest leader in Patrol. That is generally where the toughest and most frequent challenges will arise. Of course, if there are major issues elsewhere in your department, that is where your strongest leader should go. All of this is part of your effort to put the right people in the right seats on the bus, as Jim Collins would say. It also includes the harsh reality, previously noted, that one or more "riders" may have to get off the bus if your intent as the new driver is for the conveyance to reach its destination in one piece.

Extend every courtesy feasible to those you must let go. It goes back to the Golden Rule of leadership: treat others as you would want to be treated. You may want the same courtesies one day. Going away events are a big deal at most police departments. Assuming he or she is willing, arrange for a going away event for a departing staffer. If the individual is not interested, you have made a good faith effort.

Once you have your top staff in place, it is time to move ahead with your agenda. Be sure that these leaders know where you are going and what is expected of them. They will be responsible for helping you get the message out to the rest of your employees. Encourage your staffers to ask you clarifying questions. Get their ideas and input. Then, move ahead. Time is wasting.

You cannot hope to lead your police department successfully without the assistance of a loyal, solid command staff. These are the people you personally supervise, your "direct reports." No matter how talented and devoted to your job you are, you cannot do everything all by yourself. You will need these people, and you will need to know that they are doing their best. Share your plans with them. Get them the formal leadership training they need to excel. Always serve as an exceptional role model for them. If you seek their loyalty, be sure that you always treat them well. Coach and mentor them, as required. Take care of them. Be fair but hold accountable. Don't murder them when they make mistakes, as they will. Ensure that they have the tools and other resources they need to carry out the tasks you have given them. Supervise and lead them as they seek to excel. Be prepared to step back and get out of the way when it appears that they are ready to forge ahead in following your plans.

GET TO KNOW YOUR PEOPLE

As the leader of a small police agency, you have at least one advantage over the chiefs of departments employing hundreds if not thousands of cops: it is a lot easier to get to know your people, perhaps on a first-name basis. At least as important, your people get to know you and what you are all about. That is a good thing.

It's practically traditional for a new chief to hold one or more all hands meeting with his or her employees. That's a good idea and it helps everyone get at least an early snapshot of the new boss. Many new chiefs invite their personnel to come talk with them one-on-one to share their ideas and gripes. Fewer new bosses actually follow up the invitation. Extend the invitation more than once if you must in order to get results. Be sure to do an excellent job of listening without interrupting or pontificating when employees take you up on your invitation. The word will get around pretty quickly that the new boss is (or isn't) willing to listen. That will have a big impact on just how much your people will talk with you in the future. Listen attentively. First of all, that's what smart and considerate leaders do. Second, what you learn will help you learn a lot about the organization and its people that you are now responsible for.

Do not restrict yourself just to talking with your people within the confines of your office. Whether they will admit it or not, many cops like to see the Chief out on the street from time to time. Do not restrict yourself to riding along during the daylight hours. As one senior chief put it: "It's amazing what will come out of someone's mouth at two o'clock in the morning." Avail yourself of the information that is out there. Talk–and especially listen–to your people. A lot.

SUPPORT YOUR PEOPLE BUT DON'T PANDER

One more of your most important tasks is to support your police personnel. How you do it is important, too. Obviously, you talk about how good your people are, no matter what forum you happen to be in at the moment. It is also vital that you do your best to answer whatever questions come from the public regarding something your officers did or didn't do. Often non-police individuals do not comprehend the how and why of your profession, no matter how many TV cop shows and on-line videos they have watched. They may have a grossly inaccurate picture of what police work is really like. It is up to you to help educate them for the sake of your employees. This holds true whether you are conversing with Ralph the Rag Man or Hizzoner the Mayor. Be tactful. Tell the truth. But do defend your people when it is appropriate to do so.

Of course, supporting your people does not mean sheltering them when they have done wrong. Listen courteously and carefully to an aggrieved citizen's story of events. Ask some clarifying questions, if you need to. Promise to get back to the person after you have checked carefully into the matter. Then, honor your promise after you have completed your inquiry. If your cops have done nothing wrong, tactfully explain that fact. If your people have erred in one way or another, acknowledge the mistake and give the citizen an idea of what you are going to do about it. For example: "I'm sorry that we did not handle that as well as we should have. You have my apology on behalf of the Department. We are going to use this as a learning experience for our folks and do some training to ensure that it doesn't happen again." Do not forget to thank the individual for bringing the situation to your attention, regardless of the outcome. You cannot fix what you do not know about.

Always speak up loudly and clearly for your officers' needs. But to maintain credibility with your boss, first be sure the needs are legitimate ones. Sometimes that will get down to "need to have" versus "nice to have." Very few towns and cities have sufficient funds to fulfill every desire their first responders can come up with. Do not expend political currency or nail any of your key body parts to the wall over "wants" that are neither critical nor realistic. Keep your reputation for credibility with your boss intact for those occasions when a need truly *is* critical.

You always want to advocate for the real needs and concerns of those who depend upon you as their leader. That's what good leaders do. But you never want to leave the person that you work for with the impression that your primary goal for your actions is to secure the affection of your subordinates, perhaps at the expense of the other employees of your city or town. Pandering and support are not the same thing. You must never confuse the two.

WATCH YOUR COMMENTS ABOUT "CHANGING THE CULTURE"

The stark truth is that, in more than a few cases, you were selected for your leadership position because a person or persons in authority felt that the culture of the police department *did* need changed, or at least tweaked a bit. You are, in fact, expected to alter the culture, perhaps just a little, maybe a whole lot.

The definition of "culture" can vary considerably depending upon who is doing the defining. A good, common sense definition might refer to culture as "a group-shared body of beliefs, ethics, informal rules or understandings, and language." It can get more complicated than that, of course, but the group's "beliefs and informal rules or understandings" can prove key to explain what is happening in your department. The core of all this is the determination of what is acceptable and unacceptable behavior to most if not all of your people. What is to be praised or rewarded and what will result in either formal or informal sanctions, including powerful peer pressure? Culture plays a big role in determining that. You will be seeking to learn these things through your personal observations and inquiries in the department of which you are the new head.

You very likely have been placed in your position to make some changes. Some may be very minor; others may feel drastic to the ones they affect the most: your employees. Even if everything appears to be functioning pretty smoothly, you doubtlessly are going to want to change *something* in the department that you are now 100% responsible for. You are going to do that while being careful not to implement change more quickly than your people can handle it.

Most if not all of your people are proud of their organization, even if they may verbally blast it from time to time. While they may or may not think of it in terms of culture, they do think of the ways things are, what they do, and *who* they are. When you come in, particularly as an outside chief, and announce that you are going to change the culture, you well may be offending many of your people. They may interpret your culture change proclamation as saying that they, or at least some of what they have been doing, are not good enough. This easily can prove offensive even to employees who recognize the need for change and would otherwise support you in accomplishing it.

One new chief was greeted early in his tenure by this comment from a long-term employee: "Please don't tell us we need to change the culture, Chief. We have a good culture here. It's just that a few of us have forgotten it." The officer was right. The agency's primary problems arose from unethical and immoral behavior by a small handful of employees. Instead of broadcasting a statement that would come across as an agency-wide condemnation, the new leader focused his efforts on the problem-causers and over time witnessed the needed change in behavior take place department-wide. This he accomplished without ever referring publicly to "culture." But beware. Change will not occur overnight. Be consistent as well as patient and settle in for the long-haul. In time, you will begin to see the results you must have.

The message for you in all of this? Do whatever you need to do to shore up any areas in which you find less-than-stellar performance, whatever the challenge happens to be. Just don't descend from the mountain and show off the stone tablets you have labelled "culture change."

STAY OUT FRONT DURING TROUBLED TIMES

The members of your community and the members of your department want you to be a high-visibility leader. Visible as a leader for all the right reasons, not in the news because of some ethical error you committed. Your people in particular need to see you as the strong leader of the department, not someone who only surfaces on Groundhog Day.

If things are not going well, if the department is front page news because of some kind of alleged misconduct, such as a questionable officer-involved use of force, it is absolutely vital that you are the one speaking for the agency. It is your job to face the cameras, microphones, and insistent reporters and self-appointed police experts who already have decided that the cops are in the wrong. This is not the time to send a Public Information Officer or some other member of your department out to face the music. This is *your* job. Your cops will not be favorably impressed if it looks like you are hiding out, to say nothing of what the news media and the general public will think and say.

This is not a one-and-done affair for you. You must remain out front and readily accessible until the crisis passes. Speak for your officers and agency, but speak only the truth. Remain visible throughout the period of tumult, but be careful of issuing proclamations until you are sure that you have got it right. Remain very visibly in charge.

Again: remain highly visible and easily accessible, especially to your own people. State as fact only what you know for sure to be factual. Keep a positive outlook and hopeful demeanor in front of your people. Make clear that you are not running away, and never will. Stay out front. Perform as the exceptional leader you are.

NEVER MAKE YOURSELF INACCESSIBLE

Most everyone has an occasional day when he or she feels overwhelmed or otherwise out of sorts and just does not want much human interaction. That is not abnormal so long as it doesn't become ingrained as a habit. But as the leader of your employees, you cannot afford to allow those times to come very often.

Your people need to see you around the station and–on occasion–on the street. Most want to know that they can approach you without the wrath of God descending upon them, either from you or someone else. They need to know that they can converse with the Big Boss, whether the topic of the conversation is about football, kids, or how unhappy they are with something work-related. Naturally, if your employee is talking with you about a work-related issue, it is fair to ask him or her if a supervisor is in the loop. As a first-line leader, you probably were not too happy when a subordinate went around you to get to the boss. Your subordinate leaders very likely feel the same way. Endeavor to see that they are kept in the loop, ideally by the same employee who just reached out to you.

In remaining accessible to your personnel, make some extra effort to stay in touch with your late nights crew. Some of those folks may already assume that they are the forgotten orphans from the dark. It is important that they realize that they have access to the chief, too. If it means coming in early or staying late on occasion, the extra effort should be worth it for the additional exposure it brings you. It is especially vital that you show up on occasion when there is nothing special going on. That way your appearance will not be automatically associated with a problem or crisis of some kind. There is also a lot of value for *you* in these off-hours interactions. You may get a whole different perspective on departmental affairs from your Night Stalkers. It's definitely worth the extra effort.

YOUR PEOPLE ARE ALWAYS THE BEST

It is important enough that it's worth saying yet again. Your people need to hear directly from you that you are proud of them. Certainly you can and should offer sincere praise in their presence. But it is just as important that you talk about how good they are in various venues around the community. Make it a habit to do so. Word of what you are doing will get back to your employees, just as it will if you are saying derogatory things about your people or your department. The mandate to utter positive comments publicly remains in effect even if you—or your people—have had a bad day. It's important that you let people know that any negative happenings are an aberration. It is not what you and your people are all about.

Commendatory texts and e-mails from you are great and will be appreciated by most of your people. One-on-one, in-person kudos can be even more effective. Most normal human beings want to hear from someone important to them that they have done a good job. That someone should be you.

Praise for your officers should not be confined to within the walls of your department. The elected and appointed officials who make the big decisions—especially the budgetary ones—inside your city or town hall need to hear about the good work being done by your officers. Sometimes city and town managers become accustomed to hearing only complaints ("We have to get the pay up before everybody quits!")

from their police chiefs. Be sure that these decision-makers are exposed to a steady diet of news of the exceptional work turned in by your people. Your not-so-subtle message: Their cops are worth that boost in salary.

Your people are always the best. Let them know that.

LITTLE THINGS ARE IMPORTANT

You want to be seen by your people as something more than the man or woman at the top of the organization chart. You want them to see you as a decent, caring human being, too. You accomplish that goal by living your life and doing your job as the ethical, compassionate professional you are. By treating everyone fairly you contribute to that earned reputation. But there is even more that you can do.

Remembering the personal touches, acts that show people you care, will help cement that reputation. Personal touches can cover a lot of ground, but often included are personal notes or cards from the Chief to an officer who has done a good job with an investigation, arrest, or project. Some chiefs also send cards on employees' birthdays or employment anniversary dates. Naturally, if an officer has a birth, serious illness, or death in the family the Chief also needs to reach out. Be sure that your organization's subordinate supervisors know that they are to keep you advised of such happenings.

Funerals are important. If an employee has suffered a death in his or her immediate family, give very serious consideration to representing your department for the services, assuming it is within reasonable traveling distance. The same naturally holds true for current or retired members of your own department as well as those of close-by police agencies. Oftentimes, with funerals it works like this: You may or may not be given credit for being there. But it is even more likely to be held against you if you are not. Besides, showing up is the *right* thing to do.

One chief takes each new employee to lunch on his or her first day of employment with the department. Another over-achieving police boss makes it a point to learn the first names of every employee's spouse and kids. Yet another personally presents the department's challenge coin to each new hire. Of course, every organization is different. Apply your imagination in thinking about little personal touches that you may be able to apply in your own agency. Whatever special attention you come up with is almost certain to be appreciated by your people. And the special touches *do* matter. A small department chief reports that his people almost universally opined that the boss's notes didn't mean all that much. But later, during his wanderings through the department, the chief discovered that a number of his missives were posted on the desk bulletin boards and locker doors of his officers. Yes, the little things are very much worth doing.

SUMMARY

It has happened that chiefs who had great plans for leading their departments were shown the door before having the opportunity to fully implement their plans. Sometimes it happened because of a major, personal misstep. Other times the invited departure occurred due to events beyond the chief's control or due to that familiar, old nemesis: politics. But too often it happened because of poor relations between the chief and his or her employees. That is something that you as a caring, savvy leader should never permit to happen.

Getting along reasonably well with your people is absolutely within your abilities. It requires the willingness on your part to treat your followers in the way you want to be treated by your own boss: with empathy, fairness, accessibility, and common courtesy. At the same time, you also will provide your people with your example of what a police officer and a true leader should look, act, and sound like.

In working to maintain a positive working relationship with your people you will strive for respect, not affection. (Consider it a bonus if you get that, too!) You will be out front during tough times. You will recognize the importance of officer safety practices and good equipment and ensure that each are present in your department. You will meet with your people and listen to their ideas and concerns. You will be sure that your expectations of them are both reasonable and clear. You also will remember the "little things," like sending words of commendation or sympathy, as appropriate. You will remain friendly, courteous, and approachable to all, but you will never overdo it and come across as insincere.

Your police department's success will happen because of the human support structure you have constructed to bolster your own capable leadership. The positive relationship you have nurtured with your people will help ensure that you have built that framework strong.

Chapter 7

HOW TO WORK FOR SOMEONE

There is little doubt that you will have a lot of priorities during your tenure as chief of a small law enforcement agency. Few are more important than maintaining an excellent working relationship with your boss. That relationship will have a lot to do with whether or not you succeed as the leader of your department. That reality remains true whether you work for a mayor, town administrator, city manager, or board of elected officials.

The good news for you is that there are things you can do to help ensure that the working relationship is a mutually supportive and effective one. That kind of relationship should help you remain in your position long enough to take your department where you want it to go. It also may help you ensure that you eventually leave your position on *your* time schedule and *your* terms. Here are some ideas for helping turn those career plans into reality.

WHAT YOU OWE YOUR BOSS

As chief there are things that you expect of your subordinates. It should come as no surprise that your boss has similar expectations of you. There may be certain things that are important to your supervisor above all else. You may be able to identify some of them through observing what he or she says and does. Beyond that and in addition to remaining alert to those things there exist some time-proven "boss relationship" rules that are pretty much universal, no matter who you are working for or where you are working. They include the following:

Do not surprise or embarrass your boss. This is one more of those cardinal rules. You would not appreciate your people letting either of these things happen to you. Your own boss won't like it, either. Endeavor to do nothing, on-duty or off-duty, that will bring embarrassment upon your leader. Bringing embarrassment or shame to your boss and your organization will not bode well for your continued employment. If, in spite of your best efforts, you cause embarrassment to your supervisor anyway, be quick with an explanation and an apology. Try hard to reach your boss with the bad news before someone else does. Your displayed openness and personal accountability may help you survive the foul-up.

Over-inform your boss, at least until you get a feel for what he or she wants to know about. If you think that a crime, incident, or personnel issue in your department is apt to come to your supervisor's attention, be sure you put him or her in the know, once again before anyone else does. It is the right thing to do, and it will help preserve your boss's faith in your loyalty and credibility.

Share credit for your successes with your boss. You have heard it before: never hesitate to share the credit. That includes sharing it with your boss, even if he or she had very little to do with it. Once again, you are banking relationship currency for future interaction with your leader. If, for example, the number of serious vehicle crashes goes down because you were permitted to invest in some additional traffic law enforcement resources, give the boss some credit when you are citing the improved traffic safety picture. Do not award credit to the extent that it strains credibility ("Thanks to the boss, we have beautiful clear skies today!"), but give it when it is even remotely deserved.

Prove you can be believed and trusted. Your credibility is among your most precious assets as a leader. Your reputation for integrity from your boss's point of view will be established through your supervisor's observation that you always tell him or her the truth. You additionally must steer clear of half-truths and lying by omission. You earn your boss's trust by demonstrating personal integrity in everything you say and do. You will keep in confidence those things that your boss tells you are to be kept confidential. You are smart enough to realize that trust, once compromised, may be virtually impossible to rebuild.

Never show fear or self-doubt. Your boss wants to know that he or she can count on you to be an immovable rock when crisis strikes. The boss wants to know that you will keep your head when everyone else is losing theirs. He or she wants to be able to turn to you for advice and support when things get scary. And the boss wants you to accomplish all of this without ever displaying panic or even uncertainty. As far as your boss is concerned, you are his or her safe port in a storm. You may have to call upon your best acting skills to do it, but you must always convey to your supervisor the picture of a confident, in-control, courageous leader who has things well in hand or will have, shortly. After all, you are the police chief!

Let your boss know you will take care of him or her. As noted, your boss wants to know that he or she can turn to you for help when things get dicey. He or she wants to know that you will be absolutely loyal to your supervisor, so long as your leader is not doing something unethical or unlawful. One small department chief observed that his relatively young city manager was getting visibly quite tense while he and his department heads were meeting in the Emergency Operations Center during a flooding event. After the others left the room, the chief walked over, put his hand on the shoulder of his supervisor, and said: "Don't worry, Boss. Your A-Team is here. We got this." The man visibly relaxed. It may sound corny or even contrived, but it worked. Something similar could work for you and your boss under similar circumstances.

Don't hesitate to volunteer. Maybe a well-intentioned individual once told you never to volunteer for anything. If so, it is not good advice for a police chief. Your supervisor is looking for someone to make his or her life better. If you can do that by taking on a task for your supervisor, you have just put more currency in the bank for your boss relations account. Depending upon the work for which you volunteered, you may be educating yourself towards doing your boss's job one day. At the very least, you may be a more competent leader as a result of your volunteering to do something that you now know more about.

Don't be seen by your boss as pandering to your employees. As the police chief you sometimes will find yourself walking a fine line between your employees and your supervisor. You obviously want your people to know that you earnestly represent and support them in all of their legitimate needs. This is a vital role for you and one that will earn you the trust of your employees if they know that you truly care about their welfare. The key for you is not to go so far in advocating for every single thing that your people desire that you lose credibility with your supervisor. One city manager said this about a departed chief who had been immensely popular with his officers: "His cops would ask him for four bazookas and he would turn around and ask me for eight. I knew what he was doing, and I didn't appreciate it." Ouch. Represent your people well. Ask them what they truly need and advocate for it. But do not overdo. You cannot help your employees if you are no longer in a position to do so.

Do not worry excessively about what your boss is thinking. Naturally, you want to please your boss. You want him or her to have a high opinion of you and your decision-making abilities. Indeed, it would be helpful for you to know what your boss is thinking. But there is a limit to how much effort you should put into that endeavor. An insecure chief could worry so much about what the boss was thinking that paralysis in the chief's decisions and actions sets in. You are not insecure. *Do* stay aware to the extent reasonably possible what your supervisor's thoughts are on topics that pertain to you and the department you lead. But never concern yourself so deeply with your boss's thought processes that you can no longer make decisions or take action in a timely, confident manner. A good boss will expect that of you. You should expect it of yourself.

There is at least one more thing that you owe your boss. You need to show him or her that you are a good *follower*. You are clearly a good leader. But a good leader is also a good follower. Followership is sometimes defined as the ability to take direction well, support a program or goal, be a contributing member of an effective team, and deliver what the leader expects.

A good follower exhibits a number of qualities. They include:

- Good judgment
- Solid work ethic
- Absolute integrity
- Personal courage
- Unquestioned loyalty to a cause or organization
- Ego management
- Professional competence

In other words, a good follower displays many of the same traits expected of an outstanding leader. And that person is you.

An exceptional follower assists the leader by volunteering his or her talents to help the leader accomplish tasks or goals. A good follower shows willingness to take on tough assignments. This same follower demonstrates loyalty, but not blind loyalty, to the leader, team, project, and the larger organization. That follower maintains a positive attitude under stress and never ceases to function effectively as an active team member. He or she offers suggestions for improvements or positive change and serves as a knowledgeable resource for the team leader. He or she consistently displays an upbeat, "can do" attitude. The talented follower shows personal courage when faced with opposition or other difficulty. Finally, the exceptionally talented follower strives to maintain a strong, trusting relationship with his or her leader.

You are already a competent leader. By serving as a loyal and supportive follower you have added yet another competency to your leadership profile.

WHAT YOUR BOSS OWES YOU

Your boss has a right to expect a lot from the person who holds arguably the most sensitive, important position in his or her leadership corps. But that street runs both ways. It is reasonable for you to have some expectations, too. Almost certainly your boss realizes that. None of this means that on your first day on the job you present your supervisor with a list of your boss requirements. (Actually, that would be a really *bad* idea.) You should, however, remain alert to your boss's behavior to see if some things that a good boss exhibits and does are in evidence in your own supervisor-supervised relationship.

As you know from your experience as a seasoned leader and boss, a good supervisor serves as an exceptional role model for his or her people. He or she tells the truth and lets employees know where the organization is going and how it's going to get there. A good boss also has faith in his or her employees and lets them know when they have done well. A good boss praises in public and corrects in private. That same good boss coaches and mentors his or her people. The exceptional boss looks out for the welfare of his or her employees and truly cares about them. You do all these things as the leader of your people. It is not too much to expect them from the individual you report to. If you find after careful observation that too many of these things are missing, you may want to re-evaluate whether or not you want to continue to work for this individual. That would indeed be a drastic solution to the problem. But you owe yourself a positive working environment where you can lead and prosper.

At the same time, however, remember that you, too, have a major role to play in the supervisor-supervised relationship. Be open with your boss. If you have questions or concerns about what he or she expects, tactfully voice them—at the appropriate time and place. As life experience has taught you, failed communications and simple misunderstandings have resulted in long-running feuds and ill feelings. International wars have started from the same causes. Do your part to see to it that similar battles do not erupt between you and your supervisor from a simple failure to communicate and comprehend. You and your boss each have too much at stake to let that happen.

THE RELATIONSHIP YOU ARE SEEKING

The ideal supervisor-supervised relationship you want to establish with your boss should be one of mutual trust, understanding, and support. That's a must for any important relationship to work well. If you and your supervisor actually like each other, consider that a bonus.

Your boss probably hired you for the same reason you hire people: to make the organization run as smoothly and problem-free as possible. That will, at the same time, make the boss's life better. When his or her telephone or e-mail is not lighting up with policing issues and complaints, his or her life *is* better. These are the things your boss wants *you* to handle.

Your goal of improving your boss's life does not require you to do anything that you would not already be doing as an ethical, effective leader. You will display loyalty to your leader, tell him or her the truth, and avoid gossiping about the boss or criticizing your supervisor's decisions behind his or her back. You will carry out the assignments your boss gives you in a timely manner and ensure that they are done right. You will keep your boss advised of important events in the police department or community that you become aware of. You will seek to over-inform rather than the opposite. You will defend your boss and his or her appropriate policies and decisions in discussions with others, even when those "others" turn out to be police employees who may have a less-than-clear picture of whatever issue is at hand. It will be your task to provide whatever clarification you can for them.

You are aware, or should be, that you are responsible for capably and ethically leading the department that has the most potential for causing the most issues for the average town or city manager. That puts considerable pressure on you to do your job well. Hopefully you considered that when you accepted the chief's badge. If not, you must be conscious of the responsibility now.

None of this requires that you do anything inappropriate to support or cover up for a boss who has done or asked you to do anything improper. You do not cheat for your boss or otherwise bend the rules for him or her. One small town chief went to jail because he thought it was a good idea to engage in unlawful electronic eavesdropping upon his mayor's electoral opponent, at the politician's request. More often, however, "favors" that the small department chief may be asked to deliver will not reach quite that level of gravity. Nonetheless, the boss doesn't get his buddy's ticket "fixed" or have a less-than-laudatory police report concerning the city manager's relative vanish from departmental records. That's not what taking care of the boss is all about.

If you feel that your boss is asking for a "favor" that would amount to unethical or unlawful behavior on your part if you granted it, your response should be the same as if some other local notable asked you to do something similar. It might go something like this: "Boss, I know you would never ask me to do anything you knew to be improper. If I did that for you it could get both of us in serious trouble. One of my jobs is to protect you. That's why we can't do that." Or something along those lines. Most bosses will get it and desist. Regardless, stand your moral ground. It's that important.

Your boss very likely brought you aboard for the same reason you hire people: to take some worries off his or her back and smooth out any rough spots. You meet those requirements when you are keeping your department functioning smoothly and your boss is not getting a lot of complaints about the police department. That is making your leader's life better. Again: a relationship of mutual trust, loyalty, and support between you and your supervisor is what you are seeking. It gets even better if the two of you develop a genuine liking for each other in the process. That makes for a truly positive working relationship.

ALL KINDS OF BOSSES

As your work life probably has taught you by now, the world is populated by all varieties of bosses. The good ones range from the really exemplary to the practically saintly. The not-so-good types stretch from the simply irritating to the virtually venomous. Most, of course, can be placed somewhere on the scale between the extremes. Every supervisor you have ever worked for is at least a little different from all the others. It will be up to you to identify as early in the relationship as possible your leader's priorities, hot buttons, interests, and eccentricities.

You also may be able to identify some boss characteristics and leadership style based upon his or her age and level of experience. Sometimes an older, more experienced leader is more assured of himself or herself. This boss may be quite set in his or her ways and what he or she expects of subordinates. Some city and town bosses are not interested in every detail of what is going on in the police department and only want to be notified of major happenings. (It will be your responsibility to determine what your boss considers "major.") The young or less-experienced manager sometimes will require more of your attention. This boss may worry a lot that a crisis or scandalous event will somehow result in his or her termination. That boss is likely aware that police departments tend to produce more than their share of crises and "issues." He or she may want to know much more about the goings on in your department. You may need regularly to reassure him or her that you have things under control and it is going to be alright. Do not hesitate to do that but without sounding like you are talking down to someone who is afraid or unknowledgeable. Your goal is to inform and comfort so that your supervisor is suitably equipped to support and defend you and your people, if need be.

Of course, generalizing always has its attendant risks. The "old lion" boss could turn out to be a nervous house cat; the new kid could be extremely self-assured and comfortable in his or her role. By carefully observing your boss in action and listening to what he or she has to say you should be able to learn a lot. By getting to know your supervisor well you will be better able to identify his or her strengths, challenges, peculiarities, and interests. That knowledge should enable you to provide your boss with the help he or she needs to do his or her job with confidence and competence. That in itself should contribute to a mutually supportive supervisor-supervised relationship.

SURVIVING THE "DIFFICULT" BOSS

First of all, you should not begin a relationship with your supervisor by assuming that the association is going to be a difficult one. (You've heard about self-fulfilling prophecies!) Instead, look on the bright side and assume that things will go well. They probably will, to one extent or another. Virtually every relationship, personal or professional, has its rough moments. With a little patience and some extra effort on the part of both parties very often those breakdowns can be repaired. But what do you do if that benevolent state of affairs appears beyond reach?

Bad boss behavior can be displayed in any number of ways. Some bad bosses lie routinely. Others belittle their employees or embarrass them in public. Some play favorites and mercilessly pick on whomever they deem to be particularly vulnerable. Some lack the backbone to do the right thing, and perhaps show no sign of knowing what the right thing is. Yet others permit or actually engage in discrimination or sexual harassment. And others take all the credit for good work done by their subordinates and seldom utter praise for the excellent work done by their people. Bad bosses have been known to commit all these offenses and others. There appears to be no limit to the organizational havoc that these characters can wreak.

Some of your colleagues have attempted to deal with bad bosses by avoiding them. That may work to a limited extent, but eventually you are going to have to meet with and talk with your boss, however obnoxious he or she may be. Others have worked to learn the boss's hot buttons, whether they happen to relate to politics or a request for something. Again, that may work for a time, but eventually that hot topic (such as a request for funds) will have to be broached. And a few of your peers simply have decided that they could not work for that poisonous a personality and quit their jobs, thereby removing their needed leadership skills from their department.

Clearly the decision on the action to take if you are saddled with a truly bad boss is yours to make. Before taking a more drastic approach you may want to try a solution that has sometimes worked for others. You may have successfully applied it yourself. Try talking with your boss in a private, quiet, nonthreatening manner when there is nothing urgent going on. As hard as it may be to believe, some bad bosses don't *know* that they are bad bosses. In some instances, they may have worked for a leader who yelled, bullied, or otherwise mistreated his or her employees. Your boss may think that is just normal boss behavior and doesn't see anything wrong with it. By gently confronting the behavior you may be able to at least mitigate it.

It might start like this: "Boss, I respect you a lot and I know you would never intentionally do anything to hurt me. But when you ________________ (fill in the blank, as appropriate), it really hurts. I know you don't mean to put me down and I know you'd want me to tell you the truth about how I feel." There. The boss didn't *mean* to do it. He or she is really a good person whom you respect. It was all a misunderstanding. The boss is thereby given a face-saving way out if he or she wants to take it. No, it won't work every time. But it won't fail every time, either. Even if your supervisor expresses surprise and denies the existence of a problem, you may nonetheless see a change in behavior. As you know, people can alter how they act towards others without ever acknowledging that they may have been at fault. Things may get better, a little or a lot. You have to decide if confronting the boss issue is a good idea when balanced against what you know about your leader. In truth, however, it is unlikely that unchallenged bad boss behavior is going to get better.

You will not be proud of yourself if you do not make at least some effort to change disruptive or just plain unpleasant actions by your supervisor. By recognizing and then diplomatically confronting his or her shortcomings you may be able to mitigate bad boss conduct. And there are other things you can do. You may, for example, learn from your observations that there are particularly bad times to bring a problem to the boss's attention (Monday at 8 a.m., for instance). You can then plan accordingly. And there's this: If your boss truly is a bad leader, there is a good chance that you are not the only one who has noticed. By doing your own job well and not being driven off by bad boss behavior you may outlast him or her.

There is a lesson for you in all of this. If you have ever worked for a bad boss, you know what it feels like. That knowledge should aid you in resolving never to visit bad boss behavior on your own subordinates.

DETERMINE WHAT YOUR BOSS KNOWS ABOUT POLICING

Some city and town managers, often the most experienced ones, have been around law enforcement and law enforcement personnel long enough to know something about the profession and culture.

Others, sometimes the newest managers, do not. Some managers are willing, even eager, to learn more. Yet others are not terribly interested in law enforcement and will leave it almost entirely up to you to handle the department and its accompanying worries.

Through your interaction with your boss, you should be able to find out how much your supervisor knows about your work, and *wants* to know. It will be beneficial to you and your employees if your boss has at least a basic grasp (beyond what he or she sees on the TV cop shows) of what police and police chiefs do, and why. You do not want to directly question your boss about his or her policing knowledge, of course. And you don't want to force feed your supervisor or make it appear that you are trying to educate him or her, although that is in fact what you are doing. But do take every opportunity to answer questions and share your knowledge with your supervisor.

Do not hesitate to gently challenge obviously incorrect impressions your boss may have about your work. One new city manager could not grasp why his cops needed four-wheel drive patrol vehicles, even though his city was exposed to extreme winter weather conditions. His chief was eventually able to convince him of the necessity. Another new chief recalled having some early "intense" discussions with his boss because the manager expressed the view that the police department was too picky, perhaps even arrogant, in its hiring process. Over time, the chief was able to demonstrate the problems his predecessor had brought to the police department through a careless officer selection process. The manager admitted that he now understood the need for a careful hiring process.

You will be helping your supervisor do a better job by gently and gradually increasing his or her knowledge of law enforcement and law enforcement people. At the same time you will make it more likely that you will have your boss's vital support when policing issues are the focus of attention.

SUMMARY

Being unable to work with their boss is a leading cause of why small department police chiefs lose their job. Understanding what your own boss expects from you is critical to surviving and prospering in your role as police chief. None of that means that you should ever do anything unethical or unlawful to back your supervisor. Far from it. But by displaying loyalty and supporting your boss in his or her legitimate goals and decisions you are doing what a reliable and trustworthy subordinate does.

You know the most important rules for working for someone. Tell him or her the unvarnished truth. Do not subject your boss to surprises or embarrassments of your making. Share with your supervisor the kudos you earn for doing a good job. Never publicly criticize your supervisor or in any other way display disloyalty. Always give him or her your best work. Determine what your boss knows about policing and fill in the gaps for him or her when necessary.

Honest, open dialogue between you and your supervisor can solve many supervisor-supervised issues. By directly but diplomatically confronting boss problems you may be able to reduce them to tolerable ones or even remove them entirely. In the end you will have to decide if the resultant working relationship is an acceptable one.

The good word for you is that very few bosses are impossible to work for. Like police chiefs, most city and town managers and mayors are pretty good people. Odds are that you can help each other succeed.

Establishing a positive working relationship with your boss is critical to your success as a police chief. It will not always be easy. But as an effective leader you are quite capable of getting it done.

Chapter 8

YOUR ROLE IN THE COMMUNITY

Like it or not, you are now a community leader. You are the police chief. People are going to seek your opinion on everything from how to raise semi-domesticated teenagers to the death penalty, and every topic in between. You are going to be invited to all kinds of local events. Civic clubs and churches may seek your membership. You might get asked to pen a piece for the local newspaper or be a guest on a radio talk show. You are a highly visible member of your community. You will have to conduct your off-duty as well as on-duty behavior accordingly.

As a consequence of your position as leader of the police department in your city or town you will be ideally positioned to do a great deal of good for your organization. The opposite also holds true. It is up to you to see to it that you are bringing only credit and support to your police department. By serving as a positive and admirable community leader you also will be garnering support for your department and yourself. Obviously, you cannot do good things for your department if you are no longer employed there.

Some chiefs are quick to confess that they are introverts who would much prefer going home and watching television over appearing at yet another community event. That is OK. There are some not-too-difficult things you can do to become extrovert-enough to ably meet the challenge of being a "leading light" of your community.

STAY INVOLVED

To be successful as the head of the police department you must ensure that your employees and your community have good cause to view you as a leader. They need to see you not as a faceless bureaucrat but as a real person who does good things for your community and department alike. But none of these people will see you as a leader if they don't see you at all. That means that you have to "get out there." A lot.

Whether you are a new chief or a veteran leader, you must stay engaged with your community to the full extent that you can while still leaving vital personal time for yourself and your loved ones. But beware: in many communities the chief can attend an after-hours event every day of the week, including weekends. Realize that you will have to send regrets sometimes. It is also important that you protect your own physical and mental health by getting enough "down" time. One veteran chief from a small department put it this way: "At least every 90 days you need to take some extra time off just to keep from going crazy." It might amount to good advice for you, even as you strive to remain closely involved in your community.

ADVOCATE FOR YOUR VERSION OF COMMUNITY-ORIENTED POLICING

There may be as many varieties of community-oriented policing as there are law enforcement agencies in this country. Over the years the definition of this common sense mode of policing has grown wider and wider. A department may put a cop on a bike and call it community-oriented policing. Another may buy a dog that the kids can pet without being eaten and call *that* community-oriented policing. And both departments may be right, to one extent or the other.

As long as you and your officers are working to interact proactively with your citizen-customers in one way or another you are probably safe in saying that you are engaging in community-oriented policing. The fact is that community-oriented policing is not a unit or a program. Rather, it is a philosophy or way of doing business. To work properly, it has to involve everyone in the department, from the chief, who sets the example, through the greenest rookie and the clerk in the Records Section. Your command staff has to buy into it. So do your first-line supervisors, as community-oriented policing cannot possibly succeed without their positive role modeling and support. Community-oriented policing is an all hands on deck thing.

As the chief it is your responsibility to institute and support opportunities to bring community-oriented policing into the department you now lead or expand its footprint if it is already present. This you can do through programs like Coffee with a Cop, a Citizens Police Academy, and a Junior Academy for Kids. You also can do it via a well-run Citizens Ridealong program. Certainly there are other programs that you and your officers can initiate based upon your local needs. It is also perfectly alright to copy programs that are working well at other law enforcement agencies. In doing so you are saluting their successful efforts. Meanwhile, give your people the freedom and encouragement to come up with their own ideas for implementing community-oriented policing. As you well know, really good ideas often come from those closest to the work.

Programs that support the concept of community-oriented policing are important. But even more so are the attitudes and actions of your frontline employees. For your connections to the community to work well, the officer on the street and those answering the telephone at the police station must buy into it. You and your in-the-trenches employees must accept the fact that your citizen-customers are not interruptions to your work. They *are* your work. They are the reason that all of you have jobs. That may sound trite, but it is absolutely true. It is up to you to get that message across to your people. It is something you must model in your own actions.

Pass along to your frontline cops that there is nothing particularly new or fancy about community-oriented policing. It's not an effort to be warm and fuzzy or soft on crime. To the contrary, it is what good cops have been doing for a long time. It calls for stopping to visit with the kids at the playground or Dad mowing the lawn on a Saturday afternoon. It involves pausing at a local business to chat when there is no other police business at hand. It is doing what most people, cops included, generally enjoy doing: visiting with other human beings. In the process cops and citizens alike get to see that the other soul is not greatly unlike themselves. The interaction actually can prove enjoyable.

You should not over-formalize the process so that an officer ends up forcing himself to talk to someone just to score numbers on his activity log. Forced contacts are unlikely to go well. Just set the example yourself and acknowledge good community-oriented policing work when you spot your people doing the same.

REMAIN VISIBLE AND ACCESSIBLE

On occasion police chiefs have tried to keep themselves totally out of the public eye and away from the local news media. They are just fine with the fact that 99% of the local citizenry have never met their police chief and have not the slightest idea who their Top Cop is. Unfortunately, this is a strategy that in today's world is both impractical and inappropriate. It is a strategy that, sooner or later, may well have bad consequences.

You are a public figure in your community. A lot of people will recognize you on sight. As your community's head law enforcement officer, you will be invited to community events. You will be asked to speak at some of them. Your opinion will be sought on matters pertaining to crime and law enforcement. Particularly in a relatively small town or city, a lot of people will know who you are and want to hear what you have to say. Hopefully you realized that before you took the chief's job, because being the public face and voice of your department is now your responsibility. In that role you will have the opportunity to do a lot of good for your people and your agency.

As the chief you cannot make yourself hard to reach, either for a telephone conversation or an in-person chat. Your citizens expect you to be reasonably accessible and will be put off if it appears that you do not have time for them. That doesn't mean that you have to spend time with every obvious nut that comes down the road, but very few of those who want some of your time will fall into that category. Be willing to meet with everyone you reasonably can. That does not mean that you have to grant every request or agree with every argument or complaint that you hear, but you still need to allow your visitors time to make their case. You can listen courteously without promising the moon.

Especially when you are new to the chief's job, accept every invitation that you can. People will want to see you and meet you. This will present you with an excellent opportunity to connect with your constituents and permit them to determine that you deserve their support. You may need that support at some point in the future.

If you really don't like rubber chicken, try to cultivate a taste for it, anyway. As the police chief you are likely to be asked to civic club breakfasts and lunches. Attend every one that you can. It is not a bad idea to let their program chairpersons know that you are good for a quick talk almost anytime they are in need of a program. The offer will be appreciated and may result in all the speaking engagements you possibly could want.

STRIVE FOR OPENNESS AND ACCOUNTABILITY

It is popular today for various officials at all levels of government to trumpet that themselves and their actions are both open and accountable. Some of them even mean it. The truth is that in today's world it is absolutely necessary that you *do* mean it when you make that claim. The self-appointed law enforcement critics are quick to leap on any police official or agency that they can label as lacking openness and accountability. The allegation does not even have to be true. Some of these cop-bashers are not above constructing their accusations from total falsehoods.

You frustrate those who would denigrate you and your department when you deny them evidence for their claims. You do that by releasing every scrap of information on police-involved happenings that you lawfully and appropriately can. You answer requests for information in a timely manner, whether you honor that want or deny it for cause. Your news media policies and practices invite coverage by the press of your police operations, events, and programs. Your standard mode of operation should be to look for a way to release requested information as opposed to seeking an excuse to hold it back. Be sure your subordinates know that.

You also make clear to the public that you and your people are accountable to those you serve. Citizen complaints are accepted, honestly investigated, and fairly resolved. Citizen complainants are notified promptly regarding the status and eventual resolution of their concern. In addition, you as the head of the agency are willing to meet personally with constituents who have questions, concerns, or complaints regarding police employees or police service. That kind of genuine openness can win respect from a citizen complainant even if, in the end, you do not ultimately agree with the individual. From that at least some degree of trust can be built over time.

As the chief, you lead an ethical and professional police agency. There is no good reason why you should not welcome public scrutiny of what you and your people do every day and night. You have everything to gain and nothing to lose from such sincere openness and accountability.

SPEAK UP FOR LAW ENFORCEMENT

It borders on stating the obvious, but unfortunately it is all too true: police and policing are under attack today more than at any other time in memory. At least partially activated due to criminal conduct by a very few thugs wearing badges, the cop-haters and self-anointed law enforcement experts have been at full-throat across the nation. Opportunistic politicians have added their shrill voices to the outcry, and highly biased media outlets have willingly served as amplifiers for the verbal (and sometimes physical) assault on peacekeepers. Frustrated cops are leaving the profession. Disillusioned, potential applicants are turning away to avoid the perceived ill will. Some of the long-term supporters of law enforcement are left wondering if the faith they have invested in their uniformed public servants is misplaced. What can you, the leader of a small law enforcement agency, do in the face of an ugly situation?

Actually, there is much that you can and must do to serve your people and your profession in tumultuous times. What you *cannot* do is remain quietly on the sidelines. Your officers expect you to be seen and heard in difficult moments. The supportive citizens of your jurisdiction (and there are a lot of them!) expect the same. Whether the critical focus is on law enforcement for something that happened two thousand miles away or an event that occurred in your own community, you must continue to display a positive, upbeat attitude in the face of criticism. And you must speak up.

In order to preserve your reputation for absolute integrity and credibility, you must freely acknowledge that cops can and do make mistakes. Sometimes the mistakes rise to the level of criminal conduct. But it is equally important to emphasize the rarity of these mistakes, unintentional or otherwise. It is worth noting that with the literally hundreds of thousands of police-citizen contacts that occur in the U.S. every day, very, very few end badly.

During tough times take every opportunity to speak to community groups, whatever the topic might be. Know that, whatever the planned subject, queries regarding the latest police-involved controversy may have a good chance of surfacing. Be aware of that reality and be sure to have thought about your response in advance. Be prepared to answer questions about all sorts of topics, realizing that not all of the questions may be friendly ones. Thank the members of your audience for their support. Let them know how damaging to law enforcement the misinformed and hateful voices can be.

Take advantage of an opportunity to pen an opinion piece for the local paper or do an interview on a radio talk show. Again, realize that not every caller with a question for you will be a police supporter. When you appear in any public forum, do not allow hostile detractors to punch your buttons and elicit an unprofessional response. Remain calm and in control in the face of verbal assault. It will greatly frustrate your attackers and favorably impress the average citizen.

Realize that social media are very public platforms for every human being with an opinion to unload. They provide daily recreation for an ever-growing part of the populace. You or someone in your agency needs to keep track of what is being said. Respond with clarifying or corrective information if attacks are being launched against your agency based upon clearly false information. But remain careful and restrained in what you decide to post. You do not have to respond at all to hateful or moronic diatribes. You must avoid endless back and forth exchanges that only serve to keep the issue, whatever it may be, in front of the public. Realize that you will never convince every doubter of the truth. Don't try–it only will lead to frustration on your part. It's not at all unlikely that the friends of law enforcement will take up the battle on your behalf. For you, social media exchanges represent an instance when little said can be more beneficial than a lot.

Your citizens want to believe that their officers are unlike bad cops that may have gained infamy somewhere else. Even if one of your own employees has made the news through improper or allegedly criminal behavior, most of your constituents are willing to believe that he or she is the exception in a group of good people. It is up to you to reinforce that accurate assumption by what you have to say publicly. Assure your citizens that they are OK–that your good people will continue to protect and serve them with honor. Assure them that *their* cops have nothing in common with a "bad" cop they may have heard about. These are *their* officers whose kids go to the same schools that theirs do. They shop at the same grocery stores. They are *their* cops, and they are good people.

Your officers and your citizens need to see and hear you when law enforcement is questioned or under assault. Never disappoint them.

KNOW THAT YOU CAN'T PLEASE EVERYONE, BUT LISTEN

You have learned from working with cops that you cannot please them all at any given time, and probably never will. Often your officers realize that but may simply want you to listen to their concerns, whatever they may be. You will find the same to hold true with the members of your community. They may know or at least suspect at the outset that you cannot do exactly what it is that they want you to do. But they want you to listen, anyway. That's only fair, at least from the aggrieved citizen's point of view.

Do listen patiently and empathetically to concerns, but don't be too quick with pronouncements, promises, and/or proposed solutions. It is a good idea to ask questions and clarify statements. But remember that you may be hearing only one side of the issue at hand. Indicate that you will look into the situation and get back to the complainant. Then, keep your promise. Experienced chiefs often throw a lot of "hmmm" and "interesting" comments into the conversation without necessarily agreeing with the speaker. They avoid choosing sides or reaching conclusions until they know more. Meanwhile, they employ patient, active listening skills.

Not all the things that you are told need fixed are actually broken. They do not really require action from you or your troops. Listen, anyway. Then, accept that you can never make everyone happy and be able to live with that reality. That realization should contribute to your own mental and emotional health.

NEVER BECOME COMPLACENT

There is a mistake that some chiefs make that you will not. They slack off on their community involvement as their tenure increases. They mistake what turns out to be public apathy for overwhelming public support. That support or may not be the case. If they are not paying attention to the pulse of their community and staying in touch with its members, it is all too possible for an issue to emerge out of the dark and bite them somewhere sensitive.

During your law enforcement career you have, at one time or another, probably encountered a retired-on-duty chief. You likely pledged that would never happen to you. You may even have promised yourself that you would do your job until the last minute of the last day that you were on the job. Hopefully you meant just that. Ceasing active participation in your community may be a signal to you that it is time to give serious thought to your future. If you are truly losing interest in what you are doing, it may well be time to hang it up. There is no shame in culminating a life's work well done. But if you do not see retirement in your immediate future, it is way too early to curtail your involvement in your department or your community. In other words, complacency on your part can quickly hurt both your department and the people you all serve. If you plan to stay employed, also stay involved. You have heard the old homily about the "quiet before the storm." Keep your hearing sharp for that still-distant thunder. Stay involved and engaged so that the storm doesn't surprise you.

Just as you learned in officer safety training, complacency in your business is a very dangerous thing. It can lay you low in more ways than one. By remaining present and involved in your town or city oftentimes you can avoid that nasty ambush. That's called self-survival.

SUMMARY

You are not "just a cop." You are a recognized leader in your community. That status, as you probably have recognized by now, most often will feel like an honor and occasionally like a burden. As your town or city's Top Cop, you may feel that considerably less of your time is entirely your own. You will be highly visible in the community and will be expected to always comport yourself as the ethical and responsible person that you are. You will be expected to serve admirably and effectively as the face and spokesperson of the police department in your community. You will have to be very involved in that community and be accessible to the people who will want to bend your ear on a whole host of issues. Some of these "issues" you will not be able to solve but you will have to listen attentively, anyway. You will need to come across at all times as open and accountable.

None of the things your community expects of you is beyond the abilities of an exceptional leader. You *are* that exceptional leader.

Chapter 9

DOING DISCIPLINE RIGHT

The real world is not made up of sunshine, rainbows, and perfection 100% of the time. You know that. Sometimes things go wrong. On occasion the problem will be caused by a failed or broken piece of equipment or a defective policy, procedure, or practice. Oftentimes these will be the easiest difficulties to address. At other times, however, the source of the problem will have a face and a name. That individual did not intend to create the troublesome issue. There was certainly no malice or ill intent involved. A leader's counselling or additional training may be all that is required to keep the problem from recurring.

Then there is the other variety of problematic human behavior. Someone through negligence or intent has done something wrong, perhaps seriously wrong, which will have a negative impact on the organization and, perhaps, others outside the organization. *Now* how is the transgression to be handled? In this case you are likely going to respond with *negative discipline*, which often means punishment of some kind. (More about that shortly.) The problem may have arisen in the first place because a *positive* form of discipline was lacking. Positive discipline such as self-discipline.

SELF-DISCIPLINE IS BEST

You have heard all your life that self-discipline, personal discipline, is a very good thing to have. But exactly what does having it entail? For one thing, showing self-discipline means that you do the *right* things because you know they are right, not because you fear bad things happening to you if you do wrong. Self-discipline involves the personal, internalized rules of conduct that you impose on yourself and attempt to follow scrupulously. Whether rooted in religious faith, a personal moral compass, or some combination of the two, these internal rules of conduct and way of looking at life cause you to do what you believe to be right *because* you believe it to be right, not because you fear punishment. Self-discipline causes you to do things in what you perceive to be the proper way even if no one would ever know exactly what you did.

You have and display self-discipline as the leader of your organization. You rightfully expect the members of your organization to follow your lead. A police organization staffed by people displaying ample self-discipline is most often an organization that does not have to rely heavily on negative discipline–punishment–to achieve compliance with the rules. That is the situation you are seeking to establish, nurture, and maintain in your agency.

People who accept personal responsibility are routinely exhibiting self-discipline. They make it a point to do the right thing. When you regularly serve as an exceptional role model for exemplary self-discipline, you make it that much easier for your people to do the same. Practicing excellent self-discipline brings you the added benefit of depriving anyone of the opportunity to claim truthfully that you practice a double standard.

WHY DO IT?

It is no secret that most people neither like to receive discipline nor dish it out. That being the case, the question may arise: Why discipline at all?

The answer to that query can be found in a maxim that should be taken to heart by every competent leader: "Fail to deal with the bad ones, lose the good ones." It simply means that if your employees who are doing the right thing see that those who are not doing their job properly suffer no consequences for their bad behavior, eventually at least some of those who are doing it the right way will cease doing so. Your employees generally know who is carrying his or her share of the load the right way and who is not. They expect you to know it, too. If you or your subordinate supervisors fail to take action to correct the problem, you should expect diminished confidence in leadership's ability to run the department in a competent manner.

The vast majority of your police employees want to do their jobs well. They deserve your respect and support for that. Both they and your citizen-customers have a right to expect that you will not let them down by failing to deal appropriately with shoddy work or unethical or otherwise improper behavior by other members of your agency. In some instances, that will call for an appropriate disciplinary response. But there is more than one way to respond to off-the-rails job performance. That calls for looking at *intent.*

MISTAKES OF THE HEAD VS. MISTAKES OF THE HEART

Mistakes are going to happen. Everyone makes them from time to time. Even you. They are inevitable in the real world. Many of them are understandable and fixable. Oftentimes this kind of error or improper conduct is referred to as a *mistake of the head.* The mistake is made as a result of an accident or lack of knowledge for doing something the right way. An example of a mistake of the head may be found in the case of the officer who puts a scratch on the side of the police vehicle while in pursuit of an evil-doer. Or it may be seen in the instance of the cop who loses or damages an expensive piece of equipment while in a foot chase after that same bad guy. These are uh-ohs that occurred while an employee of yours was trying to do his or her job but in the doing made an honest misstep. There was no ill-intent involved. It was a mistake of the head for which negative discipline, or punishment, is probably not deserved.

On the other side of the coin is the *mistake of the heart.* In this case the employee knew that what he or she was doing was wrong, but through extreme carelessness, negligence, or plain ill intent did it or allowed it to happen, anyway. Obviously, an action that amounted to an unethical or even unlawful act would fall into the category of a mistake of the heart. It would call for a negative disciplinary response, perhaps a very serious one. Other examples of mistakes of the heart could include lying to a supervisor, intentionally and repeatedly sleeping on duty, and physically or verbally abusing a citizen. Not unlike mistakes of the head, these kinds of mistakes will happen, hopefully extremely rarely, in even the best police departments. When they do happen, a prompt, firm, but fair response is mandatory. And that is where *you* will most often be involved.

Mistakes will happen. When they do, you are the one ultimately responsible for assuring that appropriate redress takes place. A word of sage advice, formal counselling, retraining, or all of these may be needed to ensure that a similar mistake of the head will not be repeated. In dealing with the heart-based mistake, a warning notice, letter of reprimand, suspension without pay, or even termination from employment may be required. In weighing all the relevant information concerning what happened you likely will be the one to make the final disciplinary decision. It probably won't be something you will enjoy doing, but you recognize the importance of your role here and will not fail to carry out your responsibility.

WHAT EFFECTIVE DISCIPLINE REQUIRES

Doing discipline right requires that you and your subordinate supervisors follow some basic guidelines. Discipline must be appropriate and measured for the transgression involved. It should be neither too lenient nor too harsh. It should be fair and should not be administered until all the relevant facts are known. The accused's version of events and reasoning must always be heard. Discipline should be timely, meaning that it must be carried out while what happened is still fresh in everyone's mind, not six months later. Putting it off unnecessarily will not make it easier on anyone.

Administration of discipline is not a spectator sport. The employee disciplinary meeting will, in most cases, require the presence of only the disciplinary authority and the individual being disciplined. An exception may be encountered if the agency's policies and procedures permit the presence of an employee representative. Another exception may be found if the disciplining authority is concerned that correcting an employee of the opposite gender feasibly could result in some kind of allegation of sexual impropriety on the part of the supervisor. Then, the presence of a second supervisor serving as a witness may be advisable.

Your goal is for the individual being disciplined to perceive the process and result as being just. This, of course, will not always be the case. It is what you are seeking, nonetheless. Discipline, in order to be perceived by its recipient as being fair, should be consistent with what has been done before in similar circumstances in the organization.

In other words, Betty should get the same discipline as Bobby for the same misconduct, assuming that their previous disciplinary records are identical and the misconduct by each truly is the same. This is known as *comparative discipline.* Your officers, their attorneys, and their police union reps will be looking for comparative discipline as evidence of fairness and consistency. Practicing comparative discipline is also the right thing to do.

The concept of *progressive discipline* also should figure into your determination that any and all discipline issued in your organization will be both appropriate and just. The phrase simply refers to the disciplinary concept of "start light, get heavier if the desired change in conduct is not occurring." For example, a first, unexcused failure to appear for a scheduled court date might draw an oral warning, the second instance a written reprimand, and the third a day's suspension without pay. That is assuming, of course, that there are no extenuating circumstances that would mitigate the seriousness of the third failure to appear.

But beware. Like most everything else in life, there are exceptions to this general, progressive discipline guideline. For example: Perhaps in your department the first time an officer damages a patrol car in a preventable accident he draws a warning, oral or written. The second time he earns a formal letter of reprimand, and the third time he gets a suspension without pay. Now, your officer has his first preventable crash and expects a warning, as is the department's practice through progressive discipline. But it turns out that his very first at-fault accident totaled the police vehicle he was operating, did the same for the other vehicle, and sent three people to the hospital with serious injuries. And, oh. He was driving 50 mph over the posted speed limit. It would be ludicrous to give him a "don't do that anymore", first accident warning speech and call it good. In determining the appropriate discipline in any situation, you also must take into account the *consequences* of the employee's bad act. This holds true regardless of the employee's intentions. As important as the concept of progressive discipline is, it can be trumped by the consequences of the employee's misconduct. It can work in the other direction, too. It could be that your officer missed his third court appearance because he had to rush his injured child to the ER. It would be equally ludicrous to punish him for the act. Common sense must prevail. You and your subordinate supervisors must have the authority to deviate from the scripted disciplinary response when you are faced with an unusual set of facts. When you do that, you should be able to clearly explain the reason for moving away from the "expected" to both the concerned employee and anyone else situated to question the decision.

When you are directly involved in the disciplinary process, as most often you will be, realize that you do not have to make the call alone. The employee's immediate supervisor, assuming it is not you, also should be expected to weigh in with a recommendation. If need be, you can seek the opinions of your outside peers or your boss. But make it clear when you are talking with these people that you are not asking them to make a disciplinary decision *for* you. The final call should be yours to make once you are satisfied that you have sufficient information.

Adequate information always should include what the proposed recipient of the corrective action has to say about what led up to the pending discipline. Even if no change in the disciplinary decision results, as often it won't, many of your people will at least feel better that they had the opportunity to give their side of the story to the Big Boss.

There is yet one more thing that discipline must be in order to be effective. It must be *documented.* Discipline that was not recorded in some fashion did not happen, at least not for the purpose of future discipline or an employee performance appraisal.

On occasion a well-meaning supervisor, perhaps even the chief, will decide to give an employee a break for a significant "first offense" by letting the miscue go with an oral warning without in any way documenting the event with an employee log remark, computer entry, or some other means of memorializing employee performance, good or bad. Sometime later the employee moves along to a different supervisor who eventually detects the same sort of negative performance. Finding no record to the contrary, he or she assumes another "first offense" and fails to document the problem. This process could go on for some while without supervisory intervention in a situation that needs addressed. Documentation is a part of the problem resolution process. Record problematical performance and its correction and require your first-line supervisors to do the same. Doing that could serve to prevent a lot of problems in the future. Be sure the employee gets to review the documentation and make a written response, if he or she chooses. Once more, it is the fair thing to do.

When employee discipline is your personal responsibility, you will want to know as much as you reasonably can about the individual to be disciplined before you take the corrective action. That may help you anticipate how he or she will react. You can then plan your approach accordingly. One employee may be embarrassed and apologetic while another might be angry and aggressive. It may be helpful to allow the unhappy employee to vent without interruption. Be empathetic. Be patient. Try to avoid a massive display of authority. ("Because I'm the chief, that's why!") But in the end you have to impose the discipline, regardless of opposition or disagreement. You and your employee may have to agree to disagree. Seeking to end on a positive note by finding something to commend the individual about is a good strategy, but you have been around long enough to know that will not always allow the meeting to end with blue birds and shared ice cream. Try for a positive conclusion in which the two of you can agree on *something*. But be prepared to go forward without it. You have done your part and are willing to proceed with no bad feelings. The rest is up to the recipient of the corrective action.

You would be, at best, unusual if you enjoyed disciplining someone that you may have worked with for some time and know well. The recipient of your discipline may be someone you really like. But you will do your job all the same. Whether your employee concurs at the time or not, your actions most likely will be beneficial in the long term for both the individual and the organization you both serve.

THE EDUCATIONAL VALUE OF DISCIPLINE

Actions you take in the name of discipline seldom stay confidential for long, even if you do your best to see to it that they do. That is not necessarily a bad thing, because discipline is a great educator. A fair and well-crafted disciplinary action may be at least as beneficial to the rest of the organization as it is to the recipient. That is another good reason for doing discipline in the first place.

Corrective action is intended to notify the "offender" that his or her conduct is unacceptable and will draw official sanctions. In the process, all your other employees learn what is and is not acceptable behavior. They do not have to have discipline visited upon them to learn this; they get it from someone else's disciplinary experience. The choice is still theirs as to whether to engage in misconduct or not. But now they have some idea as to the likely consequences if they do.

Discipline has a unique ability to teach. It can prevent misconduct as well as address it when it occurs in order to prevent a recurrence. As the leader of your organization these are the things that you should be most interested in seeing discipline accomplish.

THINKING OUTSIDE THE BOX

Police officers and police chiefs alike tend to like structure. They also favor predictable, structured discipline in response to improper conduct. There is nothing wrong with that. Employees may feel at least some degree of comfort in knowing that a specific transgression will result in a specific penalty. There is nothing wrong with doing discipline in that way. Standardized, predictable disciplinary responses are not a bad thing. At the same time, there is also nothing wrong with straying from the well-worn path a bit. It is perfectly alright and sometimes preferrable to try something new, perhaps something that feels a little less like being taken to the woodshed. Maybe instead of negative discipline for rudeness to citizens the offender is dispatched to customer service training that includes a section on basic courtesy to other human beings. Or maybe Officer Bob who just damaged his third patrol vehicle gets sent to defensive driving class instead of buying a day off without pay. In each of these instances the offending party is likely to gain more knowledge and benefit than he would get from a piece of paper placed in his file or a day to sit at home and meditate over his sins. The idea is not to embarrass or belittle anyone but rather to secure a positive change in behavior.

You call on your creativity and willingness to do something different in many of your other duties as your organization's leader. Be willing also to step outside the box, as appropriate, when employee discipline is the issue. That's not to say that more "traditional" means of discipline will not be the appropriate response in some instances. But reaching outside the disciplinary toolbox may at times be exactly the right thing to do.

SUMMARY

You are well aware that self-discipline is by far the best kind of discipline and is to be found in quantity in healthy organizations. But you are equally aware that sometimes other varieties of discipline must be imposed. You know that all discipline must be fact-based, fair, documented, and measured for the infraction involved. And that means first determining whether the misstep was brought about by a mistake of the head or a mistake of the heart. It additionally means that the principles contained in both progressive discipline and comparative discipline are applied appropriately. You also have the ability to "step outside the box" regarding discipline when the facts indicate that you should. And you never overlook discipline's ability to educate the entire organization.

It is important that you, as your organization's leader, resist the very human impulse to put off administering or watering down discipline to mollify the involved employee and his or her peers. Staying the course is as important in disciplinary matters as it is in the very many tough challenges you face. No one expects that you should enjoy imposing negative discipline on your subordinates. All the same, you recognize the value to the organization of discipline that is decisively, promptly, and justly administered. Discipline represents one more area in which you can serve as a role model for doing it properly. That amounts to doing discipline right.

Chapter 10

YOU WEAR A LOT OF HATS

If you have served previously as the leader of a law enforcement organization or do now, it will come as no surprise to you to find that you are now responsible for a lot of different police functions, all at the same time. But if you are more accustomed to running Patrol, Investigations, or some other single operation at a police agency, graduating to having multiple breeds of cats to herd, all at the same time, may feel a bit intimidating. Have no fear. By calling upon your personal courage, abilities for organizing and planning, and time management skills, you can handle it all just fine. It starts with identifying your responsibilities in each area of police work.

PATROL

You probably have said it often throughout your law enforcement career: Patrol is the backbone of any police agency. It is the single most vital function of your agency. It is the one your citizens are most aware of. Every other law enforcement function, in one way or another, exists to support Patrol. Because of the very nature of the Patrol officer's job, that division of your agency usually will be the one that has the potential for causing you the most "trouble" while taking the lion's share of your time. It is just logical, then, that Patrol normally will be the focus of your almost constant attention and concern.

Especially if you have come into the department as an "outsider," you will need to familiarize yourself as quickly as possible with Patrol's operations and personnel. Often that will mean seeking the answers to some important questions. Questions such as:

How many Patrol officers do you really need, and how should they be deployed? Particularly in small police departments, sometimes officers are deployed based on supervisors' intuition and past experience. Sometimes they are hired and assigned based on what their employer can afford, budget-wise. Still other times Patrol staffing depends on the reality that "we've always done it that way." There is likely some merit in each of these ways of deploying your uniformed officers. But to do it well and put your people where and when you need them a scientifically based work analysis study is the most reliable route to take. It will be based upon number of calls for service, desired response time, crime rate, and other variables. It will include the consideration of what you and your elected representatives *want* your people to be spending their time doing. If you do not have anyone on board who can do the relatively complex work needed to produce a reliable and useful report, it may well be worth the cost to hire a public safety consultant to do it. These folks are out there and accessible via the Internet, but "shop" carefully. Your chief colleagues may be able to point you in the right direction. Over time, the study should pay for itself through a more effective, efficient, and cost-effective Patrol operation. Having that professionally developed data also will come in handy when you need to ask your boss and/or elected officials for additional resources.

Do your Patrol officers know their mission and goals? Hopefully, you already have set and disseminated a mission and goals for your police department. That's good. But your Patrol officers deserve more direction than, perhaps, a sergeant's instructions to "be seen, take reports, write tickets, and stay out of trouble." Supervision certainly has a huge role to play here, but your first-line leaders cannot give their people sufficient direction unless you have first given it to *them.* Lay it out in plain language. If reducing crashes and car burglaries is a priority for you due to what is happening locally, say so. If you want your Patrol officers to spend time on the highway to slow motorists down or get into the neighborhoods to practice community-oriented policing, say that, too.

Share the blueprint for what it is that you want your police department to achieve. It is almost a certainty that your Patrol force will have a major say in getting it accomplished. Spell out clearly what it is you want them to do.

Are your Patrol officers properly equipped for their difficult job? If you want your officers to do a job that both they and you can be proud of, they will need to have the tools to do it with. The best way to find out what they need is to *ask* them. His or her vehicle is extremely important to almost all Patrol cops. It is, after all, his or her office for an extended period each shift. Try to keep their vehicular equipment the very best. Particularly if your jurisdiction cannot afford great pay, it's a way of showing that their employer and their chief really do care. The same holds true for weapons, lethal and less-lethal, and body armor. The latter should be the most comfortable available that still provides for a Patrol officer's safety. Consider issuing the external, load-supporting vests if your people do not already have them.

Patrol officers in one agency will invariably voice differing equipment needs from the troops at a nearby department. Those needs can range from emergency medical and self-rescue supplies to fire-fighting gear to breaching tools. Do everything your budget will allow to satisfy your Patrol staff's legitimate, practical needs.

Do your Patrol supervisors focus on *output* or *outcome*? As you know, there is a big difference. Output most often can be quantified, such as in the number of traffic tickets written. Outcome, on the other hand, refers to results, such as a reduction in the number of vehicle crashes. You want your Patrol supervisors to look at numbers as a means of seeing what their people are doing. That is a legitimate interest for a Patrol supervisor, so long as that leader does not become *too* numbers focused. What you are all more interested in are the results. If Officer Jones issues a lot more warnings than summonses yet there are very few accidents in his beat, you might safely assume that he is doing his job. Many cops believe that most supervisors are numbers-obsessed. Try to assure that it's not the case in your department. Your Patrol officers and their first-line bosses need to focus on outcome, not output.

What is the quality of Patrol supervision? Can it be improved? Observe carefully how your first-line leaders interact with their subordinates and each other. The success of your organization will depend a great deal on the ability of those leaders to transform your directives and the department's stated goals into action. Visit a roll call briefing from time to time. How do these leaders respond to their people? As you know well, the sometimes abrasive and dictatorial supervisory practices of a generation or two ago do not go over well with today's young employees. Do your sergeants realize that? If they have held their rank for some time, have they adjusted to the changes in today's workplace? Observe and find out.

The day has passed when a new supervisor could learn everything he or she needed to know about his or her job by riding along for a bit with a senior supervisor. This sort of training still can be immensely helpful, but it needs to be preceded by formal, classroom training under the tutelage of qualified, experienced trainers. Your first-line Patrol supervisors are too important to the well-being of your organization not to have exceptional and continuing leadership training. Supplement that schooling with your own coaching and mentoring efforts.

What are your Patrol officers doing in the way of community-oriented policing? Most if not all police chiefs like to say that their agency is deeply involved in community-oriented policing. Today it is the law enforcement equivalent of Mom and apple pie. But what is it that your people are actually *doing*?

Community-oriented policing is not a program or a specialized unit, but rather a way of doing business by your entire department. It calls for getting out in the community, visiting with the members of that community, and finding out just what the problems and concerns are. You as the chief must be directly involved in that endeavor. Owing to their visibility and daily presence in the community, so must your Patrol officers.

Let your Patrol people know that they are the key to the success of your department's community-oriented policing philosophy. Encourage them to get off the main drags, get into the neighborhoods, and get out of their rides to meet the citizens. Encourage them to visit informally with your citizen-customers when there is nothing official to visit about. Encourage them to find out for themselves that interacting with their citizen-customers can, on many occasions, be enjoyable. Then encourage them to do a lot of it. It is your uniformed guardians who can make community-oriented policing work.

How do your Patrol officers spend their time? Some chiefs who felt that they had a good grasp of what their people were doing eventually discovered that they really did not. You can learn quite a bit by simply listening to your officers' activities on the police radio on a regular basis and at varying hours. Your first-line supervisors should be able to tell you even more. You not only need to know what your people are doing but also how much of their shift time is spent doing it. In other words, how much *uncommitted* time do they have at their disposal? Modern police management practices suggest that all of that "free" time should not be spent on random patrolling. Your Patrol personnel deserve more direction than that. Your officers should still have a great deal of discretion about what they are going to do and when. But they still need direction from management on what their objectives are and roughly how much of their time and effort should be devoted to each. For example, get in the neighborhoods, enforce the traffic laws, keep a lookout for evildoers, and apply the elements of community-oriented policing all could be parts of a Patrol officer's day. His night shift opposite might have a slightly different set of directions. By knowing what your Patrol people are doing you can make adjustments in the direction of what you *want* them to be doing in the interests of effectiveness and efficiency. You owe them that much direction.

Can you identify certain paperwork or other onerous tasks that you can take off of your Patrol officers to improve their workday without sacrificing their effectiveness? There are aspects to every cop's job that he or she dislikes with a passion. For many officers it is the completion of reams of paperwork for relatively insignificant events. Call upon your Patrol supervisors and their officers to acquaint you with the paperwork and other "routine" tasks that need to be completed as part of the job. Ask what they feel could be eliminated without detracting from the legitimate needs of the organization. See if your Investigations supervisors agree. Remain alert for things your Patrol officers do because "we've always done it that way," yet no one actually can identify a purpose for. You will earn the thanks of your officers when you identify paper burdens or other procedural albatrosses that you can remove from around their necks.

What can you do to make the job more rewarding for Patrol officers? No, you can't cook pancakes every morning and burgers every evening for your Patrol crew. (Actually, you *might* be able to do that on occasion!) But when Patrol cops leave small departments for larger ones it is not always about pay. Sometimes job satisfaction figures into the picture big time. It might be worth your while to *ask* your Patrol officers and supervisors what would make the job more rewarding for them. Are there scheduling modifications that might work to virtually everyone's benefit? How about rules that have no identifiable, legitimate purpose? Undoubtedly, some things your people might like to see happen cannot for some very good reasons. But that will not always be the case. Keep an open mind as your Patrol people let you know what is on their minds. Do what you can to help them gain as much satisfaction as possible from what they are doing.

Some police chiefs would acknowledge that Patrol is the most vital part of their organization, but then fail to act like they really believe that truth. You will not make that mistake. Spend time with your Patrol officers and supervisors. Show genuine interest in what they are doing and what their concerns happen to be. Look for small "perks" you can do to make their day (or night) better. Praise them publicly whenever you can. You may just find yourself and your community rewarded with a more content, more effective Patrol force.

INVESTIGATIONS

Finding out what your detectives or investigators are doing is another of your priorities as the police chief. You can learn a lot via your own observations and a review of your department's policies and procedures covering Investigations operations. But an even better source of information for you will be the investigators and their supervisors who are actually doing the work. It also will benefit you to accompany them occasionally on an investigation or a visit to the prosecutor's office to discuss or file a case.

Find out what your investigators' day looks like. Gain at least a basic grounding in what they do, even if in the past you have worked as a detective yourself. Do not hesitate to ask what you might be able to do to make their work better, easier, more rewarding. It is unlikely that you will be able to fulfill their every want, but you won't know if you don't ask. Just like the other members of your department, your investigators will be favorably impressed if there is even a "small victory" of some kind that you can grant them. Some small agencies permit their investigators to take home a department vehicle or wear standardized, "soft" uniforms as perks. Do what you can.

You should be able to get an honest and independent assessment of the quality of your investigative unit's work through a casual sit-down with your district attorney and prosecutors. Ask about where your people could do better. Couple what you find out with your investigators' own comments about their training needs. Today's criminal investigations are more complex than ever. Your detectives must stay abreast of what is new in both crime and investigative response. Be sure new detectives receive basic investigative skills training in addition to working with a senior partner. All your investigators must have access to the specialized training (cybercrime, human trafficking, child abuse, domestic violence, victims' rights, etc.) that they will need to be effective at their difficult jobs.

Ascertain that you have the right personnel assigned to your Investigations unit. The supervision must be top-notch, and the detectives assigned must be competent self-starters who can work well, when necessary, without close supervision. Your investigations section must never be a sort of modified rubber gun squad made up of cops who are physically capable but can't or won't do the job of a full-service law enforcement officer. In addition, especially in a small agency, each detective must have a uniform, body armor, and all necessary equipment ready to go in case Patrol needs immediate help in an "all hands on deck" response. A detective should always be able to perform a Patrolman's job if the situation requires. The same holds true for Investigations supervisors.

Take a careful look at the caseload carried by your investigators. Of those cases, how many are actually assigned to be actively worked? What sort of case screening process do your Investigations supervisors use to determine which cases merit additional effort? Use your own expertise to determine if changes need to be made in the case assignment process. Finally, be prepared to make the call on whether your department truly needs more or fewer human resources assigned to the investigative function. On occasion, police agencies assign additional personnel to the Investigations unit to cover some special, perhaps short-term need and somehow the assignment never gets undone. Shrinking the size of an Investigations section won't necessarily make you popular with everyone assigned there, but sometimes it must be done. If the unit truly has become bloated over time, the rest of your non-detective personnel will applaud your move. By the same token, be willing to add resources to the unit if solid evidence convinces you of the need.

Be sure your agency has in place a formalized, known, and *followed* process for assigning personnel to Investigations. It is important that proven competence is the sole means for winning a highly coveted investigator's badge. This is not the place for favoritism or personal relationships to play a role. It is also important that any individual assigned re-earns that position every day. This is not the place for retired-on-duty cops. You quickly will lose the respect of your employees if you even *appear* to be permitting unqualified people to serve as your agency's detectives. Be prepared to re-assign anyone, including a unit supervisor, for poor performance. Even beyond what your staff tells you, keep an eye on your Investigations function. It amounts to good self-survival advice for a wise police chief.

Be especially attentive to any buy or confidential informant funds that are kept in your Investigations unit (or any other department unit, for that matter.) A close receipting and accounting process needs to be maintained for these monies. More than one person should be responsible for keeping track of them. A regular audit of funds should be done, preferably by an outside authority. Once more, your actions are intended to protect both the department and you. Law enforcement leadership careers have ended due to mismanaged funds.

Check to be sure that your agency is adhering to the FBI's Uniform Crime Reporting System's definitions and standards in recording crime and case clearance statistics. One new chief learned that his investigators were labelling as "Exceptionally Cleared" any and every case in which they had run out of leads and could not solve. That is not the appropriate classification. His people said that they were doing it because "we've always done it that way." It was a practice almost guaranteed to one day bring on the allegation that the department was "cooking the books" on the agency's crime-solving effectiveness.

Good communication is, of course, important to maintain throughout your department. But clear and regular communication among your Patrol and Investigations leaders is especially vital. By staying in close touch, they can make the jobs of their respective employees easier. These exchanges also can help minimize the sniping and backbiting that is all too common between these two very critical sections in many police departments.

As you know well, a small law enforcement agency cannot do everything by itself. That holds true for its Investigations Division operations. The short answer and solution? Again, *ask for help when you need it.* Once more, it is vital not to let ego get in the way of securing the help that you need. You and your investigators should strive to maintain excellent relations with your neighboring police agencies, especially the larger ones that have more resources than you do. You may need their assistance tomorrow or a year from now. Additionally, know who to contact at your state police and federal law enforcement agencies in the event you need their assistance on a complex or geographically wide-ranging case. They have both the financial resources and the people power to help you if you just ask. Your investigators also should maintain close contact with such non-law enforcement but often helpful and influential groups as victims' rights organizations and child advocacy associations. Doubtlessly there are other such non-police organizations in your area that are willing to lend support, if asked. Stay in touch with these people.

Your investigators are an important part of your organization. Be sure you stay in touch and take care of them.

SUPPORT SERVICES

Any function of your organization that does not belong in the category of Patrol or Investigations likely would fall under the very broad label of Support Services. The duties and responsibilities of those functions can vary widely, but each is important to the effective and efficient operation of your agency. Depending upon such factors as the size of your police department, you may not have each of these specialized units. But for the ones that you do have, there are some things to think about to help ensure the smooth functioning of each. Many small police agencies staff such support units as the following:

School Resource Officers. In today's world these positions are becoming more important than ever. Do not make the mistake of taking officers who are not doing a good job elsewhere in the department and anointing them as SROs because someone feels the assignment will be less challenging. Your very best people are needed for this challenging position. At the same time, do not force the assignment on someone who really does not want to be there. He or she is unlikely to do well. Remember, too, that the School Resource Officer must have the ability to step back into the role of Patrol first responder anytime necessity calls.

Especially if your school district pays all or a part of the SRO's salary, the school administration may wish to have a say in who serves in that capacity. That is a reasonable expectation that should be honored. But if the officer is your employee the final decision of who is to serve (or continue to serve) as an SRO should be yours. Be sure that you stay in periodic touch with school officials to ascertain how the relationship is working. Perhaps even more important, a first-line supervisor should be responsible for day-to-day supervision of the SRO(s), to include unannounced drop-bys. One chief eventually discovered to his chagrin that his SRO spent most of her time on the Internet with the door to her school office closed. The school officials didn't complain because "we liked her," even though the officer was neglecting those she was supposed to be helping. You do not want that kind of surprise happening to you.

Evidence/Property. This is another one of those functions that can result in your sudden "retirement without cake" if you don't pay attention to what is going on there. If you are the new chief, it would be advisable for you to have an inventory/audit done. You should explain truthfully to your evidence custodian that this is being done to protect him or her as well as the department and yourself. Money, drugs, firearms, and other high-dollar items that should be there must draw extra scrutiny. Any significant discrepancies discovered must result in a prompt and thorough inquiry.

Ensure that your evidence/property custodian has been adequately trained for an exacting job. Make that employee's life a little easier by very closely limiting access to the evidence/property storage area. Most chiefs do not even consider themselves to be someone needing unfettered access to the area. Meanwhile, continue to watch for any vulnerabilities in your evidence booking and storage procedures. Promptly address any weaknesses that you or your people detect.

Criminalistics. Who processes crime scenes for your department? Who *should* process them? Both questions need asked and answered. Some small departments, complaining of a shortage of personnel, do not process what they consider minor crime scenes, such as vehicle burglaries, at all. While understandable, this may not leave a great impression with a victimized citizen who is paying taxes for police services. Some small department chiefs address the problem by equipping each Patrol officer with a crime scene kit that permits him or her to dust for and lift latent prints to accompany photos taken with a cell phone. It may not be an ideal solution to the crime scene processing challenge, but it tends to leave the victimized citizen with the impression that he or she has received at least some crime-solving effort from the local cops.

Many small agencies call upon their investigator(s) to do the processing of major crime scenes. It is important, however, that you have agreements in place with larger agencies that have the personnel and equipment necessary to handle a major criminal incident, one perhaps involving widely dispersed or multiple crime scenes. These arrangements must be in place *before* they are needed. It is unlikely that you will find these organizations unwilling to help you. If such mutual aid agreements or understandings are not already in place and kept up to date, whether formal or informal in nature, it will be up to you to get it done promptly. You may need that help next week–or tonight.

Recruitment and Selection. Your police officers are your best recruiters. Be sure that they have sufficient, accurate information on your department to enable them to recruit actively among the people they interact with daily. Your direction to them should be to seek out only those with whom they would be comfortable in sharing a beat or a patrol car. Of course, your officer-recruiters will be most effective in drawing new talent to your department if they are themselves being treated well by their employer. That is a situation that you can do something about, because that's *you.*

You also will rely heavily upon social media to disseminate your recruiting message. While you likely cannot afford to hire professional services to prepare slick recruiting messages, you almost certainly have people in your department or your town/city government who are really good at producing such work, and enjoy doing it. Avail yourself of their talents. Also consider relying upon communication students at a community college or university to help you, assuming you have one within reaching distance. Often these people will be more than willing to work for free on a real world project.

Take care in crafting your recruiting message. In today's world you are not really trying to appeal to the run and gun, blow things up audience. Rather, you are seeking the (often) young man or woman who is wanting more than a job but rather an opportunity to help and serve others. Design your message to grab the attention of these people. Also be sure to feature the human diversity of your department in creating your message.

Your officer selection process is, of course, just as vital to the health of your organization as is the recruitment effort. Sometimes small department chiefs desperate to fill vacancies and unable to compete salary-wise with larger agencies lower their standards and take big risks in hiring. This you must not do. The trouble you could bring into your organization from hiring "questionable" candidates is not worth the risk. When in doubt as whether to hire or not, your answer should always come out in favor of the organization: don't do it.

Once more because they may be desperate to fill vacancies, on occasion unwise chiefs take shortcuts in the hiring process. Sometimes that translates into not looking too deeply into an applicant's background for fear of finding an obvious disqualifier. Again, that is not something you can afford to do.

Watch out for the "suitcase cops" who have bounced around a lot from one law enforcement agency to another. There is often a reason behind their frequent job changes. Be at least a bit suspicious of the applicant who lists "political reasons" as the cause of his or her departure from a sworn position. Sometimes "political" reasons can turn out to be anything but. "Personal reasons" often mean about the same and must be very carefully explored during the selection interview process.

Naturally, the process will vary from one police agency to the next, but parts of a comprehensive selection process often include the following:

- Completion of a detailed personal history packet
- In-depth background investigation
- Oral board interview
- Polygraph exam
- Psychological exam
- Physical exam and drug screen
- Interview with the Chief

Yes, you need good people and getting hired as an officer for your department should not feel like an impossible quest. But you owe your employees and your community only the very best to serve as your guardians. Reaching for that goal should balance out the negatives of working short-handed at times.

Traffic Enforcement. Many small agencies are not sufficiently staffed to operate a dedicated traffic law enforcement and/or accident investigation unit. That should not keep you from requiring that your Patrol officers carry out the duties of traffic law enforcement and crash investigation. In reality, every one of your uniformed officers is a traffic officer. Each needs to know that, as a generalist, working traffic is among his or her responsibilities as a peace officer. While you do not want your subordinate supervisors setting quotas and demanding a set number of tickets, each supervisor is accountable for assuring that his or her people are contributing to the accident reduction cause. Outcome, not output, is the goal. A reduction in both violations and crashes is that desired outcome.

Revenue generation through the issuance of buckets of traffic tickets should never be the objective of what your people are doing, even though some of your citizen-customers will believe otherwise. Take the opportunity via social media or in-person appearances to let the community know what your officers are doing and why.

Cooperation and collaboration is the name of the game in traffic law enforcement and accident investigation, just as it is in your many other areas of responsibility. You might contact the chiefs of nearby departments to see if they may be interested in joining your agency in some coordinated enforcement efforts. It also would be a good idea to arrange with another, larger agency such as the highway patrol to loan expert assistance when accident reconstruction or other traffic expertise is required. If at all possible, try to send one or more of your own personnel to an advanced accident investigation course. Upon return that officer should be able to further the accident investigation skills of your other personnel, whether they are members of Patrol or a specialized traffic team.

Your department does not have to have a traffic enforcement unit to be effective in traffic law enforcement. But if you are fortunate enough to have one, ensure that your traffic cops have the equipment and training required to do their job. Try to keep them from getting regularly siphoned off for non-traffic assignments. Attempt to create a sub-culture that says it is a special honor to be part of a hard-working traffic unit. Always recognize these people for their good work.

Traffic law enforcement is a legitimate responsibility of a local law enforcement agency, regardless of its size. Your citizens will expect that you do it.

Training. You owe your people the preparation they require to do a difficult job, and do it safely and well. Too often, cities and towns look first to employee training as something to slash when the budget looks tight. That is a recipe for disaster. Do everything you can to keep that from happening to your department.

Ascertain that your first-line supervisors realize the value of training and their obligation to provide it whenever and however possible. Some of the best small agencies require time to be given over to training *every* roll call briefing, even if it is just three minutes' worth conducted by a member of the Patrol team. In addition, meeting the in-service training requirements of your state's Peace Officer Standards and Training (POST) licensing authority is critical. Assign someone from your leadership staff to coordinate your agency's training program and ensure that the training and reporting requirements of your POST are met. Do not overlook the need for training in the so-called "soft skills" to be included in your agency's training curriculum. Topics like de-escalation tactics and working with special populations are important, too. Offer to host area or regional training classes, even if you have to utilize a venue outside of your own facility. (You should find community organizations such as schools glad to furnish locations where their cops can train.) Specialized training elsewhere is important, too, even if travel and lodging can get pricey. (Sometimes grants can help pay the tab.) If you have the ability to send people away for specialized schooling, require that these employees share their newfound knowledge upon their return. Do not overlook leadership training for you and your top staff, as well. Unfortunately, too many chiefs cease their own learning efforts once they reach the status of Top Cop. There is always more that you can (and should) learn.

Your Field Training Officers (FTOs) fill a critical role in your department's training endeavors. Beyond the technical skills and procedural routines that they teach your new hires they represent everything your department stands for. Attitude is at least as important as the ability to teach for an exceptional FTO. Your newbies will be absorbing the culture of your department during the extensive time they spend with these role models. You want them to see, hear, and learn only the best. Field Training Officer is no place for a lazy, jaundiced, tired, poor attitude police officer, no matter how lengthy his or her time on the job. You must mandate that your trainees observe and experience only the positive traits they will be expected to emulate. That means placing them under the tutelage of only your best.

Professional Standards. Perhaps you call it Internal Affairs in your department. Whatever you call it, this unit will be responsible for receiving, processing, and, where necessary, investigating commendations and complaints concerning your personnel. Depending upon the size of your agency, the individual or individuals assigned may have other duties in your department. Meanwhile, you are responsible for guaranteeing that your Professional Standards investigator(s) will have the specialized training required to do an excellent job of fact-gathering for review and final disposition by you and your command staff.

It is important to complainant and complained-against alike that a resolution to a complaint be reached as quickly as possible. For some situations an explanation or apology may be all that is needed to smooth a complainant's ruffled feathers. At other times, a serious complaint, perhaps even involving a criminal allegation, will require a full-scale investigation. Although considerably more work may be required, a timely resolution is nonetheless desirable. But a complaint must never be minimized or ignored.

There are more things that you as the department CEO can do to ensure that the Professional Standards function runs smoothly and justly for all concerned. First, be sure that your agency's policies, procedures, and rules regarding Professional Standards or Internal Affairs investigations are up-to-date, complete, and clear from the time a complaint or inquiry is received until a final disposition is reached. It is vital that first-line supervisors have a voice in determining whether or not there was wrongdoing, and, if so, what is to be done about it. By sharing in decisions of this magnitude your supervisors have the opportunity to grow as leaders.

Even if he or she only fills the role of I.A. investigator part of the time, the officer or officers assigned must be well-trained for the responsibility. New court decisions can affect what they can and cannot do. Plenty of I.A. training is available, and some of it is on-line. Ensure that your investigators are prepared for their work. A lot of people are depending on them.

As the chief, it would be a good idea for you to keep a "reminder" file, even if it is only in your head, concerning in-progress Professional Standards investigations or final reports. Certainly you want to take the time to do an I.A. inquiry right, but both the complainant and any personnel named in the allegation deserve a prompt resolution of what could for all be a very troubling event. These investigations and their disposition must not be allowed to "rest" and gather dust just because someone has other tasks or is uncomfortable having to make a tough decision. Once a final determination has been reached, everyone involved needs to know the outcome and any further action contemplated.

Some chiefs place the handling of "Response to Resistance" or "Use of Force" reports under the purview of Professional Standards, even though these reports do not of themselves normally indicate misconduct of any sort. Agencies vary as to what sort of police action should result in one of these reports being completed by the officer using the force and his or her supervisor. One department may require a report and its review be completed any time a police weapon, lethal or less-lethal, is displayed. Others require the documentation only if the weapon is actually applied. Most all agencies require the report any time someone is intentionally injured by an officer, even if the injury is only claimed and cannot be verified. You will have to set the guidelines for your agency. The point is that *some* kind of documentation of use of force is required and then reviewed by leadership staff for any indication of unnecessary force that may require further investigation, additional training, or even discipline. The process also is necessary to determine possible patterns of questionable officer conduct or potentially defective policies, procedures, training, or equipment. Equally important is the need to protect the officer who has responded correctly and ethically in a use of force situation. You must personally participate in each Response to Resistance or Use of Force review and have the final say in its disposition.

Finally, keep your boss in the know concerning complaints and Response to Resistance instances that might reverberate beyond the walls of the police department. That harkens back to the "no surprises for the boss" rule. If a problem has been detected, he or she will need to hear from you what you plan to do about it.

Detentions. Very few police chiefs want to run a jail if they can possibly avoid it. Lockups are a high-risk, high-liability operation. Rely on the county or a larger agency that is willing to house your detainees if you possibly can. It is worth just about whatever you have to pay to not be in the jail business. In other words, contract for the use of jail space if that is an option.

But perhaps you have inherited a jail operation or for whatever reason cannot avoid operating a lockup. Jail operations represent a complex function that require directions far beyond the scope of this book. Nonetheless, some very general guidelines for detentions operations may be of use. The first and most obvious rule? Scrupulously follow your state's laws, rules, and regulations for operating a holding facility of any kind. Ascertain that your personnel assigned as detentions specialists have adequate training for their difficult job. The training, like that of your officers, should not be one-and-done but continuing. Avoid bringing in street cops to fill in for jailers–that is not what they are trained for.

If you must house prisoners, do everything possible to minimize the time that they are in your custody. Ensure that they are kept under constant *human* observation while they are in your facility or being transported by your people. The days of leaving a prisoner alone with perhaps a camera or two to "watch" the general area are gone–or should be.

It is a reasonable assumption that very few police chiefs look forward to the responsibility of running a jail. Nonetheless, if your agency maintains such an operation, it *is* your responsibility. Big time. If you have a jail, it is not enough that you (hopefully) have really good people to supervise its operation for you. In addition, *you* must keep a close eye on the detention function yourself. Physically inspect the facility regularly. Talk to the people who work there. Just as important, talk to those who are "guests" there. Thus armed with first-hand observations, you will have a much-improved chance of avoiding any unwelcome surprises.

SWAT. Special Weapons and Tactics (SWAT) teams have something in common with jail operations. They are both high-risk, expensive operations. Even if done responsibly, both can be challenging for a small police department. As you know, the times are long past when a group of guys could get together with their camo gear and deer rifles and call themselves a SWAT team. But just like a bigger police agency, on occasion you will have need of a group of properly equipped, well-trained specialists to handle tough assignments ranging from a barricaded gunman to a hostage-taker to warrant service at a residence known to harbor an armed and dangerous fugitive. If you are able to commit to spend the time, money, and training to equip and maintain a skilled group of SWAT operators, that is the way to go. Normally this will be a group of officers who have other duties in your department. For them, SWAT will be an as-needed, collateral assignment. If that is your situation, insist that your team members have gone through a rigorous selection process that includes a test for physical fitness. Ensure that those selected undergo extensive and continuing training under the supervision of well-qualified instructors. Training, to include education on your agency's use of force guidelines, should be a weekly event. Be certain that your team members have the right equipment, including advanced body armor, to do their job in safety. Monitoring of team members' performance should be conducted by mature, highly knowledgeable supervisors, from your own agency or from outside. These leaders will prove critical to the success of the unit. Their total interest and engagement in this highly specialized team is a must.

For you another approach may be to reach a mutual aid agreement with a nearby agency that has a solid SWAT team. Or you might consider forming or participating in an already-existing regional SWAT unit made up of qualified and motivated members from multiple police agencies. This would be a collateral assignment for team members who would mobilize from their usual assignments to train or conduct an operation. The team would be on call 24 hours a day, every day.

It is very good that you have competent people who are willing and able to lead your department's SWAT function. But as in the case of running a jail, this is a unit that will call for your personal attention. Stay in close touch and stay in the know. Commend good work as it occurs but intervene when what you learn concerns you.

K-9. Properly handled, canine-handler teams can be terrific assets to field operations and excellent public relations tools for your department. They also are relatively expensive and are yet another of those units that can bring about headaches for you and your department if not handled well. If you have inherited a police working dog unit, you will need to determine the level and quality of training and supervision the team has had. Review your agency's policies and procedures for K-9 applications. Determine if they are in line with your department's use of force guidelines. You also must be comfortable with the kind of supervision the unit is receiving. Additionally, you will have to ensure that the dog and handler team receives competent training on a regular basis, whether it occurs within your own agency or elsewhere. You also will ensure that all K-9 deployments are carefully documented. Any encounter in which the dog causes injury to anyone also must be carefully documented (including photographed) in detail and reviewed by command staff as a use of force.

If your agency is without a K-9 program but you are considering starting one, look to colleagues nearby who have such a program and get their views on the pros, cons, and operational wrinkles involved. Before you proceed, be sure you have one or more officers on board who are very interested in taking on the extra responsibilities of being a handler and the dog's at-home parent. Also be certain you have the green light from your own boss to expend the extra funds and effort required for the dog, training, special vehicular equipment, home kennel, and other equipment and supplies needed to support a viable program. Your supervisor needs to understand that the program involves much more than allowing Officer Schmuck to have his pet poodle Muffy ride around with him. You, your boss, and your elected officials need to be comfortable with the "visuals" of fielding one or more dogs in your community. In other words, will they be viewed favorably by your populace? The key for you is to deploy a well-socialized animal that can be petted by the kids, not a land shark.

Finally, before launching a K-9 program you must determine how you want the animal to be used. Do you want a drug sniffer or a well-trained Patrol working dog that can be used to search buildings for bad guys, track fleeing felons, and search open areas for evidence? Or are you seeking a multiple-purpose dog? A competent K-9 provider and trainer should be able to enlighten you on what is both possible and advisable for your needs. You also need that expert's help in obtaining a dog for police work. It is a lot more difficult (and expensive) than going to the local animal shelter and saving a mutt from euthanasia, as noble a cause as that may be.

Dog and handler teams can be extremely useful in helping you and your agency fulfill your public safety mission. Just look before you leap and be sure you are comfortable with all of what you are getting into.

Communications. If your agency contracts with another governmental entity to provide your 911 answering point and dispatch center, some chiefs would say you have an ideal situation. They would offer that in so doing you have avoided the staffing challenges, officer complaints, equipment malfunctions, and other issues that can be part and parcel of operating a ComCenter. If that is your situation, you nonetheless have work to do. Whether it is you or another member of your staff, someone needs to maintain a close liaison with the management of the Center. Information, including complaints and kudos, can thus flow freely between the service provider and your department. In addition, that someone can keep an eye on costs vs. service delivery and help ascertain if you are getting adequate service for the money you pay. In other words, allowing someone else to handle the day-to-day operations of your ComCenter does not absolve you of the obligation to do your best to ensure that your officers and your citizens are being well-served.

You have additional obligations if you operate your own Communications Center. First and foremost, you need to determine if you have the right people in the right numbers working there. Because of the sensitivity of the information handled, your ComCenter personnel must be carefully backgrounded prior to hire. Once again, "the tie goes to the runner." That is you, the employer. Do not hire someone you have any doubts about. In addition, do not scrimp on the number of personnel needed to safely and adequately staff a Communications Center. That is a must. Finally, do not staff a ComCenter with sworn personnel who can be better used on the street. The exception would be the officer who is temporarily assigned there while recovering from illness or injury. But the ComCenter is not the place for an officer who cannot or will not do his job long-term.

Supervision of the Center is also a key issue. Both sworn and civilian supervisors have been assigned to oversee ComCenters and have done a creditable job. The question for you is whether or not to spend badly needed sworn assets by putting them in a ComCenter that could be supervised by a competent civilian leader. The key word here is *competent.* In the end, you are responsible for assuring that any Communications supervisor receives appropriate leadership training in addition to remaining current on the technical complexities of the job.

If you run your own ComCenter you also are accountable to ensure that the ever-changing technology of the Center is up-to-date and adequate for your employees' needs. You can help yourself determine this by spending some time there. Plug in and sit in with your call takers and dispatchers. Show some sincere interest in what they are doing. Ask questions about the adequacy of ComCenter policies, procedures, and equipment. Those actually doing the job are your best sources for information on each of these topics. Then, make good use of what you learn.

As with the rest of your employees, come to the defense of your ComCenter personnel when they are under unjust attack. Let them (and your officers) know just how important Dispatch is to the success of your organization. Praise your ComCenter staff when they do a good job. It is important that your officers realize the value of a well-run ComCenter that serves as their lifeline in a crisis. Some chiefs have assigned new officers to spend a shift in Communications as part of the field training process. It often gives the officers a whole new appreciation of the difficulty and importance of the dispatcher's role. It would be a good practice for you to emulate if you can possibly afford it.

Finally, you may want to determine if your agency is following radio traffic protocols identical to the agencies around you, especially those you may be sharing a radio frequency with. It makes little sense for each department to adhere to a different set of radio codes and procedures. Additionally, you might consider the fact that many public safety agencies today rely on clear speech and very few codes in order to promote better interoperability among agencies and increase ease of understanding among their own employees. It just makes good sense.

Your agency's 911 answering and radio dispatch functions are vital elements of your police department. Your agency literally cannot function without them. Be sure you give them the attention they deserve.

Records. Your Records Section has at least one thing in common with your Communications unit: it is indispensable for the operation of your organization. Like Dispatch, it should be staffed by civilians and, preferably, supervised by a non-sworn manager.

Once more, like Communications, your Records employees should be carefully backgrounded before they are hired. The danger of security breaches is ever-present in this operation, and leaked information can cause you no end of serious trouble. In addition to getting the right people, you must check to see that you have adequate security measures in place to protect both the paper and electronic records you have stored in your Records Section. One very basic measure for securing your records is to make known to all your personnel (post it!) that this is a restricted access area. This is not the place for cops to gather to socialize.

The key to Records effectiveness, efficiency, and security is, of course, having quality supervision in place. Your Records leadership team must be kept up to date on statutes and procedures pertaining to this vital function, and that requires continuing, comprehensive training for these leaders. It is particularly important that these supervisors and their people are knowledgeable concerning records release and public information requests and their appropriate handling, as your Records Section is likely where these diverse requests will be received. Your Records supervisors also will need to ensure that state and federal crime reporting for your jurisdiction is appropriately and accurately handled.

Just as with Communications, you should not be a stranger to your Records people. Check by regularly and pay attention to them. Recognize their good work. Get a grounding in what they do. Ask what you can do to make their work better and easier. It is practically guaranteed that they will appreciate your attention.

Not unlike so many other parts of your organization, Records can cause you some major headaches if the job isn't done well. Beyond that, most likely some really good people are working there who richly deserve your attention. Don't disappoint them.

There are a lot of special units and functions out there that can help you achieve your most basic goals of policing: service to and protection of your community. There are some that are particular to your locale that may not be needed or appropriate somewhere else. Water safety units, beach patrols, air support, gang intervention squads, and multi-agency tasks forces all come to mind. It will be necessary that you periodically review all the support or specialized units that exist in your department. Sometimes a police agency will create a special unit to satisfy an operational or political need of the moment. Then, the team, unit, or program continues to exist simply because "we've always done it that way." You and your staff should examine your organization's structure at least annually. Perhaps you need to add a support unit of some sort to increase the effectiveness and efficiency of the agency, or for some other valid purpose. But you also may find you need to drop some support function or special unit. Or your agency may be made more effective by combining two or more support units. By doing any of these things your objective should be to help the individuals who carry out the most directly impactful functions of the department: your Patrol force.

CARING FOR YOUR CIVILIAN EMPLOYEES

You have been around law enforcement long enough to know that in too many police departments the non-sworn employees sometimes feel they are treated like second-class citizens. You also know that this is unfortunate because civilian law enforcement personnel provide incredibly valuable and absolutely necessary support to the badge-wearing members of the agency. This sense of being less important than the other members of the department is detrimental to both these employees' feelings about themselves as well as the overall health of the department. And it does not have to be that way. You as the chief can change the way these good people are regarded if that is even a minor issue at your police department.

As in so many of your other functions, it is your job to be the positive role model for how civilian employees are treated in your agency. Spend some time with them when there is absolutely nothing important to talk about. Visit with them, anyway. Get to know something about them. Find out more about what they do in your organization. Be sure that you and your subordinate supervisors acknowledge the good work your civilian employees do. Include your civilians in your award and recognition events. Be cognizant of the fact that your civilians face job-related stresses, too. They should have access to the same mental and emotional wellness support that your officers enjoy. Advocate for your civilians' pay and benefits as much as you do for your cops' salary and perks. Don't forget the personal touches, such as birthday cards and personal notes from the boss when you become aware of major events in their lives, such as births and serious illness.

Encourage your sworn personnel to engage with your civilian employees, too. Your own interactions with your civilians should provide direction as to what you expect. A few chiefs actually have discouraged their officers from associating with their civilian employees, apparently out of fear of romantic entanglements that may develop. Number one, that won't work to forestall normal human behavior. Number two, that sort of misguided policy will only serve to contribute to a sense of isolation on the part of your civilians. That will not be healthy for your civilians or the organization as a whole. Your job as chief is to encourage an atmosphere of welcome and inclusion in your department, not something else entirely.

Like your cops, your civilian employees are your ambassadors to the community. They are the personnel that your citizens hear and see when they walk into your building or telephone with a question or request. You want those citizen visitors and callers to be left with a very positive impression of your agency. That's why you need exceptional people filling those public contact positions. For that you need to hire and retain only the best. In hiring civilians, do not overlook the in-depth background checks and careful interview process. Once they are on board, do not lower your expectations for ethical and otherwise appropriate conduct, on and off the job. Do not neglect the training of your civilians, either. You owe them adequate preparation for the work that they will do for you. Whether these people are dispatchers, records clerks, evidence technicians, or something else, their jobs can be difficult and stressful, too. If they do not do them well, big problems for you and your organization can result.

Civilian employees are a contributing and important part of your police department. Hire the right ones and then do your best to keep them aboard and well-prepared to do their work. You will harvest significant benefits for your organization.

PULLING IT ALL TOGETHER

To state the obvious: there is a big difference between running a single function or division, even in a much larger agency, and being responsible for *all* of the operations of a smaller police department. You do, indeed, wear a lot of different hats. And you have to ensure that each one of them fits you well.

You will have to make it your business to know as much as you can about each of your agency's operations. You will need to show genuine interest in each. While one function may draw more of your attention and, frankly, more of your personal interest than others, you must follow a careful balancing act of sorts and focus on the operations and people of each. It is not unheard of for cops to state their opinion that "the detectives are the chief's pets" or "Patrol is where the boss's heart is," or words to that effect. As one chief put it, perhaps with tongue slightly in cheek: "Dad loves all of his kids equally."

You will do your best to support all the diverse units of your department and give careful attention to the problems and needs of each. You also will be sure to commend good work done anywhere in the department. Do not overlook your civilian employees in the process. Meanwhile, you will endeavor to remain highly visible in all quarters of your agency. That includes the units that do not work the same schedule that you do. Also, continue your practice of demonstrating personal touches in your interactions with all your people. That could include sending "good work" cards, birthday greetings, and whatever else your imagination may come up with as acknowledgments that you care about your people and appreciate what they are doing.

You are the chief for *all* your people. Stay abreast of what they are doing to the extent reasonably possible, especially when they may be facing extra challenges. Represent the interests and sing the praises of all of them, as appropriate. That can aid you considerably in assuring that everyone is pulling in the same direction.

SUMMARY

You really do don a lot of different hats as a small agency police chief. You must be a contributing member of your boss's top staff. You must take an active role in the community and your profession. But you also have a major role to play in serving as the very interested and supportive leader of your own organization. All of this you must do without either ignoring or showing favoritism towards a particular element of your department.

You obviously will need to stay well informed in the activities of your most visible arms of the department: Patrol and Investigations. But the other, more specialized and perhaps less-known sections of your agency must share your attention, too. The employees working in each function of your agency must be able to feel your interest.

Your organization is almost certain to be a more effective and efficient one when you remain knowledgeable about the people and goings on in each part of the whole. At the same time, you will be less likely to be ambushed by surprises that you definitely won't find enjoyable.

Remember: You love *all* your kids a lot!

Chapter 11

YOUR OFFICERS' WELFARE IS PRIORITY ONE

You have a great many responsibilities as the leader of your police department. None is more important than your obligation to aid your people in staying safe on the job. It is accompanied by your responsibility to serve as an alert risk manager in monitoring and supervising your employees' work to prevent actions or lapses that could expose them and your employer to civil or criminal liability. Street survival is vital, but so is financial and career survival. You are obliged to do everything you can to help keep your people safe from ALL threats.

Serving as your department's lead safety officer will require that you be an exceptional role model for officer safety through your own practices. If your people witness you acting in an unsafe manner, it is doubtful that they will believe you when you lecture them about the importance of officer safety. In addition, you will have to serve as a safety instructor, inspector, advocate, coach, and, occasionally, disciplinarian. Officer safety is *that* important. You also will recall and teach that the very first rule of officer safety is to treat others in the way you would want to be treated. An individual you have humiliated or otherwise maltreated may feel he has no alternative but to fight you. Your officers need to get *that* message, too.

But before you can help shield your officers from always-present danger, you must have an idea of what those dangers are. You heard a lot about those things in your officer safety training, perhaps a long while back. It's worth refreshing your memory on just what those hazards are.

WHAT ARE THE DANGERS?

The safety errors that have contributed to the violent deaths of many, many law enforcement officers over the years are well-documented. It is no secret that the same errors that have resulted in the deaths of peacekeepers in the past are still killing cops today, and almost certainly will be killing them tomorrow. Some of these errors have been committed by a few cops for so long that they have become ingrained as habits–bad habits. It is your job, with the assistance of your sworn supervisors, to seek out these dangerous practices and bad habits among your people and see to it that they are eliminated. Your cops' lives may depend upon your success here.

But just what are the fatal errors that too often result in the death or serious injury of a police officer? They include the following:

Complacency. Often included here is apathy, general carelessness, or the hopeless attitude of "whatever will happen will happen and I can't prevent it." That, of course, is unadulterated nonsense. An officer who sleepwalks his way through his duties, works in a sloppy manner, or is apparently brain dead to the dangers of his or her job is on track to be in that neurological condition for real. He or she is dangerous to his or her peers, as well. Complacency has been referred to as the umbrella under which all other officer safety errors gather.

Dangerous assumptions. An assumption can be thought of as anything regarded in one way or another without being based on fact. Rather, something is *assumed*, whether true or not. For a police officer, a dangerous assumption might be that all alarms are false, big dogs don't bite, or all drunks are harmless. The only safe assumption that an officer can make is that virtually *any* individual or situation could prove hazardous.

Failure to detect and react to danger signs. Every experienced law enforcement officer should be able to construct his or her own list of indicators of potential danger ahead. Those red flags could include furtive movements, hands kept out of sight, intoxication, and many others. The list can prove a lengthy one. Very bad things can happen to an officer who misses one or more danger signs. Even worse, too many officers have been seriously injured or killed after picking up on danger signs but not doing anything to alter his or her tactics in response.

Improper use of backup assistance. Failing to summon help when needed can have fatal consequences for a law enforcement officer; so could having adequate help on-scene but not using it wisely. Having three burly backups on-scene who are focused only on standing around gossiping helps no one. The officer blessed with readily available assistance must use it for maximum benefit.

False courage. The cop who routinely proclaims his ability to do his job without assistance, regardless of the nature of the call or contact, is serving as a great example for false courage. This malpractice is sometimes referred to as "cowboy" or "cowgirl" policing, and it can prove deadly. This officer may be trying to convince colleagues (or self) of his or her bravery. Whatever the case, committing this grave safety error has resulted in far too many law enforcement casualties.

Underestimating an opponent. Some bad guys are just as good at street survival tactics as are the officers they go up against. Any given offender may have much greater physical strength than the officer trying to arrest him. He may be a better shot, too. Or the frail-looking, mentally disturbed individual may seem to display superhuman strength when tested. A cop who downplays the risk of danger from a potential opponent may be headed for a hard fall, and a painful one.

Poor approach or positioning. Standing between the rear of a violator's car and the front push bumper of the patrol vehicle on the street provides a classic example of poor positioning by a police officer who is inviting crushed legs, or worse. So would standing directly in front of a door while knocking at the scene of an "unknown risk" call. And marching right up the front walk at a house where violence is known to be occurring would furnish a great example of a poor (and dangerous) approach. In each case the potential victim officer would be guilty of failing to remain constantly aware of his/her surroundings and the location of possible threats.

Failure to utilize safety equipment. There is no acceptable excuse for an officer not to utilize his or her safety belts while seated in a moving police vehicle. Likewise, there is no good excuse for failing to don a high-visibility vest when directing traffic or body armor while working the street. Basic safety equipment saves police lives on a regular basis.

Poor weapon retention practices. Every year one or more American law enforcement officers is murdered with his or her own handgun. Every call or contact experienced by a police officer includes the presence of at least one firearm: the officer's own. If that officer is careless, that weapon could end up in the hands of an enemy.

Failing to look for the next threat. Sometimes this dangerous error occurs because a good cop relaxes too soon. In other words, the officer lowers his or her guard thinking the danger has passed, when in reality it has not. An example can be seen in the case of an officer who has ceased watching for threats because he or she has just captured and secured a robber or burglar, oblivious to the fact that an accomplice—or several of them—may be nearby.

Poor use of cover. On occasion officers have taken on armed offenders while positioned in the open, even though there was excellent cover nearby. Sometimes those officers quickly became victims. Other times, officers have mistaken mere *concealment* with cover and rapidly became casualties when projectiles pierced their "cover."

Being ill, sleepy, or asleep on the job. Anything that keeps an officer from being at his or her best while on duty increases the likelihood that the officer will become a casualty. For everyone's safety, an officer who cannot be 100% present and engaged on-shift should not be at work.

Poor handcuffing. Sometimes cops are attacked because they failed to double-lock the handcuffs, put them on too loosely, or applied them too tight. Other times bad things happen because an officer failed to realize that handcuffs are a fallible, temporary means of restraint. And yet other times, a peace officer is badly hurt or killed because he or she handcuffed a prisoner in front instead of behind, or, worse, failed to handcuff at all.

Sloppy search practices. As hard as it may seem to believe, on occasion an officer dies because that officer failed to search an individual he or she had taken into custody. Other times tragedy has occurred because the search was sloppy, hastily done, or otherwise incomplete and a concealed deadly weapon was missed. Time after time, a poor or no search results in police fatalities.

Careless prisoner handling. Apparently a few officers believe that once the arrest is made and the subject is in custody, the potential danger is over. If that were true law enforcement would not have lost the number of cops it has due to the murderous actions of in-custody offenders. To the contrary, an officer remains at risk from a prisoner's attack until that officer is totally removed from the offender's presence.

Being out of shape physically or mentally. Cops have died because they gave up after receiving non-life-threatening injuries. Others have died because their opponent was in better physical shape and had a mindset for winning that the officer may not have possessed. Not only physical fitness but a winning mindset and a powerful drive to survive should be parts of each of your officers' survival kit.

Failure to realize the potential for accidental death or injury. Simply because of the nature of a law enforcement officer's job, he or she faces the potential of accidental death or disabling injury absent some careful precautions on the officer's part. Bloody experience shows that not all officers realize that. It is up to you to help them grasp the realities of the job.

Fatal errors are made by rookies and veteran officers alike. Indeed, the seasoned "old salt" who thinks he or she has seen it all and done it all may be at greater risk than the rookie who is concentrating on doing everything just right. It is important that you and (especially) your first-line supervisors ensure that all of your officers are conscious of the dangers of the job and what they can do to mitigate them. That comes next....

PREVENTING OFFICER INJURIES AND DEATHS

You have made your troops aware of what some of the threats to their safety are. You have made clear that these dangers and behaviors are things that they must avoid. But a fair question for your cops to ask is "what would you have me do, instead?" To counteract the fatal errors, you and your first-line supervisors should provide some of the following officer survival tips:

Keep learning your job. There is no room for complacency in law enforcement. Your officers must continue to learn from their training and experience and never cease striving to get better (and safer) in their sometimes-perilous line of work. Carelessness and complacency have killed enough cops.

Maintain a survival mindset. You have read or heard of incidents in which seriously wounded police officers have fought through their pain to take out a would-be cop killer. Be sure that your officers are aware of some of these incidents and the need to harbor an "I will always survive and win" attitude. It *does* matter.

Banish Tombstone Courage. Your people have nothing to prove to themselves or anyone else concerning their willingness to do a sometimes-dangerous job. There is no reason to look for a chance to be a hero. Chances are, over a long law enforcement career there's a good chance it will happen on its own. Do not reward foolish behavior.

Never stop looking for one more. Your people must never cease their continuing threat awareness and detection practices. If they find one weapon in their search of a prisoner, they secure it and start looking for the next one. If they apprehend one suspect hiding in a building, they must immediately start seeking an undiscovered accomplice. None of this means that they must become paranoid. It simply means that they must avoid relaxing too soon.

Always think about cover. A street-smart cop is always thinking about where he or she can quickly find solid cover–not mere concealment–on any call or contact that suddenly sees a weapon appear. All of your people need to be cover-conscious because you have trained them that way.

Use backup help wisely. You know how the practice of contact and cover works: one officer does the primary work of the contact while the other serves as a vigilant lifeguard. Your officers must know how it works and practice it, too. Backups can never be permitted to loiter around daydreaming or gassing with other cops while the primary officer essentially works without covering protection. Backup help is too precious an asset to be wasted.

Maintain a "reactionary gap." Your officer needs time and space to effectively defend against a surprise attack from a subject he or she is dealing with. That officer is more likely to be overwhelmed if he or she has allowed that individual to stand too close. Many safety-smart cops regard five to six feet as an adequate reactionary space. Circumstances, such as an obviously hostile subject, may dictate increasing the distance.

Listen to the "little voice." That inner voice is probably originating from your training and experience. If it is telling you that something just isn't right with the individual or situation you are dealing with, believe it. Take additional precautions, do something different instead of bulldozing ahead and hoping for the best. Something like going to cover, calling for assistance, or presenting a weapon, for instance. Your officers need to hear this survival tip from you, their leader.

Handcuff and search properly. Your people need regular hands-on practice in doing it the right way. Handcuff first, search second. Search as many times as necessary to be convinced that nothing dangerous remains on the person of the arrestee. Both actions have to be performed correctly *every* time for everyone's safety.

Stay fit for the job. Set a positive example for your people by the way you take care of yourself. Have the courage to say something if you observe one of your officers neglecting to do the same. It may be an uncomfortable conversation, but it also may be saving the life of someone important to you.

Spot and respond to the danger signs. Your cops must be alert to the commonly seen indicators that the danger quotient is rising with the individual or situation they have encountered. Just as important, they must be prepared to respond effectively when one or more of these hazard flags is present. Every officer may have his or her own list of danger signs, but some often-listed ones include the following:

- Hands intentionally kept out of sight
- Subject visibly angry or agitated
- Subject hiding or fleeing
- Subject ignoring instructions
- Subject attempting to move in closer
- Individual clinching fists or taking a "fighting" stance
- Individual verbalizing homicidal or suicidal intent
- Weapons present or indicated (Example: bulge in clothing)
- Subject intoxicated, drugged, or obviously mentally unstable
- Subject hallucinating or delusional
- Individual has known history for violence or assaults on police
- Situation includes multiple offenders present

Mentally play out threats and responses. Remind your officers that real world experience has shown that cops who have played potential threat scenarios through their minds *before* the danger appears for real tend to do a better job of defending themselves if one day that situation or a similar one goes down. No matter how busy they are, your cops have some down time, particularly if they are working deep nights. At least a little of that time should be devoted to thinking about "what would I do if" scenarios. Doing that just might save an officer's life one day.

Encourage an atmosphere where honest critiques are welcome. This one is directed at you and your top staffers. It is important that all your people become comfortable with getting together to dissect particularly dicey or complex incidents and discuss what went well and what might be done differently next time. These sessions should not be conducted as exercises to affix blame. Instead, they should be seen as learning opportunities in which everyone involved feels safe to speak up without recriminations. You personally can do a lot to establish the atmosphere of these debriefs as learning experiences as opposed to blame sessions. The goal in all of this is to learn from what has gone before in order to do a better (and safer) job the next time. With you visibly taking the lead in this effort you will be developing self-confident and safety-savvy employees.

YOUR ROLE AS RISK MANAGER

In addition to all the other roles that you fulfill in your organization you also must be an alert risk manager for your agency. Along with the other leaders in your department you shoulder the responsibility for saving both lives and money by preventing or correcting unsafe behavior by your employees. It is the humane thing to do because you are thereby preventing pain and suffering among your people. It is the financially responsible thing to do because unsafe employee behavior can result in big money flowing out of your employer's bank accounts to satisfy settlements and losing civil suits brought about by unsafe, negligent, or unlawful employee behavior. Doubtlessly you can think of better uses for those dollars.

You cannot do this alone. Your top managers and first-line supervisors must be made keenly aware of their duty to watch for unsafe equipment, policies, procedures, practices, and employee actions and then promptly intervene to address them. It is especially vital that your first-line leaders identify and "fix" dangerous officers who routinely drive recklessly, disregard safety rules and equipment, and otherwise act in an unsafe manner. These people, unless they cease their unsafe behavior, pose a danger not only to themselves but to others around them and the organization as a whole.

You cannot afford employees who are causing heightened, unnecessary liability for you and your employer. It is fair to say "you" here, as you are likely to be named in any civil suit that originates out of irresponsible and unsafe behavior by one or more of your employees. Depending upon what such an employee is doing or failing to do, he or she may be endangering your other employees or the community at large. This, of course, is the most compelling reason for repairing or removing this hazardous employee. If you wait until there are really bad consequences from his or her irresponsible behavior, you will have waited too long.

DON'T OVERLOOK YOUR PEOPLES' MENTAL HEALTH

Your employees have a great many needs and in your role as a caring and effective leader you doubtlessly spend a lot of time and energy working to satisfy them. But there are yet other important needs your people have that do not involve pay, equipment, or shift schedules. Your employees' mental and emotional health needs also will need addressed. You already know that the line of work that you and your people have chosen can be highly stressful and emotionally taxing. The stresses that your people encounter are likely a little different from the ones you face, but your people can feel them just as intensely if not more so. You do your best to protect your own mental and emotional health so that you can continue to serve as an effective leader. It is only right that you do everything possible to keep your people equally healthy.

Your employees' troubling issues can range from financial difficulties to personal relationship crises to family illness, and a whole lot more. There may even be personal physical health issues adding to the disturbing picture. You must charge your first-line supervisors with monitoring the mental and emotional health of their subordinates, as they are the best-placed people in the department to spot abnormal or inexplicable behavior in their troops. You must do the same for your own direct reports. Leaders sometimes have issues, too. What you are all looking for is out of the ordinary behavior that may indicate that the individual exhibiting it is in crisis, or rapidly headed that way. At times, a patient and compassionate ear may be all that is required to ease someone's pain. Sometimes professional help is needed. Your job and that of your subordinate supervisors is to make it clear to the troubled employee that someone cares and help is available. It is equally important that the employee hears that his or her career will not be damaged by reaching out for needed help.

Police suicides are increasing in number in this country. Ensure that your leadership team, including your first-line supervisors, is trained to spot the danger signs of pending self-destruction. Equally important, be sure your employees know that professional help is available for their asking, whether it comes from an Employee Assistance Program (EAP) provider or a police psychologist contracted by the police department. (Note: It would be well worth the cost to have one of these skilled professionals identified and quickly available to your employees.) An employee who avails himself or herself needs to hear from you that his or her future at the department will not be impacted.

But your department can experience an event much worse than the day-to-day stresses of the job. For the whole of the organization, nothing can compare to the emotional trauma created by the on-duty death or critical injury of an officer. Such an event will have a devastating impact on your entire organization. The families of your personnel may also be hit heavily. In addition to supporting the victim officer's family and assuring that appropriate tributes are made, you will now more than ever have to be the very visible leader of your department who is seemingly omnipresent to provide information and offer comfort following a tragedy.

Even as you pray that such an event never occurs you must prepare yourself in case it does. Talking now with other law enforcement CEOs who have gone through such an incident can help you learn a lot. Your colleagues can enlighten you about their personal experiences, including what went right and what went wrong in their agency's response. They can tell you what they might have done differently. The Concerns of Police Survivors (COPS) organization also should be able to alert you to things to look for in your employees and how you can best support them at such a critical time. They also can connect you with leaders who can help you plan and conduct services and other honors for a fallen officer. Additionally, they can provide advice on accessing potential federal funds for the survivors of a victim officer.

Following the death of one of your serving officers, you as the chief will have several primary responsibilities. First, you must be constantly available to the family and close associates of the deceased officer to offer condolences and continued support. This remains true even if you have appointed another member of your staff to be the primary family liaison. Second, you must ensure that all your employees and community members receive only *accurate* information about what has happened and what will happen next. Deliver this information in person to the extent possible. Such tragic events often result in inaccurate information and rumors being spread, so it is especially vital that everyone gets *accurate* information straight from the Chief of Police. Finally, if the death or injury was the result of a criminal act you will have the additional responsibility of ensuring that those responsible are identified, arrested, and prosecuted as a result of lawful, proper police work.

Next, your department's supervisors need to remain alert for the delayed emotional trauma that might not show itself for days, weeks, or longer. There may be employees who need professional counselling to deal with shock, anger, grief, or other feelings that may not emerge for some time. It will be up to you and your staff to direct these good people towards the resources they need. Keep in mind that someone not directly involved in the event may need some time away from work to recover, too. Tragedy within an organization can reveal relationships that you did not know existed.

Finally, stay in touch with your first-line supervisors and command staff members to determine if *they* may be suffering post-traumatic stress symptoms themselves. They, too, may need skilled intervention. Meanwhile, monitor your own mental and emotional condition. If someone you trust tells you that you look or sound like things are not so good with you, believe them. You, too, are human. You are permitted to experience all the emotions your people are going through. And you, too, may need some professional support. Never be hesitant to secure it. In doing so you will once again be setting a good example for your people. Your message? *It is OK to ask for help when you need it.*

Do not forget that your people can be harmed by cumulative stress—the "routine" crises that crop up every shift—just as they can be injured by a single, major event. You and your leadership team will have to remain alert for that kind of mental and emotional damage, too. Once more, monitoring your people for behavior that is abnormal for them can be important for detecting and addressing a growing problem.

Here's one more thing that won't exactly comfort you, but it is verifiably true. When asked what causes them the most stress, many cops confess that it is not the street but what happens in their own building that disturbs them the most. They talk about "the administration" and perceived unfair treatment, politics, favoritism, and other leadership abuses. That is not something you can afford to have happening in your department, and it is something that you can successfully address. By ensuring that your people are treated fairly and respectfully by *all* their leaders, *all* of the time, you can minimize or eliminate that stressor. It is your responsibility to do so.

The mental and emotional good health of your employee family must always remain a top priority for you, the head of that extended family. Remaining alert to the presence of troubling events and issues, internal and external to the organization, does much more than contribute to the effectiveness and efficiency of the department. It also shows you to be the compassionate and caring leader that you are.

YOU AS AN ADVOCATE FOR OFFICER SURVIVAL

There is yet more that you can do as a conscientious leader to help keep your people safe. You must advocate for safety and survival both within your organization and outside of it. Obviously, you must constantly emphasize to your officers one of the primary aims of the department: work safely in everything you do on the job. But you also must serve in an educator's role outside of the police organization. That role remains for you to fill whether you are talking with your boss or Bill the bartender. Included is your duty to defend your people when they have done it the right way for officer safety yet are criticized for their actions. This may require you to explain to Dad who is angry that your people handcuffed his drunk and disorderly son that cops have died at the hands of teenagers. Or it may call for you to explain to a news reporter that, yes, senior citizen drunk drivers get handcuffed and searched, too. You might even want to relate the true story of the "cooperative" 82-year-old who killed two officers with gunshots to the back of the head.

You also must be a powerful voice for your officers when the need for safety-related equipment is on the elected officials' budget agenda. Be prepared to explain to them precisely why a given policy or piece of equipment is needed to protect their cops' lives. Never come across as though you were talking down to the uneducated, even if you suspect that you are. Insulted officials are a lot less likely to grant you what your people truly need. Be direct, be forceful, but always be diplomatic.

As the recognized leader of your police department, you are almost certainly held in high esteem by your good citizens and community leaders. Your opinions are probably both sought after and highly trusted. People are interested in what you have to say. Whether you are speaking to an assemblage of three or three hundred, use the trust and respect you have earned to talk about the police officer's job and its very real hazards. Do not overstate your case or exaggerate the danger. It is real and it does not need to be embellished. Be prepared to answer questions, including the difficult ones. It is very important that your listeners understand what cops do and why. Be willing to acknowledge that law enforcement doesn't get it right every time. No one does. But it's important that the people who want to back you and your officers have the reliable information needed to do just that.

YOUR TASK AS A ROLE MODEL FOR OFFICER SAFETY

There are so very many areas in which you have to serve as an exceptional role model for your people. Officer safety is certainly one of them. The safety consciousness and practices you display in front of your people must set the standard for what they should do and avoid doing. Do that whether you are within the confines of the police building or assisting your cops out on the street. You also must demonstrate top-notch risk management practices in the way you operate your vehicle or make a decision that has civil liability or officer safety implications. Always set the example for doing it the *right* way. If you realize that you have made an officer safety error, own up to it and make it clear that you know what you should have done, instead.

Don your body armor. Religiously use your vehicle's seat belts. Qualify regularly with your weapons. Drive as if you were sane. Practice de-escalation tactics as opposed to further inflaming an already-hot confrontation. Consistently demonstrate for your people what it is that you want *them* to do.

Further, attend officer safety training with your cops. Participate and learn along with them. You are sending a clear message to all around: no matter what your rank or law enforcement experience, you can never know enough about surviving the job.

SUMMARY

As your department's leader, you have no more important a task than doing everything you possibly can to contribute to the safety and wellness of your police officers. In effect, it is you who will be your agency's primary safety officer. You will emphasize the importance you place on workplace safety by always serving as an exceptional role model for good officer safety and risk management practices. You will expect the same of your department's supervisors. Through comprehensive and continuing training, you will ensure that your officers are conscious of precisely what the dangers of the job are and how to defend against them. In addition, you will work to guarantee that your personnel have the equipment they require to do their jobs safely. Your agency's policies and procedures also will need to be carefully formulated and periodically reviewed to ensure that your people have guidelines that support them fully in their "work safely" efforts.

You and your subordinate supervisors also must serve as vigilant risk managers to detect and correct unsafe behaviors ranging from driving practices to questionable arrest, search, and seizure actions. Your people need to be shielded from physical harm, but they also must be protected from the civil or even criminal liability that can result from inappropriate or unlawful police practices.

Finally, you and your leadership corps will remain alert for any indication that your personnel are suffering mentally and emotionally from the impact of either a critical incident, cumulative stress, or perhaps some more personal issue. Your department's next step should be to offer professional assistance to those in need of help in getting through some tough times.

Take care of your work family. It is what an exceptional leader does.

Chapter 12

WORKING SUCCESSFULLY WITH THE NEWS MEDIA

You probably have observed it yourself. A law enforcement officer who would not hesitate to enter a darkened building in search of a bad guy actually quakes upon the approach of a young man or woman armed only with a note pad and a TV camera. In your leadership position, that law enforcement officer cannot be you. Reporters from newspapers, television, Internet, and radio are drawn to major crime, accident, and disaster scenes as ants are lured to a picnic. When they get there, they are looking for information. They have figured out that the person most likely to have what they need is the person in charge. In many instances, that person is going to be you.

News media representatives are an ever-present reality of the police chief's life. You will need to be able to work with them for the good of your department and your profession. The truth is that cops and reporters need each other more often than most police officers might realize. The police have the information on a crime or other event; the media control much of the access to a wide public audience that law enforcement needs from time to time. With just a little effort, cops and correspondents can work together for mutual benefit.

As the leader of your agency, you will set the standard for establishing and maintaining a positive relationship with the media. This chapter will provide you with a set of personal rules for establishing that needed positive relationship. It will equip you with guidance for doing a winning media interview, preparing a news release, putting on a successful news conference, and utilizing the local media for maximum benefit. And it will assist you in creating a useful set of policies and procedures for anyone in your agency who must interact with the ladies and gentlemen of the press. Finally, you will obtain some advice for managing the Public Information function in your department.

As a police leader, you always will have to work with the news media, like it or not. It is up to you to do it successfully.

YOU NEED EACH OTHER

It almost goes without saying that cops and news reporters are often distrusting of one another. At times, actual animosity exists between representatives of two important service providers to the public. In reality, cops and reporters may be more alike than different. Very often, both have a strong sense of justice, are aggressive in seeking information, harbor a desire to help others, and are somewhat clannish, feeling they are disliked by others. And, oh yes. Both often come equipped with oversized egos. Little wonder, then, that on occasion these Type AAA personalities are destined to clash.

One more trait that these two professions often share is a sense of the pragmatic, the practical. That shared characteristic should (but doesn't always) help them realize that each can help the other with his or her difficult job. They don't have to love one another, but they can work with each other for mutual benefit. You can help your people get that message through your own on-display relationship with the media.

That symbiotic relationship works like this: The public is very interested in what your people do for a living. That's why there are so many TV cop shows and movies. To satisfy that public thirst, the minions of the media need access to the information you and your people have about crime, crooks, crime fighting, and the good guys (that's you and your people!) Thus, you have something valuable that the media needs.

On the other hand, the media, including the omnipresent social media, have something you and your cops desire: access to the public for what you have to say. You may need to alert the public to a new scam or get help in searching for a missing person or a bad guy. You may want to disseminate some crime prevention advice. Or you may want to announce a new community-oriented policing program or get deserved attention for some good work done by one or more of your people. The point is that the reporter gets a story and your department gets assistance or accolades, as needed. Everybody can win, at least a good part of the time.

As you learned while a rookie cop, it's easier to get along than fight. That formula won't work every time now just as it didn't back then, but much of the time it will. There are a lot of benefits to be found in working well with the media. You are the one best-positioned in your agency to encourage that state of affairs for your department.

YOUR PERSONAL RULES FOR MEDIA RELATIONS

You have a personal set of rules and ethical considerations that guide you in your relations with others. They provide you with guidance for your behavior in both your personal and professional life. Many of these same guidelines will serve you well in interacting with representatives of the news media. Some are little more than common sense and adherence to the Golden Rule: treat others as you would have them treat you. In addition to these reliable guideposts that you have followed for a long time, consider implementing the following personal rules for working with the media:

Don't hide. Do not do it either figuratively or literally. Whether it is on a scene or in your office, you need to be accessible to a reporter who is seeking your attention. It is not fair for you to shove someone else out front, particularly when the news is not good. This is precisely the time when the media, the community, and your own people are expecting to see the person in charge out front. And that person is you.

Tell the truth. As a police leader your most precious possession is your proven reputation for integrity. Integrity involves credibility, or your reputation for telling the truth at all times. A media rep is likely to forgive you for not knowing, but not for knowingly providing false information. If you destroy your reputation for telling the truth to the press, you may never be able to fully rebuild it. In the process you will have done significant damage to your police department's reputation. Say nothing at all as opposed to lying to the media.

Know and follow your department's media policies and procedures. You expect your people to know and follow your agency's written guidelines for working with the news media. You are responsible for knowing and following them, too. What can and cannot be released to the media are among the most important elements of the protocol. Follow the rules to the letter.

Keep your promises. You must mean what you say and say what you mean. If you tell a reporter that you cannot give out a particular piece of information today but will tomorrow or whenever, make good on your pledge. If you promise to return a call, make sure that you do it. Once more, your reputation for credibility is at stake.

Stay humble. It isn't about you. Keep things in perspective, no matter how many microphones and cameras are thrust in your face. It is your job title and access to the information they want that have the reporters focused on you. When you are gone, the next man or woman wearing the stars will get the same attention.

Be courteous, polite, and tactful. To the media reps you are the public face of your organization. Be nice, even when you don't feel like it. In the meantime, you are continuing to build a positive reputation for your agency and yourself with the news media. It is assuredly worth the effort you invest.

Set a positive example. There is that role model thing again. If you are rude to the newspersons or make crude remarks about them in front of your people, you cannot reasonably expect your employees to do otherwise. Act like the professional you are and set the example.

Don't use the media for feuding. If you are angry with some agency or individual, do not use your access to the media to attack. If you do, you may well draw a response in kind. Remember that reporters love to highlight controversy. Settle your grievances out of the spotlight. Nobody wins in a media-enhanced mud fight.

Use "off the record" very judiciously. Once you have given a reporter a piece of information, he or she is not legally barred from using it, no matter what you may have been promised. Take the risk only if you know the media rep really well and feel that sharing the information will help him or her gain additional understanding that will be of benefit to your agency. But the safest route is not to do it at all. If you decide to go "off the record" be sure the potential for gain is worth the risk.

Ask for help when you need it. Media outlets like to take credit for the help they extend to law enforcement. If you need help in finding an offender or warning the public about some kind of scam or other criminal enterprise, do not hesitate to reach out to your media contacts to get the word out. You will almost certainly find them willing to assist you.

Pick your media battles carefully. Your goal is to get along with the media to the extent possible, not fight with them. The misspelling or mispronunciation of your name likely does not justify an angry response to the offending journalist. A serious error in the facts of a news story or a clearly erroneous quote attributed to you probably *does* require a correction. Save your objections for significant journalistic mistakes. Remain nonconfrontational when you do have to lodge a complaint or request a correction. If you get the reputation of seemingly complaining a lot, your complaining will soon lose its effectiveness.

Don't allow yourself to be rushed. When you get in a big hurry you increase your chances of missing things and making mistakes. That's something you want to avoid when working with the news media. There can be a lot going on at the scene of a media "event" and it is easy to get both rushed and rattled. But if you are pushed into giving out unchecked information that turns out to be erroneous you have just created a lot more work for yourself in trying to correct it, which you are certainly obligated to do. Resist the temptation to do *anything* with the media until you are truly ready.

Trust where trust has been earned. There are a few unethical, "bad" journalists out there, just like there are a few "bad" cops. But most of the reporters you will connect with are decent people who are trying, like you, to do a difficult job well. Allow them the opportunity to prove that to you through time and experience. Once they do, it is alright to trust a bit. After all, that is what you are asking them to do for you.

Try to enjoy yourself. It will be good for your mental and emotional health if you try really hard to take a little pride and pleasure in the fact that *someone* wants to hear what you have to say about *something.* Maybe someone important to you will get to see you absolutely sparkling in the limelight!

ESTABLISHING A WORKABLE MEDIA RELATIONS POLICY

Policies establish broad parameters by which an organization can obtain philosophy and general direction. Procedures, on the other hand, flesh out these general guidelines by detailing the nuts and bolts as to how the broader goals are to be attained. To put it another way, policy states what is to be done. Procedure tells how to do it. You will need both to establish a department-wide, positive working relationship with the media. Policy will tell both your employees and the media representatives that your intent is to lead a department that is as open and accessible to the media as is feasible while still furthering the interests of officer safety and operational effectiveness. Your procedures will provide officers and media reps alike with specifics as to what is and is not allowable police conduct. This will include directions on what kinds of information can and cannot be released.

Your news media relations policies should answer several questions, including the following:

What should be the department's "official" relationship with the news media? The principles of openness and accessibility to the media should be clearly stated in your agency's press policies. Guidelines should guarantee media access to legitimate news but include reasonable restrictions for such purposes as officer safety and investigative integrity.

What can and cannot be released to the media? Get some legal advice in establishing these important guidelines. Federal, state, and even local laws can impact on what you can turn over to the media. The victim-identifying information of a sexual assault report and the offender-identifying information of an underage subject are pieces of information most often prohibited from release by statute. A detailed listing of what you can and can't release should be provided as part of your procedural guidelines. That should prove very helpful to your personnel.

Who can talk to the media? It is important that your department speaks with a single, clear voice. For that reason, most police CEOs place at least some restrictions on who can talk with the news media. Sometimes access is limited to sworn supervisors. On occasion chiefs list only themselves and the agency's Public Information Officer as permissible media contacts. Whatever route you choose to take, realize that the more you restrict media contact the more work you will place on yourself. At the same time, you may be increasing the likelihood of frustration on the part of your media contacts. And aggravated reporters, being human, may not be your best advocates in the stories they produce.

What on-scene restrictions will be placed on the media representatives? Here you are seeking to craft reasonable guidelines that will protect the integrity of a crime or incident scene while simultaneously allowing journalists to do their jobs effectively. In the process of carrying out this balancing act you should find that at least three general rules are appropriate:

1. *Media representatives cannot through their actions be permitted to endanger officers or physically interfere with on-scene operations.* A journalist who says or shows something that you don't like hasn't violated the law. A media rep whose actions physically endanger police personnel or otherwise interfere with police operations may have done so. One common violation involves photojournalists lighting up a nighttime standoff scene, thereby ruining the night vision of SWAT operators while giving away the officers' positions. If you see that going on, you must intervene and request that the practice cease. That does not mean that you start clapping media people in irons. Most media reps will understand and follow your directions. They don't want to see your people hurt, as you don't.
2. *The media cannot be allowed to destroy evidence or otherwise alter a crime, accident, or incident scene.* Media types do not have any sort of special privilege that grants them access to an area where John Q. Public is not permitted to go. Crime scene tape applies to those carrying cameras and microphones, too. Media people know this, but that does not mean that they won't push the envelope anyhow in an effort to get a better video or story. Your proper response is to courteously direct them outside of the "no go" zone with both an explanation and a polite warning. This generally will suffice to take care of the problem. Before taking any sort of formal enforcement action be sure the media misstep was not caused by a misunderstanding or unclear police instructions.
3. *Media representatives must not be allowed or assisted to break the law.* Journalists do not get a special pass to violate the law just because they are accompanying law enforcement personnel on a scene. For example, a reporter or photojournalist who has attached himself to officers serving a search warrant in a residence has no right to be on private property unless the property owner has granted him permission to be there. Once more, a verbal warning to cease and desist normally will be all that is required to address the problem.

A final caution is in order: No one has appointed you chief of the Good Taste Police. On occasion cops' sensibilities will be rightfully offended by the cameraperson intent on getting pictures of a very gory or otherwise upsetting scene, such as a pedestrian fatality involving a mangled child. Police have no legal standing to prohibit anyone from taking pictures from a public place where the photographer has a lawful right to be. If his work is in poor taste, it will be up to his boss (or his audience) to chastise him. Deciding which images can and cannot be captured in a public place is not the job of the law enforcement leader. The era of a cop trying to clap his hand over a camera lens is long past.

Your policies and procedures regarding the media should focus on facilitating both cops and journalists being able to do their respective jobs without trodding on the other. Understanding and courtesy will go a long way. Have a solid reason for what you do, rely on your good common sense in decision-making, and just plain be nice. In most cases you can rightfully anticipate being treated in the same way.

GIVING A SUCCESSFUL MEDIA INTERVIEW

You can do this and do it well. Those legs that turn to jelly upon their owner sighting a TV camera belong to someone else. You, on the other hand, view the news media interview as an opportunity to make you and your agency look good. Law enforcement leaders who are really good at giving media interviews often follow a set of guideposts practically guaranteed to win the day. For present purposes, assume that these common sense guidelines apply to giving an on-camera interview. But they will apply equally well for any kind of media interview encounter. They include the following:

Determine who should do the interview. Ideally, the one having the most facts should do the interview. Sometimes that might be you. Other times the most knowledgeable source of information, the officer or investigator running the scene, will be too busy with other tasks to pause for an interview. In that case, it may be you who needs to gather the facts, double-check them for accuracy, and then meet the press. (That is assuming, of course, that you do not have a readily available Public Information Officer who can assume the role of police spokesperson.) There will, however, be occasions on which you do not have the in-depth expertise needed to respond to technical questions. In that case you may want to turn over all or part of the interview to someone who has the background to respond intelligently. Complex cybercrime investigations come to mind as an example of a situation requiring such expertise. At the same time, it is vital that you never create the impression of hiding behind others to avoid a media interview. Particularly when the topic at hand is controversial or one that involves issues pertaining to policy, the individual in charge (that's you!) needs to be the one responding to the tough questions.

Ask the interviewer what he is seeking and what the questions will be. It is perfectly alright to do that. A professional journalist will not be surprised or offended by your questions. He or she has a vested interest in producing a good interview, and a skilled reporter knows that giving the interview subject a chance to prepare will almost aways produce a better product.

Once you have some idea as to the topic and planned questions, pull together the information you will need and mentally organize your responses. If there are questions that you already know you will not be able to answer for whatever reason, courteously let your interviewer know that as well as the reason why. That does not mean, of course, that the question won't get asked, anyway.

Expect "surprise" questions. Do not be shocked or angered if during the interview you are asked questions that you were not told of in advance. This does not necessarily mean that your interviewer is being sneaky. The interview may have gone in an unexpected direction or one of your responses may have placed an additional question in your interviewer's head. You should expect some unanticipated questions and not overreact to them. If you don't know the answer or cannot give it, simply say so in a polite manner. But note: It is *never* OK to say, "no comment." There are plenty of better ways of saying essentially the same thing.

Prepare for the interview. If you do not already have the facts needed to answer the interviewer's anticipated queries, you will need to get to the source where they are to be found, such as with the lead investigator on the case. Double-check the facts for accuracy. Be aware of what, by policy or statute, can and cannot be given out. Remember, too, that you do not want to hand out unverified information. Follow your agency's information release policies.

Check your appearance. Assuming you are doing a video interview, you'll want to appear on-screen looking like the professional you are. It does not mean that you are vain just because you don't want to meet your audience with pizza sauce on your chin. Even a quick glance at your vehicle's rearview mirror is better than not previewing your appearance at all.

Project a relaxed but professional image. You are looking to strike a balance here. You do not want to slouch or look slovenly, but neither do you want to come across as a ramrod-stiff robot. You desire to present the image of an in-control, confident authority figure, not an egotistical prima donna. Your audience needs to know by looking that they can trust what you have to say.

Avoid distractions. Your audience should be focused on what you have to say, not your chattering portable radio or the chewing gum you are working over. Watch out for distracting hand gestures or body language. On an active incident scene, you may have limited control over your environment, but try to conduct the interview as distant from noise and visual distractions as possible.

Maintain eye contact with the interviewer. Behave in the same way you would if you were having a one-on-one conversation with your interviewer minus the presence of the electronics. Speak in a conversational-level voice. Make eye contact with the interviewer whether he or she is on- or off-camera. Realize that in some instances the individual operating the camera will also be the one asking the questions.

Be quick, be concise, be gone. The typical television interview is over very quickly. The interviewer's time constraints will dictate that some of what you had to say likely will never make it on the air. Answer the question you were asked courteously but in as few words as possible. If the interviewer wants more details, he or she will ask a follow-up question. Get what you want to say out there quickly and concisely and it is more likely to be transmitted to your audience.

Remain calm and courteous. It is OK to be a little nervous before your command performance. Even skilled interviewees often report a case of butterflies before a session. But as the old deodorant commercial used to say, "never let them see you sweat." It may call for your very best acting skills, but you need to project the picture of the calm, confident leader. That won't happen if your audience sees a perspiring, squirming, obviously uncomfortable individual who clearly wants to be somewhere else. Remain courteous even if the questions you are being asked are uncomfortable ones.

Correct any misinformation. Whether it is you or your interviewer who puts out erroneous information, the mistake must be corrected right away. That holds true even if the interview is being broadcast "live." Remain ultra-polite but correct your interviewer if his or her spoken lead-in or question contains rumor or otherwise false information. If you realize that you have accidentally given out incorrect or unsubstantiated information, correct yourself right away. You and your interviewer both have a vested interest in getting it right. Your audience deserves as much.

It's OK to ask for a "do over." It is quite normal for an interviewee to think that the session did not go well. Chances are, it went just fine. After all, most citizens do not expect their police officers to be professional speechmakers. But if you are absolutely convinced that your interview was an unmitigated disaster filled with stuttering, stammering, stumbling, and incorrect information, it is certainly acceptable to ask your interviewer for a "do over." (Unless, of course, the interview was already broadcast "live.") Your interviewer may well tell you that you did just fine. But he or she wants to turn in a good product, too, so if he or she agrees that things could have gone a lot better your request probably will be granted.

Critique your interview performance. You almost certainly will be your harshest critic if you have a chance to view your interview. Nonetheless, in watching it look for ways you could improve your performance for the next time. It is also alright to ask your interviewer for tips on how to do the job better in the future. But again: it's almost certain that you did better than you think. You get better at doing interviews by doing interviews, so start looking for the next opportunity.

There are still more interview tips to think about. You must always work to maintain your reputation as a courteous, credible professional, even if the occasional interviewer fails to meet that standard. In other words, always tell the truth and nothing but. Do not permit yourself to become provoked and remain composed, instead. Don't play favorites. If you are willing to be grilled by Interviewer Roberta, grant the same privilege to her competitor, Interviewer Robert from across town. And be careful about going "off the record" or sharing confidential information with *any* interviewer. You are a lot less likely to get burned that way.

It is entirely within your abilities to do a media interview and do it well. As the leader of your agency, you can look forward to doing more than one or two.

CREATING AN EFFECTIVE NEWS RELEASE

An effective news release is one that gets picked up and used by the media AND gets to the public with the information you wanted to present. If you have a Public Information Officer, release-writing duties often will fall to him or her. (More about PIOs later.) But if you don't have one or for whatever reason that person is unavailable, release-writing duties may fall to you, the leader. In that case you will need to know both how and when to create one that gets used. After all, a news release that ends up consigned to File 13 is of no use to anyone. Fortunately, performing that crucial writing duty really is not that hard.

When do you do a news release? Agencies that are judged guilty of generating news releases over trivial matters soon earn the reputation of news release abusers. Their multitudinous releases are apt to get filed in a media outlet's trash can without serious consideration. Although what will interest media reps will vary from one locale to the next, the subjects most often worthy of news release treatment include the following:

- Major crimes and arrests for them
- Accidents involving one or more fatalities
- Disasters, natural or manmade
- Missing children
- Major cases for which the police need assistance
- Major new programs, projects, or campaigns launched by the department
- Hirings and promotions in small departments
- Awards recognizing exceptional conduct by officers or citizens
- Any other event or incident likely to generate a large amount of media and public interest

In preparing a news release, try to put yourself in the mind of the reader, viewer, or listener. What would *you* want to know about the incident or event? Generally, you might desire answers to the same questions that a good police report attempts to answer: who, what, when, why, where, and how. These are the release's most important bits of information and they belong in the *lead* or first one or two sentences of the news release. These tidbits, which you have already double-checked for accuracy, will be the items most likely to get used by a reporter in writing a news story if he or she is short on time or space. Everything else contained in the release should be in descending order of importance and able to be omitted, if necessary, without shortchanging the media audience of enough information to comprehend what is going on. If there is time or room to include every word, so much the better. Once that is done, utilize every communication source at your disposal (e-mail, text, social media posts, etc.) to disseminate the release.

You can learn a lot about writing news releases by reviewing those posted in the past by your agency or other, larger police organizations. In addition, there is a list of news release dos and don'ts that should aid you in your journalistic endeavors:

DO be sure the release has actual news value.

DO put a head or title at the top of the release so that the media rep viewing it has a quick notification as to what it is about.

DO stick to the known facts. The writer's opinions, exaggerations, and guesses do not belong here.

DO keep it short. One double-spaced page is plenty. If a media rep wants more, he or she will contact you.

DO use the civilian version of stating dates and times.

DO keep words, sentences, and paragraphs short and concise.

DO ensure that your follow-up contact information is provided at the close of the release for use by the reporter who wants more.

DO put your release on your official web site and your social media in addition to sending it out to news reporters. That way it will be available to the public whether the reporters use it or not.

DON'T fail to proofread your document multiple times for both form and content. Your release creates an image of your department.

DON'T include police jargon or abbreviations. This is not a police report and should not look like one.

DON'T wait until the last possible moment to prepare a news release. That may be the time when everyone is busiest and things get missed.

DON'T omit sending the release to every media outlet that might be even remotely interested. You will need to keep your media contact list up to date in order to do this.

DON'T be devastated if your release does not get used. Space and time limitations and the quantity and importance of other news may bump your work aside, at least for the time being.

Sometimes looking at an example is very useful in producing a similar product. Here is a fictitious example of an initial release done on a major crime and its investigation:

NEWS RELEASE

Chupacabra Police Department
301 North Street
Chupacabra, TX 76208

Chupacabra police officers responding to a report of gunshots heard at 1234 Oak Street at approximately 2 a.m. Saturday discovered the body of an adult male lying in the driveway at that location. The man, whose identity is yet to be released by the Coroner's Office, was pronounced dead on-scene by a deputy coroner.

Arrested inside the residence was Jane Doe, age 39, of Austin, Texas. She was lodged at Smith County jail pending the filing of First-Degree Murder Charges.

Investigation continues into the incident. It is not anticipated that additional details will be released prior to Monday.

Chief Melvin Snerd
Chupacabra Police Department
Telephone 325 655-1111
e-mail: melvin.snerd@cpd.com

A news release also can be prepared to describe a non-criminal event or program which you want to announce to the community. Such a release might look something like this:

NEWS RELEASE

Chupacabra Police Department
301 North Street
Chupacabra, TX 76208

CHUPACABRA POLICE ANNOUNCE
COFFEE WITH A COP EVENT

Chupacabra police officers have invited local citizens to meet with them for free coffee and donuts at Joe's Donuts, 516 Main Street, from 10 a.m. until noon on Saturday, March 19. Residents can chat with their officers, receive crime prevention advice, and collect some swag from the cops. Police K-9 Luger and McGruff the Crime Dog will be there to meet the kids.

"These coffees provide an excellent opportunity for us to visit with our citizens," said Police Chief Melvin Snerd. "We intend to do a lot more of them. They are fun for everyone involved."

The next Coffee with a Cop is scheduled for June 19, once again at Joe's Donuts.

Officer Mark Bailey
Public Information Officer
Chupacabra Police Department
Telephone: 325 655-1112
e-mail: mark.bailey@cpd.com

This release is written to allow a news writer to drop the second and third paragraphs, if need be. The most important information will not be lost, as it is encapsulated in the first paragraph, the lead. This is the same practice the journalist relies upon in preparing his or her news story.

News releases that get used can help prevent crime, pass along important information, and highlight the good work that your people are doing. Don't fail to take advantage of releases done well.

PUTTING ON A NEWS CONFERENCE

You should consider calling a news conference when you believe that the topic to be covered will generate so much press interest that it would be impractical to distribute the details by news release or by notifying one reporter at a time. But don't overdo it. An agency that calls news conferences promiscuously for minor happenings may soon find no one showing up for an announced conference. But doing it right can greatly benefit your organization when there are major police-involved happenings in your neighborhood. The legitimate reasons for organizing a press gathering are practically limitless, but could include such things as:

- Officer-involved shooting or in-custody death
- Death or critical injury of one or more officers
- Major crime with fatalities
- Major accident with multiple fatalities
- Natural or manmade disaster and response

- Major new program being announced by the department
- Any local, police-involved incident or investigation involving nationally known "celebrities"
- Any local, police-related incident known to be drawing state-wide or national media attention

Regardless of your reason for calling a conference, some time-proven advice for making it a successful exercise includes the following:

- Someone (the PIO, if you have one) must notify your agency's media contacts of the date, time, location, and topic of the news conference, as well as who will be leading it. This is a courtesy that will let your media contacts decide if they want to be present.
- Be sure you have plenty of chairs and plenty of room in a suitable facility, assuming you are holding your conference indoors. (That is preferable due to your increased ability to control the environment.) Avoid a location with loud background noise, such as a roaring HVAC system. You likely will want a podium up front. Leave space at the back of the room for the photojournalists to set up their equipment.
- Someone needs to get there early and stay late to handle those "little issues" that often seem to arise. Again, this is an ideal task for a PIO.
- Set a time limit, let it be known, and stick to it.
- Keep your opening statement brief–two or three minutes is plenty. Your audience members want to ask questions and will get restless if you drone on and on.
- Consider reducing your opening statement to printed format and handing it out. This is especially important if there are names and addresses as well as criminal charges that you want to be sure the journalists get right.
- Open up to questions as soon as you finish your statement. Repeat the question aloud before you answer it. This allows anyone present, including those in the most distant corner of the room, to know what it is you are answering. It also gives you a little time to compose your response.
- Keep your focus moving around the group. Call on different correspondents and try to avoid concentrating on one individual who seems to be dominating the group.

- Expect surprise questions that may be off the topic the conference is about. Answer if you want, but it is also fine to politely tell your questioner that you will be happy to talk with him or her on the new topic later.
- Don't get rattled or visibly angry at awkward or just plain, stupid questions. By keeping to the high ground, you will elicit sympathy and support from your audience who likely will be able to see that your tormentor is acting arrogantly.
- Try to have some "visuals" for your media audience. They want pictures. Whether it is seized money, drugs, cash, weapons, or something else, having "stuff" on the table at the front of the room will satisfy the group's passion for visuals. You may need to get creative. One department put on a conference reporting on the solution of a decade-old murder by placing an enlarged graduation photo of the victim on an easel at the front of the room. Detectives had first received the permission of the dead woman's family. The media loved it.
- If another organization, or several of them, assisted with the event you are reporting on, be sure to invite representatives of those agencies to stand with you at the podium, if they wish. Offer others the opportunity to speak if they desire. Long-running feuds have started because someone felt left out at news conference time.
- When the questions stop, it is time to end the conference, even if the allotted time has not expired. Be sure to thank everyone for attending.
- Even if you have put on a very detailed and thorough press briefing, expect requests for one-on-one interviews. Each journalist wants something no one else has and an interview with the boss is the place to get it. Grant these requests if you possibly can. If you give an interview to one journalist, be sure you do the same for others who have the same interest. In the process you may create a needed friend or two for the future. Fall back on your "tips for giving a winning interview" for these sessions.

You are already practiced in speaking to a group of people, even when the message is not good. You can handle a roomful of inquisitive journalists just fine.

DON'T OVERLOOK THE SOCIAL MEDIA

While they may have grown up watching a talking head read the evening news, today's law enforcement leaders recognize that new generations gather much of their information (and misinformation) from what they see and hear on the social media. For them, the Internet is the new universe. As a consequence, today's police CEOs count on Facebook, Twitter, and their electronic relatives to disseminate the information that they want placed in front of the public. It is not that newspapers, television, and radio are going away any time soon. They are not. But you as the chief now have one more avenue for answering questions and complaints and distributing the word about what the local law officers are up to. Perhaps best of all, through social media you have a great recruiting tool, as that is where today's job seekers go to look for employment.

Perhaps you regard yourself as an Internet and social media expert. If so, that's great. If you have the time to do it, you can direct your agency's vital social media presence. If that's not you, you almost certainly have a young employee working for you who is quite comfortable in the on-line world. This is the individual you want to designate as your social media coordinator.

Utilize social media to tell the electronic audience about the good work your people are doing. Disseminate the crime information and prevention advice that your citizens need to stay safe. Highlight the community members who have done something in support of your agency. Swap messages with your public safety consumers. Answer questions and respond to commendations and criticisms. Post your public service announcements and news releases. Headline your department's mission, goals, and initiatives. If your officers are OK with it, post some photos and bios of your great people.

You will have to decide if you want your own personal page or site in the social media world. Some law enforcement leaders have done so with great success. Others have avoided the medium entirely and allowed the department's sites to say everything they want said. If you do decide to participate, always exercise caution and restraint in what you elect to put "out there." Once you do that, it is public in perpetuity for the world to see. You must never post when angry or otherwise emotional. You cannot come across as flippant, racist, sexist, or in any other way unprofessional. If you are thinking about posting or re-posting what you believe to be the funniest, cutest, cleverest thing you have ever seen, stop. Re-think it, at the very least. You just might be sparing yourself a world of trouble. You do not want to join the roster of cops who have become unemployed through a few, ill-advised keystrokes. You must be a positive role model on social media, too.

By assuming an active role in the world of social media your agency stands to benefit from today's "latest Big Thing" for connecting with your public. It is available to you, too. Using it wisely and well will offer you and your agency yet another opportunity for collaboration with the modern media.

THE PUBLIC INFORMATION FUNCTION

You as the chief must be comfortable in working with the media. Indeed, in your small department you may serve as the agency's Public Information Officer responsible for news media relations. But even if you are, you will need someone to fill in for you when you are simply not available. Better still, it would be advisable for your department to identify and train a member of the agency to serve as Public Information Officer, or PIO. For most agencies this will be a person who shoulders other duties, as well. Some chiefs have appointed a civilian employee to serve in this position; probably more have given the collateral assignment to a sworn officer or supervisor.

While his or her other duties may vary a bit from one police organization to the next, you should expect your PIO to handle at least the following responsibilities:

- Prepare news releases
- Respond to reporters' daily "beat checks" and queries
- Prepare Public Service Announcements
- Coordinate the department's social media presence
- Arrange or do media interviews, as required
- Organize news conferences
- Respond to reporters' queries on crimes, arrests, investigations, programs, and events
- Monitor and collect news stories, editorials, letters to the editor, and social media comments about the police department

Choosing the right person to serve as PIO is critical to the success of your agency's media relations. You are not looking for a used car salesman or a BS artist. You are seeking an extrovert who is loyal to the department and likes talking about cops and what cops do. This individual has to be a self-starter who reports directly to you but can work well without close supervision. The exceptional PIO will not wait for the media to call him or her but instead will reach out to news outlets *proactively* when he or she sees the opportunity to bring favorable attention to the department.

Your PIO must be respected within the organization for credibility and integrity. He or she must be able to write well. The PIO additionally must demonstrate patience and tact when dealing with the sometimes-demanding personalities of the news media.

In order to do his or her job well, your PIO needs to have your support and the rest of the organization must know that. The PIO will need the cooperation of your investigator, patrol officer, or supervisor from whom he or she is requesting information. But your press officer also must know to keep investigative keys and other restricted information out of the hands of the newshounds.

Help your PIO get the training he or she needs to do a good job. The International Association of Chiefs of Police is only one source of good courses on police-media relations and the PIO function. Your PIO also should be encouraged to connect with and learn from other police press officers through state and national PIO organizations. All of that added to your personal support will assist your PIO in telling your department's story to the world.

SUMMARY

Believe it or not, some of your colleagues actually look forward to a media encounter. They correctly view it as an opportunity to do a lot of good for their organization and their profession. Not incidentally, at the same time they likely are building their own positive image in the department and the local community.

It all starts with establishing a set of workable media relations policies and procedures that provide your employees with the guidance they need to help you sustain a positive working relationship with the press. Then, by thoughtfully utilizing interviews, news releases, news conferences, the social media, and the talents of a Public Information Officer, you and your people can successfully reach the public to tell your story and get credit for the exceptional work your employees are doing.

Finally, by adhering to a set of personal rules for media relations you can help ensure that your own reputation for openness, accessibility, and credibility is well-known and respected by your media contacts. That will help ensure that your agency gets media help when you ask for it and you always have the opportunity to tell your side of the story when controversy erupts.

Working successfully with the news media is an absolute necessity for a law enforcement leader. Like all the other tasks you routinely handle, you can do it well.

Chapter 13

WHEN BAD "STUFF" HAPPENS

As the famously rude bumper sticker says, "Stuff Happens." Or something like that. But when bad "stuff" happens that in any way touches your agency and your people, you as the leader are expected to deal promptly and effectively with it. Not to mention compassionately and quickly, as well.

No matter what has brought about the hard times, you in your role as leader of the organization will be looked to as the one who can "fix" it or at least make things better. At such times you will be expected to be everywhere at once, keeping people updated and letting them know that you all will get through the crisis, or a series of them. While directing your efforts toward a solution of whatever the problem at hand happens to be, you also will be focusing on what comes next: recovering from the bad "stuff" and returning the organization to a sense of normalcy.

You additionally will have a big role to play when your personnel are accused of misconduct. You will be responsible for ensuring that any allegations are properly received, investigated, and adjudicated as quickly as possible. You will ensure that the rights of the complainant and the complained-against are protected. Where misconduct is found, you will lead the effort to prevent the mistake from occurring again.

Bad "stuff" is assured to happen from time to time in every organization of human beings. The really important thing is how you lead your people in overcoming it.

YOUR ROLE WHEN THINGS GO WRONG

One police chief is famous for saying: "When things are going great, anybody could run this place. When things go south is when they need *me*." Allowing for perhaps a bit of exaggeration, there is at least some truth in what the chief had to say. Tough times are when your character and courage as a true leader will come to the forefront.

Sometimes a tragedy will have occurred because of something your people (or you) did or failed to do. A high-speed chase results in the death or serious injury of innocent citizens. An officer-involved shooting results in the death of an innocent party. Or one or more of your officers are accused of criminal acts. The initial reports look bad, indeed. What are you to do next?

The cardinal rule that you must always tell the truth is in effect here. First, telling the truth is always the morally and ethically right thing to do. Second, by lying you have just made the situation, whatever it is, worse. Once lies, by you or someone else, are injected into the issue or incident the untruths themselves may quickly become the focus of all observers. And that's not good.

Answer all questions truthfully. If you cannot answer, say so. Personally stay out front. People want and expect to hear from *you*, so do not send someone out in your stead. If you played a role in the foul-up, admit that, too. Both your people and your boss will expect that kind of honesty. Do not wallow in guilt when you actually had nothing to do with the fallout-producing incident. But neither should you try to shirk the responsibility for fixing things that are your duty to fix.

Visibility and accessibility are never more important for you to demonstrate than following a "bad news" event. Everyone needs to hear and see that you are still in charge. They also need to learn from your lips that, while things may be rough for the moment, normalcy will return. You and your people *will* recover. The compassionate yet determined face that you show your people is important for helping them recover from whatever bad thing has happened. Keep telling the truth. Don't sugar coat bad tidings. But do emphasize that *it is going to be alright.*

Do not neglect your own needs and those of your loved ones during a time when it seems you are spending 24 hours a day responding to a crisis. Eat, rest, and sleep even if none of those things feel appealing. Keep those closest to you in the know and share with them what you are feeling. Doing so won't be imposing on them. They almost assuredly *want* to help you. They may just need you to tell them *how*. Patient and nonjudgmental listeners are always welcome. Do not distance yourself from them.

You and your people must recognize one, guaranteed truth: On occasion you have to go through the bad times to get back to the good ones. It *will* happen.

KEEP EVERYONE IN THE KNOW

You already know that you must utilize every means at your disposal to keep everyone informed during and following a critical or controversy-causing event of any variety. Some of that communication can be accomplished through frequent e-mails. But to the extent possible, your people will need to see you live and in person, even if that means visits to very early or very late briefings.

Beyond your department you also will need to keep your boss fully briefed on the happenings. Some bosses will want you to contact and brief your local elected officials. Other bosses will want to use your information to make the other contacts themselves. Just be aware of what the drill is in your jurisdiction and act accordingly. It is important to the reputation of your agency that these local officials feel that they have the scoop about important goings-on. That should also boost your stature in the eyes of those same officials who can see for themselves that you are performing admirably in the face of adversity. And that is relationship currency that you can bank for future draws.

Do not forget that the news media will need to be kept informed about the event or incident if they have previously expressed interest in it. Being proactive and reaching out to them instead of waiting to be contacted can build some good will for you here, too. That good can prove especially valuable if the item of interest is a controversial one.

It is important to get information out quickly. But it is equally important to get it right the first time. If you suspect that you do not have the whole story, be very cautious about making pronouncements. Especially when your officers are accused of misconduct and you have reason to believe they are not guilty as charged, you quite naturally want to come to their defense. That's good and, knowing you, your people have come to expect it. But be careful of making "dangerous assumptions" and jumping to conclusions without learning the whole story. It is wiser (and safer) to say something like: "From what we know at this point it appears that the officers acted appropriately. We will know more when the investigation is complete." Or something along those lines.

In summary, DO keep everyone in the know. DON'T disseminate information that you do not *know* to be accurate.

RECOVERING FROM A TRAGEDY

When very bad things have happened to your agency and its people, your work family will need some time and understanding to recover from those blows. There is shock to overcome, perhaps lasting discomfort to deal with, and, potentially, post-traumatic stress that could manifest itself much later on. In other words, it is not over just because the incident or event itself has passed.

At times like these it is important for you and your people to get together with the members of their extended work family and share good thoughts and good will. You will want to be a part of those gatherings. At the same time, it is equally important to recognize that returning to a sense of normalcy as soon as possible will be healthy for everyone in the organization. Most human beings find comfort in sharing grief and recovery in the presence of trusted others. At such times *routine* can feel reassuring. Even in law enforcement, you and your personnel can take comfort in experiencing some sense of normalcy. Even the mini-crises that can define a police officer's day are something that he or she *normally* confronts. For someone who has just been through something that felt anything but normal, that feeling of "getting back to business" with friends can be most welcome.

Attempting to return to a sense of normalcy does not indicate a lack of caring for someone who has just been the victim of a tragic event, or been close to a tragic occurrence. It simply recognizes the reality that in order to survive human beings need to feel whole again as soon as they can. You are one of those human beings who must be able to function in order to lead effectively. No disrespect for anyone is contained in that need.

Not everyone heals at the same rate. While one individual may be able to recover from incredibly bad happenings very quickly, another may take years to accomplish the same, if they ever do. That does not mean that one is stronger than the other or "better" than the other. It just means that people are different. And that's OK. It does mean, however, that you will need to maintain a loose "surveillance" of your organization in the days, weeks, and months following really bad news. You should alert your subordinate supervisors to do the same.

Stay present. Remain visible. Be sure you are easily accessible. You are, once again, setting the standard for your people and community. Act normally. Engage in the activities that you normally would, ranging from attending meetings to participating in departmental and public functions. Do that even if you do not feel particularly engaged just now. Acknowledge the recent events. Accept condolences, if appropriate. Then, move on to the business at hand. Continue to lead the move back to normalcy. That, too, is a leader's responsibility.

HANDLING ALLEGATIONS OF POLICE MISCONDUCT

It has probably happened to you. You have walked into a governmental agency to make a complaint or ask a question and left with the impression that *you* had done something wrong or distracted someone from doing something much more important. Something like gossiping, texting, or surfing the net.

Or maybe your contact was by telephone and you found yourself being transferred endlessly from one extension to the next while listening to some really bad music or, worse, hearing a taped propaganda message over and over. Maybe you completed your trek to telephone hell by being parked on the voicemail of someone who it turned out was on an extended vacation to Pago Pago. Welcome to what passes for openness and customer service today, at least in some quarters.

You may be thinking by now that's not the reception citizens receive when they contact *my* organization. Hopefully you are right about that. But it should not surprise you to learn that is the treatment many citizens expect because they have been treated that way before by other governmental entities. As a good leader, your goal should be to surprise them with courtesy and responsiveness they did not expect. With very little effort, you and your people can do just that.

It is fair to assume that a citizen who wants to tell you or one of your subordinate supervisors how he or she was maltreated by one or more of your people will be somewhat upset, if not downright angry. The very first task at hand may be to calm that individual at least somewhat before the whole story can be told. There are some experience-proven things you and your people can do to accomplish that task successfully. Consider the following:

- Try to avoid foregone conclusions. It is very easy to think that you have heard it all before and know in advance where the conversation is going. You may be wrong.
- Let the complainant tell his or her story without interruption. This is not the time to challenge or question the speaker. There will be time for clarifications soon.
- Watch your demeanor, facial expressions, and body language. This is not the time or place for eye rolling, grimaces, folded arms, or loud sighs. Show the speaker the courtesy of paying attention. You would expect the same.
- Treat people as individuals and use their name. But it's Ms. Jones, not Bobbi Jo, unless she indicates otherwise. Some people, particularly ones from earlier generations, do not appreciate instant familiarity with someone they do not know.
- Stay calm and in control of your emotions, even if you feel sure you are listening to a bucketful of lies. Try to avoid raising your voice, even if your complainant does. Take some deep breaths if you find yourself overheating.
- Try hard to ignore angry, exaggerated, or rude comments made by a complainant. He or she is likely attacking the situation, not you personally.
- Smile when appropriate. Nod affirmatively from time to time to indicate that you want the person to keep talking, not that you necessarily agree.
- Allow your speaker to save face, if you can. If the complainant has made a mistake, you do not have to rub his or her face in it.
- Try to show as much empathy as you can for your speaker's situation. It costs nothing and may help defuse an angry, frustrated individual.
- When he or she is finished with an initial speech, it is time for you to ask questions and seek clarifications from the speaker. You also can seek additional details of the situation. Endeavor not to sound like you are challenging his or her version of events. You should be attempting to gather as much information as possible for any needed follow-up.

- Stress what you and your agency *can* do, not what you can't or won't.
- Tell the truth. Do not promise things you cannot or will not deliver. But do keep any promises that you do make.
- Thank your complainant for bringing his or her concerns to your attention, even if you are not feeling particularly thankful at the moment.
- Apologize, if appropriate. You will have to be the judge of that. It is possible to explain and defend your employee's actions and still express regrets that the complainant is upset about what happened. Oftentimes, people are surprised to receive an apology from a government official, especially one who wears a badge. The apology itself may be all that is required to smooth ruffled feathers. Keep it available in your leader's toolbox.
- Tell the complainant what happens next. Let him or her know if you have to do some follow-up. Give him or her some idea as to what the timeline will be. Find out if re-contact is desired. If you do promise another contact, be sure that it gets made.

It is likely that many of the questions and other "issues" that you receive in person or over the telephone you will be able to resolve pretty quickly with a bit of patience and tact on your part. But some others will require further inquiry to determine if police misconduct *did* occur and what is to be done about it if it did. You will now need to get your employee's version of events and talk with any other witnesses to the affair. Body camera images, if available, will be especially valuable. You may be able to resolve the whole issue right there. If your employee did the right thing, you can let both the employee and the citizen complainant know that. If an error was made, you can provide correction or additional direction to your employee and let the citizen know *that*, too. The idea is to fix the problem so that it does not recur.

Your citizen-complainant needs to hear back from you promptly, assuming he or she has not already indicated that no further contact is required. Courteously brief him or her of your findings. Avoid getting into back-and-forth debates. If you have found that your people could or should have done better, don't hesitate to say so. As noted, it is perfectly alright to apologize, if you feel that is appropriate. (That may be all that your complainant is seeking–affirmation that he or she was "right.") In the end the two of you may simply have to agree to disagree.

But try to reach agreement on *something*, even it is nothing more than it's a nice day outside. If your people did err, it is alright to give your complainant an idea of what you are going to do about it. "We're going to use this as a learning opportunity for all our people" is a phrase that more than a couple of chiefs have memorized.

It would be a wonderful world indeed if all complaints were of the minor variety and could be quickly and easily resolved at least somewhat amicably for everyone involved. On occasion, however, that will not be the case. That is when you will have to call upon a more formalized complaint resolution process. It is important that your agency has a detailed set of policies and procedures governing Professional Standards (Internal Affairs) investigations. It is equally vital that anyone involved in the investigative effort follows them to the letter. Doing so will help protect everyone's best interest. While by no means an exhaustive list, the kinds of allegations requiring a formal Professional Standards investigation could include the following:

- Use of excessive force
- Criminal act by a police employee
- Racial profiling
- Official oppression
- Sexual misconduct
- False arrest
- Search and seizure violations

Before your agency can launch an investigation of any sort you will have to ensure that your department's policies and procedures governing the practice are adequate and up to date. The guidelines should specify who is to do the investigation. (It should not be you, as you will have to sit as the final authority to rule on whether or not there has been misconduct and, if so, what to do about it.) The guidelines should cover how long following the alleged event a complaint can be filed. (Some agencies have a 30-day cutoff rule.) They should delineate who can make the complaint. (Some agencies say only the person allegedly maltreated can make the complaint, not a friend or relative.) Other departments require the complaining party to make a written, notarized affidavit as to their allegation. Set whatever complaint restrictions you believe are reasonable, but know this: The more limitations you place on the complaint process, the harder it is going to be for you to claim truthfully that your organization is both responsible and accountable to the public.

But it is absolutely reasonable to place certain, common sense restrictions on the citizen complaint process. For example, your agency normally should not accept a complaint because a citizen believes he or she should not have received a traffic ticket. The propriety of the charge is for a court to decide. Nor should you accept an allegation of "perjury" because a judge or jury believed the cop instead of the complainant. Again, the matter has already been decided in the legal arena.

It is important enough to say again: It is vital to have in place a detailed set of clear guidelines for conducting an internal investigation *before* they are needed. If your department does not have any, or the ones you have are weak and incomplete, it's likely that a nearby, larger agency has some for you to copy. You do not want either the complainant or the complained-against to be able to truthfully claim that you were "flying by the seat of your pants," so to speak, because your department had no direction for handling such critical matters.

Assuming that you have adequate guidelines in place, it is time to look at some specific directions for you and your assigned investigator to follow in carrying out a fair, thorough, and competent investigative and adjudicative process. You may want to consider the following suggestions:

Determine who is to do the investigation. Will it be the accused employee's direct supervisor, a member of your command staff, or someone else? If what you know of the alleged misconduct at the outset leads you to believe that there might be criminal conduct involved, it would be advisable to have the investigation done by an outside agency. Doing so will make it more difficult for anyone later to claim the investigation was biased or otherwise tainted. In the state of Texas, for example, many local law enforcement agencies call on the Texas Rangers, a branch of the state's Department of Public Safety, to do the investigation. (Many local agencies in Texas also rely on the Rangers to conduct their Officer Involved Shooting (OIS) investigations.)

Clarify what the "charges" are. Your employee deserves to know what he or she is supposed to have done wrong. Your assigned investigator needs to know what it is he or she is investigating. That needs determined and clearly stated at the outset of the inquiry. If additional allegations surface as the investigation proceeds, they can be made known to all at that time. Chapter and verse of the rules and/or laws alleged to have been broken needs to be stated.

Enforce a reasonable time limit. If your policies and procedures don't set a time limit for the investigator to complete his or her work (they should), you must set one now. You have heard the expression "justice delayed, justice denied." Everyone touched by the inquiry deserves to know the outcome as quickly as reasonably possible. Some agencies set a deadline of 30 days from the date the complaint is received. If an unusually complex investigation requires more time for completion, your established guidelines should grant you the authority to extend that time.

Review documentary or video evidence. The investigator should be able to get a feel for what needs to be done by performing a very early review of any reports or body cam video that exists concerning the incident or issue. The review may also give an early indication of what actually happened and identify witnesses, inside or outside the department.

Determine who is to be interviewed and when. Your investigator needs to figure out who is to be interviewed and in what order. In many instances the employee or employees alleged to have engaged in misconduct are interviewed last. Everyone needs to know when and where they are to show up for an individual interview. No group interviews should take place. If subsequent interviews turn up additional witnesses, they can be notified of when and where to appear later.

Choose the right interview location. Obviously, an interview location with privacy and no distractions is what you are seeking. Police employees accused of misconduct should never be interviewed in the same room used for the interview of suspects and arrestees. Doing otherwise could send a message to your people that you do not want to send. Not ever.

Record all interviews. All interviews pertinent to an Internal Affairs investigation should be audio recorded. Some agencies include video, too. What you choose to do may be at least somewhat dependent on the available facilities.

Provide necessary advisements. Most formal, Professional Standards investigations today include a *Garrity* advisement before the interview commences. The advisement mandates that the employee cooperate with the investigation by answering interview questions truthfully and completely on pain of discipline, almost certainly termination of employment, if those rules are not followed. At the same time, since the employee's responses are being "coerced' by threat of discipline, any statements made during the interview cannot be turned over to criminal investigators or used against the employee in a subsequent criminal proceeding. Most agencies provide the advisement in written format and require the signature of the interviewer and interviewee. The form often looks like this:

ADVISEMENT FOR INTERNAL AFFAIRS OR ADMINISTRATIVE INVESTIGATION INTERVIEW PURSUANT TO *GARRITY*

You are being questioned regarding an official investigation by the____________Police Department. You will be asked questions specifically and narrowly related to the performance of your duties or fitness for office, and your knowledge of pertinent events.

If you answer truthfully, neither your statements nor any information or evidence which is gained by reason of such statements can be used against you in any subsequent criminal proceeding. However, these statements may be used against you in a subsequent administrative personnel action.

If you answer untruthfully, your statements or any information or evidence which is gained by reason of such statements can be used against you in any subsequent criminal proceeding.

You are entitled to all the rights and privileges guaranteed by the laws and Constitution of this state and the Constitution of the United States, including the right not to be compelled to incriminate yourself. If you refuse to answer questions relating to the performance of your official duties or fitness for duty, you will be subject to administrative personnel action which will result in your termination from employment with the Police Department.

Interviewer________________________ Date_______________
Employee_________________________ Date________________
Witness___________________________ Date________________

Garrity is not something you will have to deal with on a daily basis. Most of the complaints you encounter will be of "the cop was rude" variety. Nonetheless, by preparing yourself and your supervisory corps for handling the more serious allegations you will be even better prepared to handle the minor ones.

Permit the interviewee to talk freely. Your people should know how to do interviews, whether they are talking with a victim, witness, suspect, or a cop. It is vital to let the interviewee tell his or her version of events without interruption. Questions and clarifications can follow. The process cannot be rushed.

Stick to the subject of the complaint. This is not a fishing expedition. Obviously, the interviewer can pursue any additional potential violations uncovered as a result of statements made during the interview(s). But this is not the time or place to ask an officer accused of causing a serious traffic accident if she still beats her spouse.

Confront obvious falsehoods. Once the interviewee has related his or her story, the interviewer can now request clarifications and, if necessary, pose probing questions that delve into the veracity of what has been said. The story may start to change.

Re-interview, as necessary. As the investigation proceeds the investigator may learn additional facts that require another interview of someone he or she has already talked with. It may need to be done because there is now an apparent conflict in what different people have had to say. In order for the investigation to be a thorough and fair one this must be done, as required.

The investigation must be summarized. At the conclusion of the inquiry the investigator must complete a summary of his or her findings. From this statement you and any other reviewers must get a clear picture of what actually happened, and what did not. Your agency's policies and procedures should dictate whether or not the investigator is required to state whether or not he or she believes there was misconduct. By this point in the process the investigator should know more about what actually occurred than virtually anyone else, so it may be helpful to you to learn his or her opinion. The final call is yours to make, however.

Determine who is to review and decide. Once again, this should be spelled out in your department's policies and procedures. Many chiefs find it desirable to have the accused employee's entire chain of command review the investigation and enter written recommendations as to the "guilt" or "innocence" of the accused. If any member of the chain finds misconduct, he or she is also required to recommend the corrective action that should be taken. Each member is thus permitted to grow by direct participation in a vital personnel process. It is also important that each supervisor is required to share accountability for the decision made.

Identify your categories of findings and then select the appropriate one. Your department's policies and procedures should provide you and your staff with the list of possible findings following the review of the contents of a Professional Standards or Internal Affairs investigation. Many police departments rely on the following categories of findings:

Exonerated–the employee did what he or she was alleged to have done. However, it was exactly what he or she *should* have done under the circumstances. For example, a parent has complained that an officer handcuffed her drunk and belligerent teenager. The complaint is classified as Exonerated because that is precisely what an officer following your agency's policies pertaining to officer safety should have done.

Unfounded–the investigation determined that the alleged misconduct did not occur.

Defective policy, procedure, or practice–the accused employee was following the department's guidelines, but those guidelines have now been shown to be faulty or inappropriate. The guidelines must be revised but the employee is not guilty of misconduct.

Sustained–the alleged misconduct occurred and corrective measures will have to be taken with the employee(s) responsible.

Misconduct not based on complaint, sustained. The investigation showed that the employee did not commit the misconduct alleged, but was instead responsible for some other prohibited conduct. For example, the officer did not steal the complainant's money, as alleged. But he or she did fail to inventory the property properly. Corrective action is indicated.

Not sustained–some departments slap this label on an allegation when sufficient evidence cannot be developed to prove what happened one way or the other. But other agencies upon reaching that state of affairs place the label "Unfounded" upon the investigation's results. Their logic is that a criminal defendant is found "not guilty" when an allegation cannot be proven at trial. They believe that law enforcement officers should have the same privilege. The final labelling decision is, of course, up to you.

Finalize the decision and determine corrective action, if indicated. Although you hopefully have had plenty of staff input, the ultimate decision on misconduct or no misconduct is yours to make. If misconduct occurred, it is up to you to determine the corrective action to be assessed. In doing that you will consider such factors as the gravity of the sustained misconduct, its consequences, and the prior disciplinary history of the employee or employees involved. You'll also want to remain mindful of the principles of *comparative discipline*: what has been done with other employees who engaged in the same or similar misconduct? You additionally want to think about *progressive discipline*: has the employee engaged in identical or similar misbehavior previously and been disciplined for it? In most cases the new misconduct will call for heavier discipline than that administered the last time. But out-of-the-ordinary circumstances always can call for a deviation from the formula.

Notify those involved of the findings. Both complainant and complained-against deserve to know the outcome of the inquiry in a timely fashion. For the complainant, a phone call, e-mail, or letter most often will be your means for communicating. A telephone call will give that individual the best opportunity to ask questions or seek clarifications. He or she may or may not agree with the findings, but it will be your task to remain courteous and avoid getting into a back-and-forth argument, regardless.

Your employee also needs to hear from you as soon as possible. If there is to be corrective action taken, he or she must know what to expect. Do not apologize for disciplinary measures, as that would undermine the whole corrective process. Remember: it was your employee, not you, who engaged in the misconduct.

Take any required corrective action. Get the corrective action done promptly and be prepared to move on. The task is unlikely to get easier with the passage of time. Be sure there is adequate documentation of the action taken.

Carefully follow the appeal process. It is likely that your department, your employer, or both have written guidelines to be followed by all concerned when an employee feels his or her discipline was unfairly imposed. This is a normal, established employee right and does not indicate that you or your department have done anything wrong. The corrective action you have decided on is much less likely to be revised or reversed if you have carefully followed your agency's policies and procedures for doing internal investigations and assessing discipline. Realize that the appeal authority may nevertheless modify the assessed discipline. Again, know that this does not mean you have done anything wrong. Sometimes, a modification in discipline is made simply because the appeal authority desires to "show mercy" or otherwise throw a bone to the employee.

Attend to any needed follow-up. It is up to you, the boss, to ensure that the entire process of complaint resolution and, if necessary, corrective action has been properly concluded. If the investigation revealed the need for additional training for one or all employees, you will need to ensure that it gets done. If it uncovered an erroneous or otherwise flawed policy, procedure, or practice, you'll need to see that the appropriate revisions are made. Finally, if the investigation and its review pointed up a need for a change in behavior by one or more employees, you must ensure that this is accomplished, as well.

Brief any others who need to know the outcome. Particularly if the allegation of misconduct was a serious one, your boss will need to be kept advised of the progress of the investigation as well as its final outcome. Your partners in HR were probably involved in the process and will want to know the final outcome, as well.

Allegations of misconduct involving your employees, particularly sustained ones, can result in turmoil within your department and beyond. Handling them and their aftermath appropriately can reduce the tumult a great deal and put your department back on the path to normalcy and good health.

SUMMARY

Inasmuch as you are the recognized leader of your police department, people both inside and outside the organization are going to look to you for comfort and reassurance when things go awry. In many cases they will be turning to you for accurate information concerning what happened and what can be expected to happen next. You will be tested. Consciously or not, others will be assessing your abilities as a leader.

Obviously, the death or critical injury of one of your officers will bring about the greatest stress of all. But other major incidents also can focus an intense spotlight on you and your agency. Tragic accidents or errors involving you or your people will result in harsh scrutiny. Remaining in firm control of your department during such times will require all of your skills as a leader. You will be required to provide leadership as well as comfort to your employees and perhaps your community, as well. You will work to keep morale up even as you answer tough questions and respond to perhaps tough criticism from both inside and outside the police department. You will have to remain highly visible and accessible for the duration of the upheaval. You will ensure that operations continue and things get done right even when everyone is tired and stressed.

During rough times your people and your community need you more than ever. They need, in a word, a leader. And that leader is you.

Chapter 14

COMMUNICATION IS THE NAME OF THE GAME

Inasmuch as you are a human being, it is practically impossible for you *not* to communicate. Sometimes you do it without speaking a word. You communicate through the affectionate look you give your significant other. You communicate something else entirely when you tell Sergeant White that yes, it's OK that he takes off Friday night, while shooting him a look that says it is not so OK after all. (In this case you may be confusing more than you are communicating.) You have to be just about unconscious not to communicate.

Communication is sometimes said to involve the exchange and, hopefully, comprehension of thoughts, feelings, ideas, and information. Clear and accurate communication is an absolute necessity for the health and effectiveness of your police organization. Excellent, two-way communication between you and your subordinates is a requirement for both efficiency and good morale in your department. The same requirement for good communication also applies to the relationship that exists between you and your boss and you and your community. Communication can be a big factor in determining whether you succeed as a police chief–or not.

A good leader recognizes the value of being a good listener. That is a trait of every effective communicator. He or she also studiously avoids committing some of the major errors that can kill effective communication. In addition, the exceptional leader has mastered the skills required of an individual who can communicate equally well in either the written or spoken word.

Effective communication makes for a more cohesive, productive, and content work group. As the leader of that group, you will set the standard for excellent communication practices. What follows will aid you in doing just that.

ENEMIES OF GOOD COMMUNICATION

In order to do anything right, it can be extremely helpful to know how *not* to do it. There are several, easily-identifiable stumbling blocks that you will want to avoid as you strive to be an excellent communicator. They include these communication killers:

Bias and prejudice. You are less likely to listen intently to what someone else has to say if you think you already know what he or she is going to speak because you dislike or distrust him or her. If you assume in advance that you are going to disagree with whomever is speaking because you've *always* disagreed with him or her in the past, it is unlikely that any useful communication is going to take place. The best way to overcome this communication failure is to try hard to set aside what has happened in the past and instead focus on what is being said (or written) now.

Rushing unnecessarily. You cannot help the fact that your job sometimes requires you to get things done in a hurry. But rushing when it comes to communicating a message can practically guarantee that the intended recipient will not get a clear picture of what you intended to communicate. Repetition is fine, but if you end up having to repeat your message you really have not saved any time. Try to slow down and get it right the first time.

Unclear message. At some point in your life, you almost certainly listened to or read a message and had not a clue as to what the message sender was trying to communicate. You don't want to be guilty of the same communication sin. If your message is in written form, read it over repeatedly before you send it forward. Put yourself in the shoes of someone who has no advance knowledge of what you are trying to say. Is the message clear? If you are speaking rather than writing, watch your audience for any indication of understanding, such as affirmative head nods. *Ask* if the message was understood. Be prepared to repeat, if need be, perhaps saying it a little different way.

Distractions, interruptions. Distractions can be physical or mental. A chiming cell phone or a chattering portable radio can make it hard for someone to concentrate on what you are saying. A mental distraction can interfere when you are already formulating what you want to say in response instead of actually listening to the speaker's message. An interruption is just what it sounds like. Your goal should be to exchange information at a time and place when you and your communication partner(s) will not be sidetracked by other "stuff."

Emotional involvement. This communication enemy can be but doesn't have to be related to the bias and prejudice villain. If you just plain dislike the individual attempting the communication you are unlikely to get the message clearly, or believe it if you do get it. But when stress or other high emotions are involved even otherwise-clear communication can also suffer. This can happen, for instance, at the scene of a critical incident, such as an officer involved shooting. In such a situation, instructions may need to be repeated, perhaps more than once. It may also be an excellent idea to ask questions during a stressful situation to ensure that your meaning was comprehended: "Did everyone understand what they are to do?"

Inappropriate Language. This goes well beyond the fact that you are going to turn some people off if you use profane or vulgar language. Not all inappropriate language consists of bad words. You also must stay away from using words unlikely to be easily understood by your audience. You should not address a gathering of your officers as if they were youngsters (even if some of them come close to being in that age group.) Neither should you author an all-hands memorandum apparently produced by a PhD for consumption by other PhDs. You are seeking to communicate clearly, not impress people with your vocabulary.

Based upon a lifetime spent communicating with other human beings, you probably can think of some other barriers to good communication. But those listed here are some of the worst offenders. Fortunately, in addition to avoiding those critical errors there are things you can do to ensure accurate, effective communication.

HOW TO COMMUNICATE EFFECTIVELY

Effective communicators are, without exception, also known as good listeners. It also has been said that a good conversationalist is one who "shuts up and lets me talk about my favorite subject: me." Be that as it may, it is no secret that you cannot be an effective communicator unless you put a lot of effort into truly hearing what the other party to the exchange has to say. And that gets down to the application of some basic listening skills. First of all, do not assume in advance that you know what the other party has to say. Let him or her speak freely. Try not to interrupt. Nod to assure the speaker to continue. Attempt to practice "full face listening," that is, focus your attention and vision entirely on the speaker, and nothing or no one else. You should not be creating the perception that you cannot wait for the other party to cease speaking so that you can talk. Practicing full face listening takes some practice and concentration, but you can do it.

Listening skills certainly are vital to effective communication, but there is more you can do to ensure that accurate transmission and reception of information, thoughts, and ideas actually occur, such as:

Ensure that the message is clear. Whether your communication is written or spoken, as the message sender the obligation is on you to make sure that the message is a clear one. Keep it concise. Keep it as brief as practical. Don't insert a fifty-cent word where a nickel's worth of clarity will do the job better. Long, complex sentences are to be avoided like Ebola. Oral presentations that drone on and on are the equivalent of a slow and painful death and are also to be dodged.

Don't try to force too many complex thoughts or directions into a single message. Your intended message recipients may lose your intentions and instructions in a sea of words, written or spoken. Tackle topics one at a time, checking to see if the first one was understood before starting off in a new direction. Remember that the average person's attention span is not without limit.

Remember the value of openness and credibility. Someone who is not trusted or believed cannot be a very effective communicator. Confirmed liars may sometimes be listened to but what they have to say is likely not taken to heart. Your reputation for integrity will be most helpful when you are the one sending the message. Remaining devoted to the truth is perhaps the best way of being recognized as the excellent communicator that you are. Your consistent openness and accessibility will complete the picture of you as an effective communicator.

Two-way communication flow. If it is going to work, communication has to be a two-way affair. If you are the one initiating the message, whether it is written or spoken, your audience needs to have the ability to ask questions and, if necessary, seek clarification of the message. This process should continue until everyone who wants to has had a chance to respond. Diatribes, written or oral, that do not allow for response from the intended audience are far too easily misunderstood. As your department's leader, you should encourage feedback from your people on just about any topic under the sun. That feedback may or may not change a decision you have made or a policy that is about to be implemented, but most people will appreciate that the boss was at least willing to hear them out. It's just one more thing that a good chief does.

Calm and controlled approach. Keeping your message delivery unemotional and factual will contribute to its being comprehended. That's not to say you cannot let your feelings show on occasion. Expressed emotions show that you are human. You certainly do not want to come across as a heartless robot. But staying in control of your expressed emotions to a reasonable degree oftentimes will remove a distraction as you work to communicate with those under your command. For example, if every time you address a meeting of your first-line supervisors you come across as angry, pretty soon that consistent anger may result in at least a part of your audience disregarding what you have to say. Save your emotions for when they are truly appropriate.

Repeat as necessary. There may not be a "magic" number of times a message has to be repeated before everybody "gets it." Sometimes it can vary depending upon the message's personal impact on the reader or listener. Nonetheless, you should be prepared to repeat important messages more than once, perhaps for the cop who hangs out on the night shift and is always quick to complain that "nobody tells me nuthin'," almost certainly untrue. To be sure an important communication is received by all hands you may want to rely on multiple avenues to get it out there: memorandum, e-mail, orally, etc. That will make it a lot harder for that cop on the night shift to claim nobody told him nuthin'.

By exercising some sound communication habits you will increase the likelihood that important information is easily exchanged in your organization. There are, as noted, plenty of things you can do to help that effective communication take place. Telling the truth tops the list. Whether writing or speaking, choose your words carefully. Keep the more-distracting emotions (such as extreme anger) out of your messages. If you are communicating orally, listen carefully to your intended message recipients and encourage a two-way exchange. Make sure your message is a clear one. Use all of the communication means at your disposal and do not hesitate to repeat the message, as required.

A leader who cannot communicate successfully commands little more than the desk in front of him or her. That leader is not you. By communicating effectively with your people, you make it much more likely that your organization's mission will be accomplished. An effective leader cannot ask more.

PUTTING IT IN WRITING

An excellent leader is also an excellent writer. In his or her leadership role the leader will prepare written communications for a variety of audiences, ranging from elected officials to disgruntled citizens to the department's employees. He or she will author letters, memos, e-mails, plans, orders, performance reviews, and other documents. These are all things that require some sort of permanent documentation. You as your organization's leader will provide that documentation.

If you recognize writing as a difficult task for you, there are things you can do to become more comfortable while producing an excellent written product. If you have a university or community college in your vicinity, oftentimes you will find a writing course somewhere in the curriculum. There are also lots of books out there intended to aid the reluctant writer (an Internet search will help you find them.) But you also can get better at the written word by carefully examining examples of well-written documents of all kinds. Get a hold of some written works produced by people whose writings you admire to get tips on how it is done. You can gain a lot by emulating the good work of others.

As you contemplate composing your written message, try to place yourself in the shoes of someone who has no idea of what you are trying to communicate. Write and, if need be, re-write for that individual's level of understanding of the subject. Be sure your choice of words is appropriate for your reading audience. Going through that mental exercise will help you get better at converting what you are thinking into the written word.

As with many things in life, you often get better at something by doing a lot of it. That holds true for producing the written word. Honestly critique your own work. It also can help to set something you have written aside for a few hours or a few days and then take another look at it. Something that seemed clear earlier may appear less so now. Read over your written product multiple times, first for content. Is the message clear? Will someone else grasp its meaning? Then, go back and dissect the document to be sure that spelling and grammar will pass muster. Make revisions, where needed. Then, give it one last reading before you send it forward. The same holds true whether you have created an e-mail, text, memorandum, letter, report, or some other version of the written word.

At some point in your career, you probably have told a young officer that you are known within your department and beyond by the written work you produce. Even more so, the same holds true for law enforcement leaders. With some diligence and close attention to detail, you can do this and do it well.

YOU CAN'T BEAT THE SPOKEN WORD

Face-to-face, oral communication skills are a prerequisite for effective leadership. You know that. You must get your message across clearly if you are to be a successful leader. This holds true whether you are speaking to a briefing room of five cops or an auditorium filled with 500 members of your community. Just as in writing, you get more comfortable and proficient at public speaking by engaging in public speaking. Many chiefs would agree that their own cops can be the toughest audience on the planet. If you can succeed in communicating orally with them, you can master speaking to any group in existence . . . and you can.

Exceptional public speakers draw on words that are appropriate. This is as true when you are speaking to a roll call briefing as it is when you are addressing the Little Old Ladies Society. You are serving as a role model here, too, when you refuse to spout gutter talk. A police department is not a bank. But neither should it be a place where obscene language becomes part of the background noise.

The spoken word sometimes does the written version one better because speaker and listener can each pick up on cues–such as facial expressions and body language–from the other. That can make it easier for each participant in the exchange to grasp if the other party is understanding a message being sent. Questions can be asked and clarifications sought. The positive result should be better communication and the benefits it brings to everyone concerned.

When you are an effective oral communicator, you help foster an atmosphere in which there are fewer misunderstandings accompanied by the bad things that can result from them. That sort of positive workplace environment is what you are seeking as your agency's leader. By setting the example as an effective communicator and expecting the same of your subordinate leaders you can make your police department a more enjoyable place to work as well as a more effective and efficient one.

SUMMARY

Words, written or spoken, can harm and confuse others just as other words can inform and support. Words can depress morale as well as elevate it. Communication, or the lack of it, can help determine which way all of these things go.

As a leader, you rely on excellent communication to increase the effectiveness and efficiency of your law enforcement agency. You have learned that an organization where information and ideas flow smoothly is more likely to be an effective work group of well-informed and reasonably content people.

As a law enforcement leader, you must be a good writer and public speaker. You will have a difficult time succeeding as a leader without possessing both of those skills. You must be a patient and careful reader and listener, too. You must be able to comprehend the meaning of a message directed to you and then be able to send an easily-understood message of your own. That is what communication is all about.

Everyone in your organization as well as the citizens you all serve will benefit from your sound communication practices. That positive state of affairs is what every exceptional leader is seeking.

Chapter 15

EVALUATING AND REPAIRING EMPLOYEE PERFORMANCE

The typical police leader, from sergeant through chief, would readily confess that completing employee performance reviews is not exactly his or her favorite thing to do. In fact, some supervisors do not like to do them at all and wish the responsibility could somehow be made to go away.

You are not the typical police supervisor. You know that evaluating the work performance of his or her subordinates is a necessary and important task of every competent leader. You realize that preparation of the review document and the following sit-down session with the employee are equally important tasks and must be allotted sufficient time and effort to benefit both the employee and the organization.

None of this means that the performance review must be fun for all concerned. Just about everyone is at least a little bit apprehensive when he or she knows their work is being examined. You probably feel some of that apprehension yourself come time for your own performance review session. But you recognize that the task is important enough that it must be done and done well. The information contained in this chapter will arm you and your subordinate supervisors with some suggestions for getting the job done right.

IS PERFORMANCE APPRAISAL NECESSARY?

If the person preparing the performance review and the one receiving it are both uncomfortable with the whole thing, does it really make sense to do it at all? The answer is a resounding "Yes." There is too much of value in the process to allow it to go extinct. You know that. You can help by letting your people know that you see that value. You also can strengthen support for the process by the effort you put into doing your own performance appraisals of your direct reports.

All employees deserve to know how they are doing in their boss's eyes. The performance review lets him or her know how the supervisor believes he or she is getting the job done. Unless the employee is a highly unusual individual, he or she *wants* to be perceived as doing a good job. The performance review can tell him or her that.

The performance review also lets the employee know where he or she can do better. If your employer connects performance to pay, as should be the case, the employee learns what he or she needs to do to earn a salary increase via a pay step raise or some other monetary recognition for demonstrated job competency. If the employee is interested in securing a special assignment or promotion at some point in the future, a well-written performance appraisal can provide evidence that the advancement is deserved.

Many employees want to know what they need to do to advance their career and perhaps increase their job satisfaction. An honest, well-crafted performance review will include clearly stated, personal goals intended to help them do that. If, for instance, one of your top staffers has expressed the desire to be a police chief one day, you might consider adding a couple of goals to his or her annual performance review:

1. Serve as acting chief during my scheduled or unscheduled absence.
2. Put together and deliver a presentation for city council.

Your subordinate supervisors should be able to come up with goals for their own people. One means for helping them do this: have them *ask* their employee what he or she would like to see as a target goal. When employees have a role in setting their performance goals, the chances increase that the targets will be hit.

It has been noted that a comprehensive performance review can assist a valued employee in reaching a personal goal. There is yet another good reason for the exercise. At some point you may need to counsel or discipline an employee for less-than-acceptable job performance. You will need evidence to do that, and that means documentation.

A well-written job performance evaluation provides that documentation. When that solid evidence via documentation is in place, it is unlikely that a corrective sanction will be overturned. Competently done performance reviews thus strengthen the organization and the individual employee by identifying the need for training, coaching, counselling, or other remedial steps. The community you all serve benefits at the same time because you have established a more efficient, effective, service-providing police department.

Performance reviews come in a lot of different formats, from a page of check-off boxes to a score-by-the-numbers sheet to a nearly blank piece of paper requiring a free narrative to describe the employee's job performance. Some reviews include a combination of each of these formats. All of them can work well in the hands of an engaged and truthful evaluator. The key is that the evaluator realizes what an important task he or she is performing and commits to doing it well.

WHAT ARE YOU EVALUATING?

Sometimes a governmental entity utilizes the same job performance appraisal form and format to evaluate the work of every employee in the organization, regardless of rank or job duties. In other words, the Patrol sergeant is evaluated on precisely the same factors as is the backhoe operator. A skilled evaluator can make this kind of system work, but it is best that an evaluation system is tailored to the specific tasks undertaken by specific employees. In other words, it is probably not necessary that the sergeant knows how to operate the backhoe in a competent manner. While both employees should be rated on their ability to "work safely," it is also important that each is assessed on his or her abilities to carry out the functions of a specific job title. A good performance appraisal system will allow for addressing those differences. What should be the most important to the employee is what *your* organization considers important.

The performance review system that your agency utilizes should allow for the differences between what a patrol officer and a captain or assistant chief does, even though the two ranks will share some things in common. Officer safety, for example, should be evaluated in the performance review of each. If you are creating or revising an existing performance review form for your own agency, you probably want to measure some or all the following if you are seeking to evaluate the work of a first-line officer, since that is the position that most of your agency's work evaluation reports will address:

Policies and procedures. The successful police officer must not only know and understand the agency's guidelines for doing his or her job properly, he or she must follow them scrupulously. Does the individual's job performance reveal a solid understanding of these directives?

Job knowledge. The employee must know the laws he or she is expected to enforce as well as the technical aspects of the position, such as how to recover and book evidence properly or how to investigate a traffic accident. Can he or she do all of that successfully? Are there weak areas that need shored up? If so, adding that knowledge might be listed as an employee goal for the next appraisal period.

Safety practices. Does the employee demonstrate good officer survival tactics and show an appreciation of the hazards to be avoided? Does the officer adhere to good risk management practices, such as keeping the operation of his or her patrol vehicle under close control?

Communication skills. How complete and well-done is the employee's written work? How clearly does he or she communicate on the police radio, telephone, and computer? Is he or she easily understood?

Interpersonal relations. How well does this employee get along with citizens, peers, and supervisors? Is he or she effective in de-escalating tense situations? In other words, does this individual exhibit good people skills?

Knowledge of the area. Is the officer capable of getting around the jurisdiction quickly and easily? Is he or she aware of the problem spots and other areas of special interest?

Judgment and decision-making. Does the employee have a reputation for exhibiting sound judgment and solid, timely decision-making? Can that employee make good decisions under stress and time constraints without seeking supervisory advice? At the same time, does the employee realize when it is time to consult a supervisor?

Teamwork. Law enforcement requires that its practitioners have the courage and confidence to work alone when required but are also able to contribute as strong and collaborative members of a team when necessary. Team players must carry their share of the load and not be disruptive to the group atmosphere or effort. Is this employee able to do that? How well?

Attendance/punctuality. By the nature of his or her law enforcement position, an officer needs to be routinely present at the appointed time. Does this employee consistently fulfill that obligation? If not, dates and times of the excess absences or late arrivals should be noted.

Self-confidence. In order to be effective at his or her difficult job, a law enforcement officer must be self-assured. But that self-assuredness must not cross the line into arrogance. How does the employee stack up to those dual requirements?

Professional appearance. This measurement looks at your officer's grooming and the appearance of his or her uniform or other clothing, depending upon assignment. Does his or her appearance bring credit to the department as a professional-looking organization–or not?

Acceptance of direction. Does the employee accept supervision well, or does he or she frequently challenge supervisory instruction? An intelligent employee should request clarification of orders when necessary, and he or she certainly should challenge instructions that are unethical or unlawful. But when challenging direction becomes routine behavior for an employee, very often big trouble is at hand. If the behavior is not corrected, this employee will not have a lengthy or happy career in law enforcement. With specific instances of problems documented, this issue must be addressed immediately.

Your agency may want to include many more work behavior traits to be evaluated, but these core areas definitely will need to be observed and rated. The idea is to produce a document that provides an accurate record of previous performance and opens the door for further discussion with the employee.

PREPARING AN ACCURATE AND BENEFICIAL PERFORMANCE APPRAISAL

If you are like many police chiefs, at one time or another you have despaired over the quality of performance appraisals completed by one or more of your subordinate supervisors. What follows is a collection of tips for preparing an accurate (and helpful) performance review report. It should prove useful to even your most challenged review writer. It might even serve as a good refresher for you as you prepare to document the performance of your own direct reports. Some basic rules of thumb include the following:

Invest the time and effort in doing it right. It will not be fair to anyone if the writer waits until the last minute and then rushes his or her way through the preparation of a performance review. The same holds true if the supervisor fails to leave sufficient time for the sit-down session in which the contents of the review are discussed with its recipient. The tasks must be recognized as the important duties that they are and never rushed or shunted aside for "more important things." If you are the evaluator, you owe your employee the same time and consideration you would expect from your own boss at performance review time.

Consider using an outline. Some review writers prepare an old-fashioned topic outline to help them produce the narrative of a performance review report. Sometimes following the A, B, C routine helps them organize their thoughts while assuring that important subjects are not neglected. Particularly if narrative preparation feels like a difficult task for you, you might want to try doing an outline to start the writing process for your next review and see if it proves helpful. You may want to offer that suggestion to your other supervisors.

Avoid springing surprises. The performance appraisal process should not be the first time an employee has seen or heard a particular critical comment from his or her supervisor. Major emotional reactions can result from such surprises. A good supervisor avoids these performance review shocks by giving his or her employee continuing progress reports throughout the review period. That way the employee has the opportunity to fix any deficiencies before the next performance review report becomes due.

Back your assertions with evidence. All cops know that evidence is required to prove a point. It is just fine to write that Patrolman Snark has an attendance and punctuality problem. That statement then needs to be followed by dates and times when the problem surfaced. (That's one more reason why smart supervisors regularly document employee performance–good or bad–at the time it happens.) Proving something by evidence and example is just as important in the performance review as it is in the courtroom.

Don't apologize for being honest. You should never have to say you're sorry for doing your job. One of a leader's most important tasks is honestly to evaluate the work of his or her people. Never make excuses for exercising your integrity.

Watch out for some common errors. No matter what their profession, sometimes supervisors make some of the very same errors when evaluating employee performance. On occasion they allow their personal feelings, positive or negative, to get in the way of doing an accurate work appraisal. Other times they fall victim to the "halo or horns" effect and cite only the good or bad work because one or the other is prominent. Employees seldom do *everything* wonderfully or *everything* poorly. Or the supervisor jumps on the "central tendency" bandwagon and rates everything as "average" or "acceptable" because it feels easier than justifying a higher or lower rating. Or he or she is victimized by the "recency" effect in which the review references only very recent observations and events, ignoring the fact that something very significant happened a few months back. Once you have educated your supervisors about these performance review bugaboos, they should be less likely to fall victim to them.

Keep it concise. When writing a narrative, keep your sentences and paragraphs reasonably short and to the point. The best job performance reviews are the ones that can be easily understood by anyone who reads them. You are writing to communicate, not to impress with your abilities as a novelist.

Check your work. You may have commented on the correctness or lack of same in your subordinates' written work. It thus would not do for your own appraisal document to contain spelling, grammatical, or content errors. Check your work for content accuracy and then read it again–very carefully–for any other errors.

Finish with a summary. Consider concluding the performance review document with a final paragraph that sums up the employee's job performance during the review period as succinctly and clearly as possible. If the contents of the review permit you to truthfully do so, try to end on a positive note, such as "Samantha had a good year of solid police work, and I look forward to her having an even better one in the next 12 months."

Performance reviews are just one more of the written assignments that you must do and can do well. You have a right to expect the same high-quality work from your subordinate supervisors. The good that results from this written work will be beneficial to your entire organization.

THE SIT-DOWN SESSION

With the completion of a well-written and comprehensive performance appraisal document the job is now at least half complete. The next and equally important task for you or one of your subordinate supervisors is the face-to-face session in which the results of the review are presented to the employee. This is the time to verbalize for the employee what are considered the most important points of the review. Many supervisors choose to give the document to the employee ahead of the sit-down session. That way the employee is able to formulate any questions he or she may have about the contents and conclusions of the performance evaluation. Reviewed and reviewer can then discuss questions or differences of opinion during the meeting. That ultimately can improve the communication that takes place.

In the best of all possible worlds the employee will tell his or her boss that the review is spot on, thank the reviewer for the accurate comments, and immediately seek to implement any called-for goals or requested changes in work performance. As you know only too well, things don't always go that way in the real world. When reality happens, a few tips on handling the session when things don't seem to be going smoothly may be helpful. Those trouble-shooting suggestions include the following:

Work to minimize emotional involvement. The fact that their job performance is being evaluated is enough to generate stress for some employees. Particularly if he or she suspects that a less-than-stellar job performance is going to be discussed, that individual may arrive at the sit-down session primed to do battle. If you are already on high alert yourself, the likelihood of the session getting tense is increased. It may help you to take a few deep breaths in advance and make an effort to calm yourself. Greet your subordinate with a pleasant demeanor that says you are not seeking a confrontation. Speak in a calm, quiet voice. Monitor your employee for any indication he or she may be getting agitated and take a short break, if necessary. Do not hesitate to commend your subordinate on things he or she is doing well.

Be prepared for outbursts and venting. An already-upset individual may have to be given an opportunity to vent his or her spleen, so to speak, before any useful communication can take place. Your best response may be to listen quietly without interrupting. Once he or she winds down (it may take a few minutes, perhaps accompanied by tears), it should be easier for you to continue with the purpose of the meeting. As you proceed, you may have to go through the vent-and-listen drill again if your employee fires up more than once. But do get back without fail to the message you have to deliver. That's the goal of the sit-down.

Don't back down when you know you are right. Some people bluff, bluster, and bully for the purpose of getting others to back down and have their way. Some employees have been known to try this routine on a supervisor who is telling them something that they do not want to hear. You cannot allow that trick to work on you or one of your subordinate supervisors. Remain patient. Allow your employee to vent. But do not permit him or her to intimidate you. Do not admit to error or unfairness when you know neither is present. Make direct eye contact with your employee. Don't raise your voice, but don't whisper, either. If you have done your research carefully and prepared a clear and accurate review, you have nothing to apologize for. Be clear on where improvement will have to occur. Do not omit something you intended to say because someone is argumentative or outright nasty. Do your job and do not permit either a whiner or a would-be bully to divert you from your purpose.

Own your work. Let your subordinate supervisors know that you expect them to be accountable for the performance reviews that they have delivered when they have met with their employees. They must own up to their fact-based opinions and not attribute them to someone else–like you, for instance. The boss didn't do the performance appraisal. They did. Make sure that your supervisors realize that they will lose the respect of their people AND their boss if they cannot muster the courage to take credit for their own work, whether well-received or not.

As an effective leader you recognize the importance of an impartial, accurate performance appraisal for employee and organization alike. You know that when evaluating employee performance you have to be an excellent observer, an impartial reporter, a skilled writer, and a great oral communicator. You realize the value of earned praise for an employee, but you also recognize that you have to demonstrate the courage to tactfully explain where improved job performance is needed. Perhaps most important of all, you will ensure that your subordinate supervisors understand all these things, too. That's what a good leader does.

YOUR ROLE AS A COUNSELOR

Not infrequently a performance review sit-down merges with a counselling session in which you or one of your subordinate supervisors addresses a need for change in an employee's job performance. But there are additional reasons for initiating a counselling session. They can include:

Improper on-duty or off-duty conduct. This could mean anything from cutting up in roll call briefing to engaging in a well-publicized extramarital affair that is bringing discredit to the police department. The fact that the conduct affects the effectiveness of the department's operations makes it fair game for supervisory intervention.

Personal problems brought into the workplace. When an employee's off-duty troubles affect those he or she is working with, the conduct becomes an issue for supervision. Whether the problem originates from financial difficulties, romantic entanglements, or something else, when the employee's work suffers and his or her peers are in danger of getting dragged into the drama, it is likely time for some supervisory advice.

Relationships with peers and supervisors. Whether it is through a hair-trigger temper, a condescending attitude towards others, a total lack of patience or some other negative personality trait, an employee who creates disruption in the workplace, perhaps repeatedly, must be reined in. An honest counselling session may be the last stop before discipline is imposed on the transgressor.

Alcohol, drug, or mental issues. Cops can fall prey to the same afflictions that plague the rest of humanity. Here the counselling meeting may serve to help identify the problem and point the suffering police person in the direction of professional help. The supervisory intervention becomes especially vital when the afflicted employee's at-work behavior may be endangering others.

You and your organization have some specific goals you are seeking to accomplish via a counselling meeting. You are naturally trying to improve the employee's work performance and behavior on the job. But you also are exhibiting compassion in trying to help your employee overcome whatever problem or problems are causing him or her to suffer, and perhaps inflict that suffering on others. Remember, however, that the responsibility for "fixing" the difficulty remains with the employee, not the supervisor. You are also seeking to help the employee maintain a positive change long-term. The end results are intended to benefit the employee, the organization, and the community served.

But the first step in confronting a problem through counselling is identifying that a problem exists in the first place. You doubtlessly have come across some of the common warning signs before. They include at least the following:

- Major change in at-work demeanor or disposition
- Repeated complaints of rudeness, discourtesy, or otherwise inappropriate behavior from both peers and citizens
- Evidence of drug or alcohol abuse
- Increased use of sick leave; repeated instances of late arrival for work
- Deteriorating quality of work
- Frequent emotional outbursts, ranging from anger to crying
- Increased instances of use of force
- Insubordination towards supervisors
- Deteriorating hygiene, grooming, or dress
- Avoiding contact with peers or (especially) supervisors
- Family members contact you with concerns about the employee

Of course, the need for counselling can exist without any of these things being noted. On the other hand, an alert leader may have already picked up on a host of them. Whichever is the case, it is now time for intervention by leadership. Counselling may be the first step.

Experience has very likely taught you some things that your subordinate supervisors may or may not know. You know that prior to any successful counselling session it is necessary to gather information concerning at least what *appears* to be going on. You will need to identify the issue (or issues) and collect the relevant facts. You also know by now that very often a troubled employee's peers are the first to know that something is amiss. At the same time, some may be very reluctant to "tattle" on a colleague. You may want to approach them in a nonthreatening mode, such as: "Hey, something seems to be wrong with Joe. What do you think is going on?" You could learn a lot that way, particularly if you talk with more than one employee. It is a reality of police life that oftentimes peers know what's happening well before staff does.

With at least some information in hand, you can now plan your approach to the employee. The idea, of course, is to transmit the fact that you want to help, even though responsibility for solving the problem will remain with the employee. You are not there to threaten, but it should become clear that action will be required. You will need to find a private, quiet spot where the one-on-one meeting can take place without interruption. And you'll ensure that sufficient time is available to prevent the session from being rushed. It is that important.

Once you and the subject of your attention sit down to talk, there are a few things you can do to increase the chances that the counselling session is a useful one, such as:

Get to the point. Certainly you want to be non-confrontational, and it's fine to begin with perfunctory pleasantries, but there is no need to beat around the bush. The employee knows he or she has not been summoned to discuss fishing or football. If the individual does not know precisely why he or she is there, that individual is naturally going to be curious. Minimize the foreplay and get to it. Be up front about the reason for the meeting. State the issue clearly and concisely, all the while making eye contact with the person across the table. Staring at the tabletop when talking will not be helpful.

Allow your employee freedom to speak. The employee may have done something that you are not pleased about. You have now had an initial opportunity to inform him or her of that fact. But he or she *is* your employee and deserves the chance to be heard in response to what you have said. Beyond that, you have the obligation to *listen* to your employee without interruptions or counterarguments. You will get your chance to talk again soon enough. By careful listening you may just find out a lot about what has been going on, perhaps including some details you did not even suspect. That ultimately may result in a much more successful counselling session.

Be careful of emotions. That includes your own. It is important that *you* remain outwardly calm if you expect your employee to do the same. Just as in the disciplinary meeting, the topic of the session may result in an emotional outburst from the person across the table. While you will not allow genuine emotions or theatrics to sidetrack you from the purpose of the meeting, you will nevertheless be willing to slow things down to allow your employee to vent. Things may go better after he or she has blown off some steam. Be patient, express empathy if you feel that is appropriate. Then, proceed to state your message and expectations.

Keep it focused. This is not the time or place for either of you to "garbage bag" and bring up every real or imagined happening or transgression since the beginning of time. If it is not relevant to the present topic of the meeting, it probably does not need to be discussed just now. Venting is fine within reason, but an employee who ventures too far afield needs to be nudged back to the subject at hand.

Focus on behavior, not people. That advice may sound odd, since people are creating the behavior. Nonetheless, it's important that your employee be made aware that it is *conduct*, not personality, that has brought about the need for the meeting. It is all too easy for a disgruntled or simply defensive employee to play the "you've never liked me" card. You may have to respond directly to that contention: "It's not about you, it's about what you're doing (or not doing)."

Make the issue clear. At times counselling sessions can wander widely, and not necessarily through ill-intent on anyone's part. People talk, and sometimes no one can predict where a conversation will go. But focus is important here. In conversing with your employee state clearly and concisely what the issue is, and what he or she is expected to do about it. It is absolutely acceptable to ask in a nonthreatening manner if your message is fully understood. Be prepared to back up and restate if necessary. That doesn't mean you cannot talk about other things that are on the minds of either of you. But it may be necessary to come back to those things another time. Right now, your planned, central message must be center stage.

Make it clear you want to help. Let your employee know that you are truly concerned about his or her welfare and future in the organization. You can express empathy and concern without loading his or her difficulties onto your own back. You *can* be there to provide a sounding board for his or her thoughts about a solution. You *can* be ready to lend support.

Don't go instantly to problem-solving mode. Law enforcement leaders of necessity tend to be structured and action oriented. You may need to remind yourself to slow down just a bit and permit your employee time to think about what needs to happen next. It is certainly acceptable to *ask* your subordinate for his or her solution to the issue. You might be surprised by what you learn. Once you hear from your employee, you may be able to offer support for the solution he or she has come up with or offer some additional options.

Set a time limit for results. If the counselling session was intended to result in a change in employee behavior, as very often it will be, it is not a good idea to leave floating in the air just *when* the action is to be accomplished. It is fine to ask your employee what he or she thinks would be a reasonable deadline for the work to be accomplished, but a date does need to be set.

Summarize and try to end on a positive note. At the conclusion of the counselling session, it is always a good idea to sum up what has been discussed and determine if your employee understands what needs to happen next. It is OK for you to ask him or her if it is clear what needs to take place. Any confusion on your employee's part needs to be dispelled by the end of the meeting. If it is feasible, you also want to conclude the session in a positive manner. Hopefully, there will be *something* that your subordinate is doing right that you can comment favorably on. You also may want to say that you know he or she will be able to accomplish what you have asked to be done. Whether your employee responds favorably or not, you will have taken the high road by trying to conclude in a positive vein.

Follow up to ensure compliance. It will be important to determine if what you called for in the counselling session has been or is being accomplished. In other words, are the called-for actions actually taking place? It is unacceptable for your employee to be all happiness and light and readily agree to what you want done—and then do absolutely nothing. Your earnest efforts have been wasted if that is allowed to happen. If you are not seeing progress following the counselling session, it is time for another sit-down with the employee. You can ask if he or she is encountering difficulties in carrying out your directives. Restate what is expected. Restate the deadline, too, unless you find a very good reason for extending it. The employee must not be left with the impression that he or she can ignore with impunity what you have directed be done.

The counselling session is a crucial component of your effort to observe, evaluate, and thereby directly affect employee performance for the better. Be certain that you and your subordinate supervisors always give it the attention it deserves.

WHAT HAPPENS NEXT?

The performance review or counselling session has not been completed when you have left the sit-down meeting. Whether the sit-down has been for the purpose of performance appraisal, counselling, or both, your next goal should be to provide your employee with advice regarding what needs to happen now. The idea is to build upon strengths, address weaknesses, and assist the individual in furthering his or her career and job satisfaction. The hope is to increase your employee's value to the organization while helping him or her get more satisfaction from what he or she is doing now and will be doing in the future as a part of the organization.

It is always best if your employee agrees that the goals you have established for him or her are worthwhile and need to be accomplished. For that reason, it's great if you can allow him or her to assist you in setting those targets. Oftentimes, they are more likely to get accomplished that way. He or she may even do your goal setting for you. But realize that you may have to tone down some more unrealistic desires. It would, for instance, be unrealistic for your rookie cop to want you to send him to the FBI National Academy next year. You may need to gently steer him or her in the direction of a more realistic goal, at least for the present: "Reduce the number of times your reports have to be returned to you for correction of spelling or grammar errors."

Weaknesses or problems identified during the performance review or counselling process call for goals intended to repair them. If, for instance, your employee has received multiple citizen complaints of discourtesy during the current evaluation period, a goal of "zero sustained discourtesy complaints during the upcoming performance appraisal period" would be appropriate.

Goal setting should be seen by everyone involved as a very important part of the appraisal or counselling process. An employee should receive well-documented credit for meeting previously set goals. Follow-up action also needs to be taken if he or she fails to meet established expectations without a very good reason. An effective leader does not permit a goal he or she has set for a subordinate to be disregarded. Perhaps more time needs to be granted for its accomplishment. You can discuss that possibility with the employee. Whatever the case, goal setting is not simply an administrative exercise to be done just to check a box or satisfy a directive. Job performance goals are intended to help, not hinder or punish, the employee. The same holds true for counselling decisions. As the leader helps his or her people get better at what they do, that leader simultaneously betters the police service provided to those paying the freight: the taxpayers of the community.

SUMMARY

You never assumed that the task of doing an employee performance appraisal or counselling session would always be easy. But you realize that these are important tasks that must be done–and done well–in an effective organization. To carry out these responsibilities successfully, you must be a careful observer, an impartial reporter, and a great communicator. You must be empathetic, courageous, honest, and tactful in executing these duties. A leader like you must be ready to praise the good work and courageous enough to confront less-than-acceptable performance or behavior. You can and will do that.

As an effective counselor you will be patient and nonjudgmental yet straightforward in your efforts to address employee issues. Once again, you will show compassion yet pull no punches in clearly lining out what will need to be accomplished by the employee in meeting your expectations. You will support your subordinate in every way you reasonably can, but you will leave no doubt that the responsibility for "fixing" any problems lies with him or her, not you. You will establish deadlines and follow up to ensure that the goals the two of you have set are met.

By doing your job as an evaluator and counselor and requiring your subordinate supervisors to do the same you will have benefitted your employees and your police organization. Those are highly significant accomplishments for any small agency CEO.

Chapter 16

HANDLING CRITICAL INCIDENTS

As a law enforcement leader, handling critical incidents–and handling them well–is a part of your job description. No, they do not arise daily. But one can explode at any time of the day or night, any day of the year. When that happens, your people, your community, and your bosses expect you to answer the bell with a timely, compassionate, and effective response. Nothing to it, right?

Actually, you can do this. Your training and law enforcement experience have prepared you for the successful handling of a critical incident, regardless of the nature of the situation you are facing. This chapter will arm you with some additional tips for doing it right.

WHAT IS A "CRITICAL INCIDENT"?

Sometimes critical incidents are thought of as events drawing in dozens if not hundreds of first responders and massive amounts of other emergency response resources. And they may, in fact, involve all of these things with large numbers of casualties added to the mix. But a critical incident might be more loosely defined as a situation resulting in a response from your agency that may pose not only serious operational challenges at the moment but also result in both immediate and long-term mental and emotional stress for some of your people. Depending upon the size and nature of the incident, it could result in mental and emotional stress for *all* of your people.

For many police leaders the officer-involved shooting leaps to mind first as an example of a major critical incident . . . and so it is. But there are plenty of other scenarios that could amount to a critical incident for you and your personnel. The possibilities are practically limitless, but could include at least the following:

- Barricaded subject or hostage-taker
- On-duty, criminal or accidental death of an officer
- In-custody death of a prisoner
- Mass casualty incident
- Natural or man-made disaster
- Violent, gruesome crime or accident scene, especially with child victims

Any critical incident also can be defined by what it requires you and your subordinate supervisors to do in response. In many instances, your initial response to the unfolding crisis will be the same, or at least similar. You will be required to collect accurate information, analyze that data, formulate a plan for response after examining risks, threats, and options, activate the response, and then review the effects of that action and make revisions, as indicated. Once things have cooled down, you will then need to conduct a "lessons learned" critique of the entire operation.

A critical incident additionally can be defined as an occurrence that will require mental and emotional support for your people, whether two or twenty of them, because of what they have just been through. This support might come from a mental health counselor two days after the incident or deeper counselling sessions with a police psychologist for one or more of your employees that may continue for weeks or months following the traumatic event. The follow-up response may call for a combination of these things.

Perhaps the safest assumption you can make based on all of this is that critical incidents come in all varieties, in all shapes and sizes. When they happen, you and your leadership team will be expected to respond and take control of an out-of-control situation. You as the leader of the organization will be expected to do this with personal courage, exceptional judgment and decision-making ability, compassion, and effectiveness. You will, in short, be a leader. That is a role you know how to fill well.

YOUR ROLE AS THE LEADER

Doubtlessly you are familiar with the Incident Command System (ICS). You know that it calls for the appointment of an Incident Commander, the top leader, regardless of the size or nature of the incident. The Incident Commander promptly will establish a command post, even if it is no more than the inside of a police vehicle. The Commander (in this case, you) will assign first-line supervisors and officers to handle specific tasks and responsibilities on-scene.

As the Incident Commander you are in charge of the handling of the incident. That needs to be made known to everyone involved in the response to the situation. Make those notifications in person, by radio, cell phone, and however else you choose, but ensure that everyone gets the message. If you are operating as part of a unified command structure, such as with the fire chief at the scene of a multiple-alarm disaster, everyone needs to know that, too. In addition, anytime a change in the Incident Commander occurs, such as when you assume command from a first-line supervisor, that piece of information needs disseminated to all. The important thing is that everyone involved knows who is in charge at any given time. As you well know, only one person needs to be issuing orders.

When you are in charge, your people need to know that. Display self-confidence. That can be contagious to others. Be the leader; do not get involved in taking the nuts-and-bolts tasks of handling the crisis onto yourself. Focus on the big picture and delegate tasks to your subordinates. Stay visibly calm and in control. That, too, is contagious to those around you. It can even be transmitted through your radio voice. This is what a good leader does.

Now that it is clear to your people that you are leading the response to the critical incident, you as the leader next will need to follow some specific steps to bring the incident, whatever it is, under control. Consider the following:

Gather relevant information. You will do a quick size-up of what it appears you are facing. You want answers to such questions as:

- What has happened so far?
- Who or what appears to be involved?
- What are the *known* threats or dangers?
- Are there casualties? How many? What is their status, killed versus injured?

- Are you facing time constraints? If so, what are they?
- What are your resources? What more do you need, including specialized personnel or equipment?
- Which laws, policies, and procedures apply in this situation? (Example: use of lethal force.)
- What is the desired outcome or goal?
- What *don't* you know about the incident that could prove hazardous?

Realize that you will virtually never have *all* of the information you would like to have about what is transpiring. Your obligation is to do the best you can with what you know.

Assess and analyze. Any incident you confront will be at least somewhat different from those you may have faced previously. Each will present its own, unique challenges. Nonetheless, your previous experience will help you in solving the latest problem. Tap your memory for what it can tell you about what may have worked for you before.

Do a quick analysis based upon what you know at this point. Beware of rumors and dubious, unconfirmed reports from "witnesses." Rely heavily on your own senses and what your personnel are telling you based upon their direct observations. Seek to clarify what it is you are facing and what you will need to do to solve the problem. Give special attention to determining what additional resources you will need and how you will obtain them.

Develop an action plan. Prioritize the problems or threats confronting you and address the most critical–the greatest threats to life and property–first. Stay flexible. Be prepared to alter your response as you gain additional information or the situation changes, as it often will. Critical incidents can be extremely fluid in nature. Your plan does not have to be perfect. It can be modified as conditions dictate.

Communicate your plan and it into effect. Use all means at your disposal to notify everyone involved in responding to the incident what the plan is and each individual's part in implementing that plan. Encourage clarifying questions to help ensure that everyone knows his or her role. Execute the plan of action. Be prepared to make revisions based on new information or a changing situation.

Get any needed help on the way. You may have done this already following your initial size-up. That early assessment should have given you at least some idea of additional resources you will need to address the crisis. Get help on the way promptly if you have not done so already. You can always cancel or send away surplus help that turned out to be unneeded. Unless you need that incoming help to do something immediately upon arrival, establish a staging area with a strong supervisor present as the place for this assistance to go to stand by for assignment. Be aware that a major incident may result in well-intentioned responders self-dispatching themselves. That is why you will need a strong supervisor present to keep your help in one place unless it is actively engaged in addressing the incident. Continue to re-assess and adjust your call for resources, as required.

Keep communication going. Information-sharing is vital as you deal with any critical incident. Remind your people to keep you as the Incident Commander advised of any changes or added difficulties they may be observing. *Ask* them for regular updates. On the other hand, share with them relevant information that you have gleaned. If it becomes necessary to alter the initial response plan, be sure that everyone gets the word. You are going to be plenty busy, but do not forget that your own boss needs to have some idea about what has happened and what you are doing about it. By periodic updates given to him or her you may be able to help your boss keep elected officials and other "interested parties" off your back and away from your scene. That, all by itself, could make your communicative efforts well worth it.

Don't forget your people. Depending upon the nature and length of the incident, you may need to plan for relief for your people from inclement weather or other bad conditions. On a long-running incident you also will need to plan for water, food, and restroom breaks for your officers. Appoint someone to be in charge of personnel relief efforts. If the incident turns out to be a truly lengthy one, it may be necessary to arrange for a shift change or changes.

Keep an eye out for personnel who may be suffering physically or psychologically from what they are experiencing. They may require emergency relief and attention. Some of your people might need emotional counselling support later, but one or more of them may need it while the event is still fresh or even in-progress. Ask your supervisors to remain alert for personnel appearing to need relief or other attention. Remind your people to keep a look out for each other, too. Do not overlook the reality that you may need a break yourself. As you know well, any of you could begin experiencing emotional fallout from what you have been through. And it may not show up until sometime later.

Plan for demobilization. Even before the situation is finally resolved you should be making preliminary plans to release no-longer-needed resources, including personnel. You eventually will account for every person and piece of equipment committed. (This is another task you may want to assign to a subordinate supervisor.) The task can feel a bit laborious, especially if the critical incident is a complex one that may have been spread over a wide area. But this final inventory is important; no one and nothing gets left behind. As you demobilize the goal is to leave the scene as much as possible as it was before the incident occurred.

While you likely will want to save a full-scale debrief and critique of the affair for another day, it would be a good idea to get all your responders together briefly to help ascertain if everyone appears to be alright. Such an informal gathering also gives people a chance to share stories and emotions. If someone knows he or she was truly scared or otherwise traumatized from the event, there is value in letting that individual learn that he or she was not alone in experiencing those feelings.

As the leader it will be your responsibility to see that all of the things enumerated here are covered. But do not hesitate to enlist others to help you all through the ordeal. If you have built a strong and competent staff, that should not be a problem.

TACTICAL CHALLENGES

As experience has taught you, tactical situations come in a lot of different guises. To name just a few, they can include:

- Barricaded gunman
- Hostage-taker
- Interrupted violent crime
- Man with a gun call
- Mass shooter
- Active sniper
- Dangerous offenders at large in a populous area

When you get down to it, responding successfully to a tactical challenge is just one more exercise in problem-solving. Certainly, there are specific tactics that you can apply to resolve specific tactical challenges. But there are also well-known problem-solving principles you can apply towards the successful resolution of *any* tactical problem. You will recognize many of them:

- Learn as much as you can as quickly as you can about what you are facing.
- Take a few deep breaths to calm yourself; when you are outwardly calm it will help to calm others.
- Apply all of your experience, knowledge, and training in analyzing the situation and developing a plan of action.
- Prioritize and triage the component problems carefully.
- Apply patience and seek to slow things down, where that is an option.
- Be willing to take *reasonable* risks as you seek a solution.
- Mix compassion with your personal courage in your handling of the incident.
- Stay flexible; be willing to revise a plan when necessary, perhaps more than once.
- If there is time, accept proffered help while controlling self-dispatched, "surplus" assistance.
- Realize that it won't end exactly the way you want every time.
- Learn from each incident and be willing to share the knowledge.

In addition to these general guidelines, there are some other, specific actions you can take for winning the day when you are facing a tactical problem.

Realize the importance of information-gathering. It's been said before, but it is that important. Information or the lack of it often will determine the final outcome of the tactical challenge you are confronting. Begin collecting data even before you arrive on-scene. Learn everything you can from your dispatcher and anyone else who may have information about what you are facing. Depending upon the nature of the crime or other emergency, that could include the number and description of the actors, known casualties, threats (including weapons) believed involved, and more. Your information-gathering should continue once you arrive and establish a command post. Remain a sponge for new information for the duration of the tactical event.

Establish a command post. You will require a secure, centralized location from which you and your assistants (if you are fortunate enough to have some) can gather to work on planning and decision-making. You will not have the time to chase down the people you need to keep nearby, so emphasize to your help that they need to remain with you and available. It is important to have this location for command and control even if it is no roomier than the interior of a police vehicle.

Plan and execute deployment. Even before you arrive at the scene of a tactical problem, begin planning how you and your people will approach, arrive, and deploy, particularly if that problem amounts to a crime in progress. If indicated, direct the creation of a protective perimeter. Communicate your instructions to each of your responding resources. Each individual must receive clear directions as to where he or she is to go.

Invisible deployment is what you are seeking. If you and your troops are responding to an in-progress crime, you naturally want to surprise the offender(s), not have it happen the other way around. Be alert for any good cover possibilities. Caution your people about positioning themselves too close or otherwise easily detectable by armed offenders. If you have trained them well, your officers should already be cover-conscious and alert to obvious threats in their environment.

Maintain situational awareness. It is vital that you remain aware of what is going on around you at all times on a critical incident scene. One chief discovered that in his haste to deploy he had set up his command post within sight (and gunsight) of the location where an armed hostage-taker was hiding. Some quick re-positioning was called for. Your situational awareness should include keeping track of where curious onlookers and members of the news media might be gathering. You may require two perimeters: an inner one to keep the offenders in and an outer one to keep uninvolved parties and traffic out.

Update what you think you know. Continue your information-gathering for the duration of the incident. The tactical situation you have encountered will almost certainly be an ever-changing one. Keep collecting fresh information and be prepared to alter your plans and actions accordingly.

Project a calm, in-control demeanor. Taking a few deep breaths before proceeding to problem-solve will do more than help you calm and steady yourself. It also will give your brain a little bit of time to gain control over a likely adrenaline dump. You will now be better-equipped to make sound decisions. Your calm, in-control approach to problem-solving should be contagious to those around you.

Act and act decisively. In most cases you will not have to make a life-or-death decision the instant that you arrive on a scene. (But if that *does* turn out to be the case, you certainly are well-equipped to make the call.) More often, you will have at least *some* time to analyze the situation and come up with a plan of action. Once you have done that, put your plan into effect without hesitation. You will not fall victim to the "paralysis by analysis" syndrome that overcomes a few leaders because they can never seem to get quite enough information to permit them to decide to do *something.* That is not you. You have the courage to *act* on the decision you have made.

Maintain flexibility. Life probably has taught you that there are few perfect decisions. You also have learned that a decision that was absolutely appropriate when it was made may need revised when the situation changes. As a consequence, you will be ready to alter your problem-solving responses as the tactical picture on the ground changes, as it often will. Your need for resources–either more or fewer–may also change during a fluid situation. Do not hesitate to make those changes, too.

Anticipate the ending. Your incident will reach a conclusion, as distant as that may feel during the heat of the incident. Your goal then will be to return things to a sense of normalcy, to the extent possible. Close-by neighborhoods and the larger community will need to be advised of the termination of a threatening situation. The news media and social media should be able to help you accomplish this task. Your human and other resources will need to be accounted for and returned to other duties. Emotions also will need to be returned to something resembling a sense of normalcy. Be certain that you have checked on your responders to be sure they are alright.

You have proven that you are very good at making decisions under pressure. That ability will not be lessened when the decisions you must make are tactical ones. You've got this.

OTHER KINDS OF CRITICAL INCIDENTS

As noted, critical incidents will arrive without warning, in all sizes and varieties. The other-worldly spaceship crashing onto the local donut emporium almost certainly would qualify as a critical incident. But there are plenty of other, perhaps less-obvious critical incidents, too.

Law enforcement officers tend to think of plane crashes, train wrecks, and active shooters as critical incidents, and they are correct in their thinking. But a critical incident for you and your people could arise in a very different form.

During a recent pandemic, many small police departments experienced the loss of one or more officers not from gunfire but from disease. Regardless of the cause of death, the resulting emotional trauma for the deceased officer's peers was not lessened. You may have experienced such a tragedy in your own organization. If so, you know how much sadness and disruption resulted within the walls of your agency. As a compassionate person, you doubtlessly shared in the pain and comforted other sufferers. All of you were hard hit by a very personalized version of critical incident. And all of you needed time to go through a recovery period in order to get back to your normal mental and emotional health. Time truly *does* heal.

Of course, localized critical incidents do not have to result from death. Very serious allegations, including criminal ones, against one or more of your officers can result in emotional trauma and major disruptions in the operations of your agency. Disciplinary actions that a significant number of your people disagree with also can cause something resembling a critical incident in your department, as can a promotion that is not universally popular.

All of these things call for an expansion of the definition of the phrase "critical incident," but all of them fit the description for the trauma they can cause in your police department. It does not require the presence of scores of first responders and a sea of red and blue flashing lights to constitute a critical incident that will require your intervention.

An "in house" critical incident will mandate that you remain highly-visible and clearly in charge, just as would be the case in any other kind of critical incident. You will need to ensure that everyone is kept up to date on what has happened and what may happen next. You must be constantly available to provide an empathetic ear or even a receptive shoulder for tears. You will seemingly have to be everywhere at all times. You will have to make the important decisions that must be made, and you will have to make them without hesitation or indecision. You will, in a few words, once again have to serve as a highly capable leader.

YOU DON'T HAVE TO GO IT ALONE

You doubtlessly have discovered that the leaders in your chosen profession are seldom reluctant to aid their colleagues by providing resources in the face of a critical incident. There's no doubt that you are quick to do the same. You should not be hesitant to ask for advice or on-the-ground help when you even *think* you might need it. Never allow a misplaced sense of pride or ego to keep you from asking for the help that you know you need. Call for it early rather than too late in the incident. It is much better to have help standing by in a staging area as opposed to having ready assistance nowhere around. You always can offer your profuse thanks and release assistance when it is no longer needed. Naturally, you always will be quick to return the favor of proffered help, needed or not.

There is another way in which you do not have to go it alone. You have known for a long time that you can learn a lot about handling problems by observing others who have handled the same or similar challenges. The same holds true when the problem to be solved is a critical incident. As in other sorts of problem-solving, you also can learn a great deal from the successes and failures of others made in response to critical incidents. These lessons are as accessible to you as the news stories and opinion pieces they generate. Today's press and social media are not hesitant about dissecting and critiquing officialdom's response to critical incidents. If you can keep your temper under control, you may be able to learn *something* from what has been published about a well-publicized incident that happened 2,000 miles distant. Keeping in mind all the while that these journalistic pieces may have been authored by someone who knows little or nothing about policing or critical incidents, you may nonetheless be able to mine some useful data from the thing.

Sometimes larger departments will produce a written report from the after-action critique conducted on a major critical incident. Most of the time the agency's chief is quite willing to share the report with a colleague. You may be able to learn a lot here, too. On occasion, law enforcement professional publications will run articles dissecting major critical incidents, noting what went well and what did not. Remain alert for these learning opportunities. The idea is to learn, no matter what the source.

There are some books out there that can teach you much about the handling (or mishandling) of a critical incident. Douglas Brinkley's *The*

Great Deluge, which highlights the leadership failures at all levels of government following the catastrophic landfall of Hurricane Katrina on the Gulf Coast in 2005, is a particularly informative one.

Handling critical incidents is not unlike so many of the other responsibilities you have mastered as the chief of a small to medium-size police department. By learning from the successes and failures of others, you can meet your own challenges that much better. You do not have to go it alone. It is one more way in which you will be serving as an exceptional leader.

SUMMARY

Your recognized ability to make sound, timely decisions amid the stress of a critical incident was likely one of the reasons you were selected to lead your organization. You should be proud of that justified recognition, because you have earned it through your good work.

That good work has included your careful information-gathering efforts and analysis of the problem you were confronting. You weighed the time and resource constraints. You then applied the problem-solving skills you had learned via training and experience. Whether your critical incident was a tactical operation or something else, you applied a solution and remained alert to consequences in order to revise, as necessary, your solution if initial results indicated the need. Finally, you learned from your own experiences as well as those of others in getting ready to handle your next critical incident.

As in everything else you do on the job, the phrase "everyone goes home" is always foremost in your mind. Nowhere is that more important than in the handling of a critical incident of any variety. When you successfully meet the challenges of a critical incident you meet that goal and keep that pledge.

Chapter 17

YOUR LIFE IN A POLITICAL WORLD

"I am a professional, not a politician."

You may have said that with pride on more than one occasion. All the same, in order to succeed as the leader of your organization you will have to be able to swim through the often-political sea that surrounds you. While you cannot be totally apolitical, you *can* always remain above any pressure from any political source to do anything clearly inappropriate. You do not have to be a back-slapping, baby-kissing hypocrite. But you must have an understanding of things political if you are going to well-serve your agency and protect both it and yourself. After all, you cannot take care of your people if you are no longer present. Fortunately, by remaining always above-board and ethical in all your relations with others—politicians included—you can serve your department and your profession without ever surrendering your integrity.

You also may have taken pride in the fact that surveys of public trust virtually always show law enforcement officers much higher on the trust chart than are politicians. That is probably unfair to the many civic-minded men and women who are serving their communities as honorable appointed and elected officials. Like you and your cops, they are good people trying to do the right thing. You can and must be able to work well with these individuals in order to serve your department and your community. You must be willing to extend trust once it has been firmly established.

You absolutely cannot be oblivious to the political world around you if you are to take care of your employees and your citizen-customers. You can do so by developing a good understanding of people and their motives. The very good news is that you can do this without forsaking either your integrity or your effectiveness as a leader.

CONNECT WITH THE COMMUNITY

You already know how important that is. You are a public figure in your town or city. Like it or not, it goes with the territory. You will be recognized at the grocery store and at the kids' soccer game. You will be an unusual small department chief indeed if you do not have someone show up at your home's front door with an "issue" he or she wants to discuss with the chief. More than one or two of your citizens know where you live.

The truth is that your boss, your employees, and your citizens want to see you active in the community. Your troops probably don't know, and some may not care, about exactly how you spend your time. Most will make the assumption that you are out there going to coffees, meetings, lunches, and community events where you will represent the police department and its interests. That will, of course, include your employees' interests. If your troops come to believe that you are out there schmoozing only to further your own, personal welfare, that will amount to very bad news for you. It is vital that your people know that you are publicly saying good things about them and the police family. (And what you are saying *will* eventually get back to them.) They also will expect that you are bending the right ears to get them the things they need, or feel they need, to be safe, to do their jobs well, and take care of their families. In this role, they will see you as some sort of politician, and that's OK. You will start to lose their respect and support if they do not believe you are doing that, politically oriented or not.

You want your people to know that you really are ably representing them to the ears that matter. At the same time, you do not want to sound like you are bragging or expecting applause for what you are doing. Your best bet is simply to matter-of-factly let your top staffers know what you are up to and the specific efforts you are involved with. The word should spread from there.

And speaking of "the word." Many police chiefs like to talk. That's a good thing, because they need to do a lot of it in representing their department and its people. *You* will need to be good at talking, too. But be careful. Sometimes chiefs become so preoccupied with talking that they neglect to listen. That's understandable, as it is part of your job to speak up for your department and profession. Remind yourself of the need to bite your lip and just listen, as often as you can. You are an important person in your community and people want to tell you what's on their mind. Most of the time it will be friendly discourse. Occasionally it won't be. Try to listen patiently without interrupting. Be empathetic, if appropriate. Most normal people will be pleased that they had a chance to spill their guts to "the Big Cheese." You may even rack up some additional good will for your department in the process.

As you go about your duties as a very engaged ambassador for your police department, you are going to meet and interact with a lot of different people. It's important that you allot some ear time to them all. But always remain mindful that a very few of them are going to have beliefs and agendas that are going to be very different from yours as a decent, ethical police chief. Mama probably cautioned you about the hazards of talking religion and politics. There are likely a few more topics that could be added to that short list. Just be very cautious about professing your agreement with a speaker whose party line sounds way outside the norm. You do not need to have this individual broadcasting to the community that "the police chief agrees with me!"

You additionally must use your good common sense in deciding which organized groups you want to be a member of, on-duty and off-duty. Yes, your off-duty time is yours–to a point. But you are a highly visible public figure, and that means that you are always under close scrutiny, including by some who may not wish you well. That does not mean you cannot be a member of the Kiwanis or the Elks or any other reputable organization. In fact, you *should* choose a civic club that appeals to you. It doesn't mean you can't support the campaign of a favorite elected official or two when you are off the clock and out of uniform. But it *does* mean that the chief of police should not be a member of the "Let's Stomp Kittens" club or some other far-out organization practically guaranteed to garner universal public condemnation. Naturally, anything that sounds like a hate group isn't for you. Just rely on your good judgment and trusty common sense and you will be just fine.

Connecting with the community also will require you and your agency to take advantage of the social media. That's important, and some people will be favorably impressed when you personally respond to messages. But again, be cautious. Know that once you have gone on an unwise rant or perhaps used inappropriate language on-line, your words are out there forever and cannot be recalled. Both elected and appointed officials have watched their professional careers crash in flames due to a post they made in a moment of misplaced emotion–or simple stupidity. You do not want to join them. Always remain as courteous and professional on-line as you are in person.

Staying in touch with the members of your community–knowing what they are thinking and saying–is extremely important for you as the law enforcement leader of that community. Talk a lot. Listen even more. You will be a better chief and do a better job for it.

LISTEN TO EVERYONE

As noted, it is now your job to lend an ear to just about everybody. That does not imply that you have to grant unlimited time to the guy with the tin foil hat who wants to tell you about the extraterrestrials who probed his private body parts last night. You should be able to identify those individuals right away. But try to accept all the requests for a little of your time that you can grant. Welcome those invitations to speak to the Rotarians or the Optimists. It will give you an opportunity to communicate your agenda and let community members see that you are a good person who deserves their support. In addition, answer as many phone calls and e-mails personally as you can. Once more, additional people are getting to know you for what you are: an honest, personable leader.

You cannot afford to be shy when it comes to meeting your public. More than a few police chiefs would confess that they had much rather go home and watch TV as opposed to attending yet another after-hours event. But as you likely know by now, an introvert can force himself or herself to be an extrovert at work, at least within reason. That is your fate now. It's an obligation you must meet in order to succeed as your community's law enforcement leader.

Especially if you are a new chief, and even if you are not, a lot of people are going to want a piece of you and your time. Give it to the extent that you can. It should pay dividends for both you and your department in the long run. Naturally, many community members just want to meet you and be able to say that "I know the police chief." Some will have their own agendas, overt or otherwise. Listen to everyone, all the while remaining mindful that the speaker may be shading the full truth just a bit in support of his or her position. That's not necessarily a terrible thing; it is normal human behavior that you are wise to by now. Just be aware that you may not be getting the whole story.

It is important that you extend the courtesy of giving an audience to members of the "out" groups, too. Politics sometimes see the strangest things happen. The "out" group of today may be the "in" group tomorrow. Your best (and most ethical) course of action is to be courteous and respectful to all. Be careful about swearing your allegiance to anything and everything any group is saying or proposing, but listen politely nonetheless. You can pick up a lot of political intelligence that way without becoming a politician yourself.

In today's world the name of the game is information. To play it well, you need to arm yourself with reliable data. Much of that you will learn from your interactions with others in your sometimes-political world. Listen to a diverse group of people. Analyze what they have to say. Consider their possible motives. These may be as pure as the driven snow–or not. Be courteous always but be careful what you take to be the unvarnished truth. Work continuously to identify your best sources of accurate, unbiased information and pay special attention to what they have to say.

You will have your hands full as you work to make and nourish all of the community contacts that you can. Nonetheless, you will be benefitting your department and yourself by doing so. But beware. Even in a relatively small town or city you can find an after-hours event to attend almost every night, including weekends. You owe it to yourself and your loved ones not to burn yourself out by trying to do *too* much, even with the best of intentions. Don't try to be superman or superwoman. Reserve enough "me" time for yourself and those closest to you. You will be healthier for it.

DON'T BREAK YOUR RULES FOR ANYONE

Your integrity, your ideals, are not for sale at any price. You must not forsake them for anyone or anything. They represent the core of who and what you are. They allow you to occupy the moral high ground you must enjoy to lead your department. Any politician or anyone else you may encounter who cannot grant you approval or acceptance for what you are is not someone you want for an ally or a friend. The crooks on the street know that. Your employees should know it by now. The players on the local political scene need to get it, as well.

One of the best ways to let the politicos know what you are all about is through what you do every day, on-duty and off-duty. Much of it may come through seemingly little things. If you are known to drive like a maniac because you think you are immune from getting a ticket, you should not be surprised when a local mover-and-shaker asks you to "fix" a summons for him or her. When word gets around that you accept expensive gifts (booze comes to mind) from local businesses at Christmas, you shouldn't be shocked when the gift-giver expects special privileges from your officers. If you are carrying on a well-known extramarital affair (and most of them *do* get known), you should not be indignant when a local official asks you to do something unethical or unlawful for him or her.

By acting in an unethical or otherwise inappropriate manner you set yourself up to be pressured or blackmailed by someone who realizes that you must preserve your image as a moral, upstanding role model in the community. By disregarding your moral compass in the quest to gain approval and acceptance from a dishonorable individual you will have started the slide down a slippery slope that will bottom out in a hopelessly damaged or terminated career. That fate must not be yours.

There may be few professions that have as many rules as law enforcement. Most exist for very good reasons. As a leader you are practiced in both following and enforcing the rules. You serve daily as a positive role model for how your people should behave in a line of work that is highly visible and closely monitored by many.

You also serve as a positive role model by obeying the rules that exist beyond your workplace. Those rules can include everything from the traffic laws to the income tax code. You are aware that there are a lot of people out there who don't take legal or moral guidelines all that seriously. A very few of those people are public officials. Over a career you probably will encounter one or two public officials or other leading lights who feel they are perhaps just a bit above the law. These may be the same people who feel that they cannot get a traffic ticket or that you will take care of it if they do. They may feel that their kid will get a warning rather than arrested when he is caught burglarizing someone's home. These same folks may expect not only special breaks but also special services for them and their friends. In other words, they expect you to break the rules for them, either a little bit or big time.

Hopefully you will never be confronted by someone asking you to do something that you know would be inappropriate if not outright unlawful. But if it does happen, there are ways of responding that do not require you to clutch your chest in horror, shriek, and flee the scene. Or something equally theatrical. It is possible for you to keep from embarrassing the individual (even if he or she doesn't deserve it) while deflecting the inappropriate request and maintaining the moral high ground. Simply and courteously explain that providing the requested information or doing the requested favor would violate the rules, law, departmental policy, or whatever else would be the case. Explain that granting the request could get the both of you in serious trouble, something you know the requestor would certainly want to avoid. (Most politicos would get that message, right away!) Perhaps he or she did not understand that the rules covered such things. At least he or she will now be able to maintain that was the case. It just might now get around that the chief doesn't bend the rules for anyone, even if the individual reporting that fact does not consider it a "good" thing. That is not a bad reputation to have.

At the same time, be sure that the local politician or community leader is not denied something he or she appropriately should have access to simply *because* he or she is well-known in the community. In other words, a local notable should not be punished just *because* he or she is "somebody." Everyone gets treated the same. Ensure that your community or political leaders have access to the same police services anyone else would receive. If in the process they convince themselves that they are getting something special because they know the chief, that's up to them. It won't hurt you, either.

In the end, whether or not you are asked to do something improper for someone has a lot to do with the way you do your job and the way you are viewed in your community. If you are seen as a straight shooter who follows the rules and sets the example for integrity in leadership, that fact will get around, especially in a small jurisdiction. That should lessen the chances that you are ever approached about doing something questionable or clearly inappropriate. In doing that you are really following a pretty simple formula. Don't break the rules for personal gain. Don't break them for the benefit of anyone else, either.

NEVER MISTAKE APATHY FOR SUPPORT

It's a classic scene from a jungle adventure film or a war movie. Things are very, very quiet, which makes the good guys nervous. Trouble may be just around the corner. You are a good guy (or gal), too. When things are really, really quiet in your community and you are not hearing anything at all about yourself, your employees, or your department, that may amount to just what it seems: very good news. If that is truly the case, savor the moment and celebrate. You all deserve it.

But it would be a mistake to assume that all is well just because there is not an angry mob in your parking lot or a gaggle of protestors burning you in effigy in City Park. Sometimes people stop talking or complaining because they feel it won't do any good. That doesn't mean that they are not still upset and will at some point explode into action. And you want to keep that from happening.

The most reliable means for avoiding such nasty surprises is to stay in close touch with the members of your community, most especially the very vocal ones. If people are angry about something you or your department are doing, you need to know. In that way you may be able to act to defuse the situation before it detonates. But first you need to know that the problem exists.

You cannot afford to confuse apparent quiet or public apathy for unqualified support for you or your agency. By treating people fairly and always keeping in close touch with the local grapevine(s) you can help forestall nasty surprises. Doing that will help protect your department and your livelihood in a political world.

SUMMARY

As a police chief you will have to navigate political waters without becoming an indebted politician yourself. You will have to labor across a political landscape without losing either your way or your ethics. You will have to maintain a nose for the political winds without being blown into doing something your integrity tells you that you should not do.

In order to best serve and protect both your organization and yourself, you will need to listen to a lot of different people who have their own desires and agendas. You will need to analyze carefully what you learn, but you also will be willing to trust where that trust has been earned. Trust or not, you will never circumvent the rules for anyone, no matter what their perceived political "clout" in the community. By adhering to the rules yourself, you will remove the opportunity for anyone to blackmail or otherwise pressure you into doing anything that your personal integrity should tell you is wrong.

As the leader of your police department, you must understand how the local politicians function and interact without becoming politicized yourself. It can be helpful to your efforts as your agency's leader to understand who has what agenda and what impact that might have on your police department. You constantly will monitor the hometown political environment for how it may affect your organization and its mission. But you will not bend or stretch the rules for promised personal or organizational benefit.

By virtue of your position, you are now part of the local political scene. How you handle that reality will help determine how well you maintain a solid grip on your ideals while best serving your agency and your profession. It can even help determine whether or not you honorably retain your position as your department's leader. Like so many of the other responsibilities you meet successfully on a daily basis, you can do this and do it well.

Chapter 18

TAKING CARE OF YOURSELF

There is a very good reason why the flight attendant tells you to put on your oxygen mask before you try to help anyone else. The harsh reality is that, unless you are well and functioning, you *can't* help anyone else. That reality holds true in the relationships you have with your family, your employees, and your community.

As an effective and compassionate leader, you are all about helping others. It is what you do every day. You truly care about the welfare of other people, whether those others are your closest loved ones, your officers, or the citizens you have pledged to serve and protect. You take that pledge very seriously.

You do much in fulfilling your promise to aid diverse others. You do not forget your significant other's birthday, nor do you miss *all* the kids' soccer games. You work hard to see to the welfare of your people. You do your best to ensure that they get the training, equipment, benefits, and support that they need to do their jobs safely and well. At the same time, you do everything you can to see that your citizen-customers are served with dignity, respect, and courtesy. You work to ensure that the police services they receive are delivered in a timely and professional manner.

In other words, you do a lot. The danger that comes with all that work is that you may be tempted to neglect your own needs in the interest of taking good care of others. One veteran police chief offered this advice: "As chief, you have got to take some time off every 90 days or so just to maintain your sanity." The chief made a good point, but today there is a lot more to it than time off, as important as that is. Nowadays it is often referred to as "maintaining a good work-life balance." That will be your oxygen mask in working to help so many others.

There are many things that you can do—and refrain from doing—to maintain your best physical and mental health while effectively leading your police department and enjoying your life. This chapter will identify some of them. It will begin by reminding you of some behaviors to avoid as much as you would a rattlesnake. Earlier you read about some ways to self-destruct in the workplace and beyond. A review of those critical errors with a few new ones thrown in should help to begin the discussion.

GUARANTEED WAYS TO FAIL

A lot is said in leadership courses about how to succeed as a leader. That's good. A lot less gets said about how to fail at leadership and life. Getting fired does not sound like a good way to take care of yourself.

Unfortunately, there are a lot of ways to self-destruct as the leader of your organization. Failing there also can make it difficult to do a good job of taking care of those at home. Falling prey to any of these critical errors will not aid you in your quest to stay physically, mentally, and emotionally healthy. Knowing what these destructive mistakes are can help you avoid them. These ways to harm your career, yourself, and, at least indirectly, others include the following. Some of them you have seen listed previously. They are important enough to see one more time.

Lie to your boss. You expect to hear only the absolute truth at all times from your subordinates. It should come as no surprise that your boss expects the same from you. Once a falsehood or half-truth you uttered is discovered it may be virtually impossible to restore the faith that your supervisor previously placed in you. With that trust gone, it is difficult to see how the supervisor-supervised relationship can survive.

Embarrass your boss or your department. There are many ways to do just that. Committing illegal, immoral, or unethical acts, perhaps repeatedly, may lead the pack of job-fatal errors. To some extent, your chances of employment survival may depend upon the gravity of your foul-up(s). Everybody makes mistakes and most everyone else knows that and are often willing to extend some measure of forgiveness. But when the seriousness or number of embarrassing mistakes pushes beyond reason, bad consequences are almost certain to follow.

Be involved in a high-profile scandal. See the preceding. Professional law enforcement demands that its practitioners, particularly its leaders, always do the right thing. Today a police leader who becomes involved in a highly visible on-duty or off-duty embarrassment ranging from a sexual indiscretion to a drunk driving fiasco can expect to see his or her career nosedive or even terminate. That is not how to go about taking care of yourself.

Be guilty of insubordination. As long as you have not been ordered to do something unlawful or unethical, your boss expects you to do whatever it is he or she has directed you to do. It's no more than you expect of your own subordinates. Argue for your position privately if you disagree with the instructions you have been given. If you do not succeed in changing the directive, unless it is clearly unlawful or otherwise obviously inappropriate, carry out your orders without revision. Otherwise, you should expect to feel the full weight of your organization's disciplinary machinery.

Engage in sexual harassment or racial discrimination. Law enforcement organizations nationwide are justly proud of shedding the reputation for routinely doing either or both of these things, as sometimes happened in the past. You can expect to be held quickly accountable if you engage in either version of citizen or employee maltreatment. That does not amount to taking good care of yourself, either.

Repeatedly do stupid things. Oftentimes really dumb behavior results from mental laziness. It also comes from disregarding everything previously learned from education, training, life experience, and the exercise of plain common sense. Other times stupid behavior springs from arrogance or a misplaced sense of entitlement. You cannot engage in stupid behavior and simultaneously take good care of yourself. The two are simply incompatible. Leadership leaves no room for stupidity.

Not knowing your job or your people. Plainly stated, ignorance is a bad thing. If you do not know thoroughly the ins and outs of your job, you probably are headed for trouble. If you are weak in your knowledge of policing, your troops will know it before your boss does. They will not be shy about spreading the word, either. At a small department, it is not difficult to know *something* about each of your people. If it appears that you have not undertaken the effort to learn something about each one, your employees are unlikely to think highly of you. That won't help when you need to call on them for support.

Displaying a lack of self-confidence or self-control. Sooner or later it is going to show if you have little or no confidence in yourself or your decision-making ability. The same bad effects will result if you cannot control your emotions at the times when a leader must do so. A chief who has frequent blowups and displays of temper towards subordinates provides an excellent example of someone who has failed at practicing mature self-control.

Blaming others for *your* errors. As a leader you are going to make mistakes on occasion. That's part of being human. A leader with exemplary integrity takes full responsibility for his or her errors. Attempting to shift the blame to someone else will cost you dearly in the eyes of your employees and your boss.

Running afoul of booze or badge worshippers. If you keep up with the news, yearly you will learn of one or more of your colleagues who are now unemployed because of something he or she did (like driving) after getting a snootful. Or you'll hear the sordid tale of a chief who is looking for a job because he or she could not resist the siren call of some poor, lovelorn soul who was impressed by a badge and an authority figure. You are supposed to be a role model for admirable behavior in your community. Giving in to the temptation to do dumb things can end that positive role model status (and your employment) pretty quickly.

Failing to practice what you preach. You don't much like hypocrites. Chances are, your diverse audiences do not care for them, either. Here is that role model thing yet again. If you are constantly lecturing your people about officer safety, you should demonstrate the same through your actions on the street. If you regularly remind your people of the need to be sterling citizens in the community, you must keep the grass mowed in your own front yard. As you tell your troops, someone is *always* watching.

Inability to trust or delegate. You may be highly competent and really good at your job. Hopefully, you are both. But no matter how good you are, you can't do it all. You need help. You must be able to trust your leadership staff and subordinates to do some of the work for you. If you cannot, these people should not be working for you. In delegating tasks appropriately, you should find that you have some very talented and trustworthy people in your organization.

Inconsistent behavior. Even if they may not admire or agree with every single thing you are or do, your employees and your supervisor want to know that they are dealing with the same police chief every day. In this respect, consistency is a good thing. If you are ecstatic one day and very grumpy the next you are going to confuse at least some of those around you and leave them wondering if you are a bit strange. Once more, it may require some of your best acting skills but try to maintain consistency with a positive attitude towards others, on and off the job.

Exercising privileges denied subordinates. This one falls into the RHIP–rank has its privileges–category. You may indeed have the ability to do or have some things that your troops do not based on the fact that you are the police chief. Taking home an unmarked vehicle every night may provide a good example. Your people probably understand that. But you should not be doing things or enjoying major "benefits" denied your police officers. Accepting free restaurant meals when your people are expected to pay for theirs is an example of such a poor practice. Neither your employees nor your boss should ever be left with the impression that you believe you are somehow special.

Reacting before knowing all the facts. You know all about dangerous assumptions when it comes to officer safety practices. But reacting prematurely and perhaps unwisely spouting off at the mouth also can prove problematical in such areas as discipline and other "employee relations" matters. Verbally "convicting" Officer Jones of inappropriate conduct before knowing all the details of the situation can result in erroneous pronouncements and generate some very hard feelings towards you by your people. Try really hard to bite your lip until you know the whole story. Even then, exercise sound judgment in what you have to say in public.

Taking care of yourself includes taking care of your job for as long as you want to hold the position. By remaining aware of the ways in which you can lose both respect and your job, you should be able to keep either of those things from ever happening to you. In that way you will be guaranteeing that you *won't* fail.

TAKING CARE OF LIFE AND LOVED ONES

You do a lot for your agency and your community. But you do not owe either your whole life to the exclusion of yourself and your loved ones. What you are seeking is a healthy work-life balance in which you preserve plenty of time for yourself and those closest to you. Make sure that you do not work late *every* night. Be equally certain that you do not go in super early *every* day. Do not find some after-hours event to attend *every* night of the week. Practicing excellent time management skills can help you avoid some of those less-than-healthy traps.

Family and loved ones must always come first. Both are vital to your emotional survival. Always have time for them. This is another of those cardinal rules. It will keep you healthier even as it benefits the emotional well-being of those who care deeply about you.

It has been said so often that by now it sounds trite. Nevertheless, it remains true: No one approaching the end of life has ever wished that he or she spent more time at work and less with loved ones. It is very easy to become engrossed in the challenges and, sometimes, the rewards of leading your department. When things are going well and, at times, just the opposite, it is easy to allow your work to become all-consuming. It is up to you to resist that temptation.

There are the feelings and needs of people other than yourself to consider in your role as a law enforcement boss. They belong to your loved ones. Many of your colleagues have confessed that they have succeeded at work only because of the patience, support, and love of those closest to them. A lot of law enforcement leaders have offered that they only have survived and prospered because of the strength of their partner. As a consequence, that is the first person whose welfare you should look to in taking care of close others throughout a long and successful law enforcement leadership career. If you are fortunate enough to have a partner, you owe him or her a lot.

Your loved ones and your job certainly are owed much of your time. That is appropriate. It is also appropriate that you save some quality time for *you*. To remain physically, mentally, and emotionally well, you must do that. Leave yourself some personal time for healthy diversions that make you feel good. If it is watching sports, that's OK. The same holds true for fishing, hunting, or any other outside activity that helps you decompress and enjoy yourself. Allow yourself time to do the things that you do not *have* to do but *want* to do. If others want to do these things with you, that's great. But it is also completely alright to balance *we* time with *me* time. As long as the balance is a just one that does not leave a loved one's feelings hurt, you are on the right track. The point is to do *something* that will distract you from the concerns of the work world.

Exercise should be a component of keeping yourself physically and mentally healthy. You might look at your busy schedule and determine that there simply is not time for it. You may have to get creative to get it done, for it is well worth it for the personal benefits that can attach. You might have to make time for a workout before work, after work, or at noon when you really would prefer to be doing something else. But ultimately the benefits should be worth the extra effort. You will likely have more energy short-term and improved overall health long-term. You will feel better and almost certainly be more productive when you return to work.

Different people have different ways of obtaining their self-preservation exercise. Some like to walk, others prefer to jog. Some enjoy swimming, others like to do strength-building repetitions followed by a little cardio work. Some of your peers prefer to exercise alone, enjoying the quiet moments in which they can think without the distraction of other human beings. Others feel that their drive to exercise is stronger when they have others sweating along with them, perhaps in the process pushing them to work a little harder. Whatever works best for you is fine.

If you are like many cops, you probably like a little structure in your life and would prefer to count on the same half-hour or hour every work day to get your exertions done. That's terrific if you can manage it. But you're busy, and you could have to resign yourself to the fact that your exercise regimen may have to include considerable flexibility. You may not be able to do it today, maybe not even tomorrow. That's no reason to abandon your endeavor to stay healthy–and alive. Again, be flexible in order to continue to exercise as best you can. The world will not end because you missed a week in the gym.

One word of caution: If you are out of shape and have not done any serious exercise in quite some time, get your medical health provider's blessing before launching an intensive exercise program of any kind. Even then, approach it in moderation. If your goal is an hour of exercise five days a week, you may want to start off with thirty minutes four times weekly. You may have known cops who have abruptly commenced a Superman-level workout program, only to injure themselves and give up on the whole effort. You do not want to be one of those souls.

Then there is the issue of diet, good or less so. One veteran chief commented that he had never met a new police chief who had not put on at least ten pounds during the first year of wearing the Boss Badge. It appeared that the temptation of too many calorie-filled breakfast meetings coupled with lunch meet and greets were too much for the average chief's willpower to overcome. No one is going to lecture you here about the evils of too many chicken-fried steak dinners or excessive numbers of power rings (donuts) consumed with your late-shift crew. The key is simply to exercise restraint and your good common sense concerning the consumables that you put into your body. It may mean that sometimes you have to order a dry English muffin when everyone else is enjoying eggs, bacon, and pancakes; or grab a salad when the rest of the crowd is digging in—heavily. Console yourself with the knowledge that you may well look and feel better than they do, later.

Then, there is the issue of you and alcohol. There is nothing that says you cannot enjoy a libation or two off-duty with friends or associates. It should be fairly obvious to you that you cannot drink on-duty, not even to share an alcoholic beverage with some local heavy hitters who have invited you to lunch. (Remember: You must not partake of privileges denied your officers.) Of course, you should never drink to the point of intoxication or to the extent that your judgment or motor skills are impaired. You do not operate a motor vehicle after drinking. As simple and obvious as that advice appears, police leaders still lose their jobs with depressing regularity after getting busted for driving under the influence. On occasion, prescription and other drugs are found enhancing the effects of the alcohol.

The law enforcement profession is merely a microcosm of society. Alcohol addiction is a worldwide problem. There are alcoholic police officers and alcoholic police chiefs, whether they will admit it or not. A "functioning" alcoholic is still an alcoholic. Functioning or not, his or her life is still heavily impacted by the condition. At least initially, only you may know that you have an alcohol problem. As you know, if you are an alcoholic, no level of alcohol consumption above zero will work to stop the downward spiral brought on by alcoholism. That's part of what being an alcoholic means. If upon making a brutally honest self-assessment you recognize that you have a drinking problem, seek help before things get worse. Help is available through professional counselors, medical practitioners, and Alcoholics Anonymous. You certainly *can* regain control and resume a happy and productive life, on and off the job. After all, you have mastered many challenges before.

No reasonable person would expect you to lead your life in seclusion and abstinence. But it is not too much for your boss, your officers, and your community to expect you to conduct yourself in a manner that you will never have cause to be ashamed of. That amounts to taking good care of yourself and your loved ones.

There is yet something else you can do to take care of yourself: Have some friends who have no connection whatsoever to police work. Law enforcement officers have been accused of "professional incest." It means that cops tend to spend their time, including at least some of their off-duty hours, talking to and associating with other cops. Police chiefs are often guilty of the same practice. It is understandable. Doctors and lawyers and firefighters often do the same thing. It's interesting and fun to hang out with people with whom you have shared interests and who can understand your worries and travails. These are the people you may have gone through some scary doors with and shared other work-related challenges. They *know* where you are coming from. There is nothing wrong with that . . . up to a point. Story-sharing is healthy. It can be very beneficial to your mental and emotional health. Keep it up. But there is more.

In order to maintain some kind of mental balance (others might refer to that as sanity) in today's increasingly complex world you sometimes need to think and talk about something besides police work, personnel issues, and the difficulties of navigating the local political environment. You need to talk about *something,* almost *anything,* besides the issues that often inhabit the police chief's world. You need friends and conversation partners who have nothing to do with law enforcement. The discourse can be about almost anything–dogs, sports, vacations, national politics, you name it. Just try really hard to steer away from cops and cop work. That can be hard, especially if your conversation partner *wants* to hear some of those crazy stories he or she knows you have a whole mental storehouse of. Tell your tale and then try to get the conversation back to something besides policing as quickly as you can.

You might be amazed at how much you can learn from someone who has nothing to do with law enforcement. One small department chief learned a lot about people from his regular lunches with a local pastor. Another confessed to both learning a great deal and enjoying his visits with the CEO of a large manufacturing firm. But there is no mandate for you to learn *anything* from socializing with non-cop friends and acquaintances. Just soaking up the positive human interaction will be good for you. There is nothing wrong with enjoying the talk and companionship of cop friends and associates. Just try to intersperse it with time spent around *normal* people!

One more thing to remember in protecting your mental and physical health during a long and successful career spent serving as a law enforcement leader. It's just this: Most crises have a short shelf life. The incident or event that looked like a career-ender for you on Monday oftentimes will appear much less grave on Friday. Often this will include any negative news media coverage that seemed destined to bring about the end of life as you knew it, as the newshounds move on to the latest plane crash or alleged bad police behavior. You probably *will* be allowed to get up off the floor, even at the time it doesn't feel like it. There are exceptions, of course. If you run over the mayor in the City Hall parking lot on Monday, he well may not have forgotten about it by Friday. But most of the time the "stale news" principle will apply. You can safely proceed with life. And should.

Take good care of yourself and your loved ones. It will pay big dividends for you and for them.

CONFIDANTS AND MENTORS

You know that talking it out is good for you. You probably have told your young cops about the value of talking about whatever is angering, annoying, scaring, or otherwise troubling them. You need to take your own advice. You must have a confidant, or several. This has to be someone you are comfortable with baring your thoughts and your soul in front of and talking with about virtually anything. For many police leaders, their primary confidant is their significant other, their unofficial, assistant police chief. But whether it is your spouse or someone else close to you, this individual must be willing and able to serve in the role of a nonjudgmental, patient, exceptional listener. You will need someone who can listen to your woes and frustrations and refrain from either judging you or leaping straight into problem-solving mode. You need someone who will listen more than talk, empathize more than criticize. Chances are, you probably already know one or more of these near-saints. Now you just need to reach out to them if you have not done so already. They can be literal lifesavers. They may help keep you from being carried out of your chief's office feet-first one day.

Having one or more mentors to reach out to when you don't know what to do next or just visit with periodically can prove extremely valuable to your physical, mental, emotional, and career survival. Your mentors almost certainly will be people who have seen and done a lot, probably as leaders of other law enforcement agencies or even organizations uninvolved in law enforcement. Often, but not always, they will be older than you. Regardless of age, by this stage in life and career they already have mastered a lot of lessons, some of them very likely learned the hard way. You can learn a lot from these people. Do not be shy about posing your problems and frustrations to them. If they are truly good mentors, they will be honored that you turned to them for empathy or advice. You will make *them* feel good.

A lot is said today about "paying it forward." Mentoring falls into that category. Mentors may well have helped you previously and are currently assisting you in handling your often-difficult job. You can "pay it forward" by offering the same mentoring service to new or aspiring leaders. Your mentee will be grateful, and you will have the comforting satisfaction of knowing that you helped build one more exceptional leader for law enforcement.

BE A LIFE-LONG LEARNER

You can never know it all. You are never too smart or too experienced or too old to learn something new. You probably have said some of those things yourself. And they are all true.

As a leader you are confronted by a lot of new learning experiences every day. There are books, professional publications, videos, and web sites available for your perusal. As the chief you may feel almost overwhelmed by what is out there. But to stay on top of your game as your organization's leader you will have to take advantage of as much of it as humanly possible.

Your challenge is to make the best use of your available reviewing and reading time. Make the time to look at the things that apply to your job as chief and pertain to the effective operation of your agency. Pass the rest of the stuff on to those whom you feel most need to see it. If you have limited time, and you probably will, pass the latest on firearms and firearms training along to the person or persons who are responsible for both. Then, expect them to brief you on the salient points if, in their opinion, changes need to be made in something the department is currently doing.

Try to keep up on current events that may impact your agency and your profession by scanning the day's news, whether on-line or on television. As you well know, something happening 2,000 miles away could impact the way you do business. You also may want to subscribe to an Internet-based clipping service that tells you what is happening in your field, nationally and beyond. Your boss or other local officials may be doing the same. Keeping up with the news could keep you from being caught short and embarrassed one day concerning a current, "hot" topic you should have known about.

College classes, online or otherwise, can help you stay on top of your profession and maintain or improve your effectiveness as a leader. Even if it is not directly related to your job, a class or degree you undertake can further your personal growth and expose you to the enjoyment of learning something new. There is evidence that a brain kept actively learning, regardless of its age, remains healthier, longer. Surely there is no better motivation for being a life-long learner.

THERE WILL BE DISAPPOINTMENTS

One small department chief compared being the leader of a police agency to being in love. "There will be extreme highs," he related, "and extreme lows. That's just the way it is." You may or may not agree with the chief's assessment. Whether you do or not, you doubtlessly have experienced a time at work when, at least figuratively, there was a rainbow in the sky, the birds were happily singing, and all your people seemed to be reasonably content. And then the next day or the next week or the next month, the bottom fell out, the wheels came off, and you wondered aloud if you were running a professional law enforcement agency or a kindergarten school. Welcome to the world of the police leader, where there almost certainly will be disappointments on occasion. Sometimes, they may be big ones.

You may be disappointed because a local official you perhaps admired turns out not to be the ethical person you thought he or she was. Worse, you may have found the same unpleasant surprise in one of your staff members, once again someone you regarded highly. It can happen because people are people the world over. Sometimes they do things that no one could have predicted. That does not mean that *you* have somehow failed with that individual. You cannot possibly know everything and do everything required to keep the rest of the world on the straight and narrow. Do your own job according to the ethics of your profession. Show others the way it is *supposed* to be done. Try hard not to be *too* devastated when others fall short.

Disappointment also can raise its ugly head when something you have spent much worry and sweat to achieve is denied or minimized by those above you. If you know that you have done everything you reasonably could have done to achieve your goal, whether it's a pay raise for your people or one more police car, try hard not to act crushed in front of your employees. Those kinds of emotions are contagious. Try to maintain an upbeat, positive demeanor around your employees. Cursing the fates (or your boss) will not benefit your health or your job security. Instead, be willing to swallow your bad feelings and resolve to come back another day, perhaps with a revised argument or proposal. It just may work this time.

Many police chiefs would agree that the good times far outweigh the bad as they lead their law enforcement organization. Most of the time they truly enjoy what they are doing and want to stay at it awhile. They know that disappointments will come, whether big or small. That's life. They are willing to accept a little bit of bad accompanying a whole lot of good. Hopefully that describes you.

But it may not. If, after careful consideration, you have reached the conclusion that the bad times outweigh the good, you have a major life decision to make. Even if receiving a regular paycheck is vital for you, its value dims considerably if you are miserable in what you are doing. Life is far too short for that. If you are convinced that making the situation better is beyond your ability to control, the career choice of leaving your current position may be the right thing to do. If a disappointment is so big or so chronic that it cannot be overcome, taking care of yourself might decree that a change of scenery is indicated. Both your physical and mental health may mandate such a drastic solution. You certainly could and should get the input of those closest to you. But in the end it is you who have to make the call. Taking good care of yourself demands it. It is vital that you know when it is time to go.

KNOW WHEN IT'S TIME TO GO

Your time as chief will not last forever. Sooner or later you deserve a break, and someone else deserves a shot at the job. The time will come when you leave the position, whether it is for a better chief's job, a change in career choices, or to go sit in front of the fireplace. In spite of the horror stories you may have heard, most chiefs are not run out of town in front of a howling mob. But some chiefs do receive "outplacement counseling" before they are ready to depart, and that is a fate you desire to avoid. You want to leave on your own terms at your own, chosen time. There are some things you can do to figure out when that time has arrived and make the transition as comfortable as possible. Exiting with your head held high is just as important as some of the other things you have accomplished as police chief.

You can find your job suddenly at risk without warning, perhaps because of something you did not have anything at all to do with. An example might be found in the case of a clearly wrongful and perhaps criminal use of lethal force by one of your officers. You were home, in bed asleep when it happened, but there is a public outcry and your boss, to save his or her own head, has to be seen as doing something. So, he or she fires the police chief. These kinds of chief terminations are not frequent, but they do happen. The situation most likely will be beyond your control and you probably could not have anticipated or prevented it. Very occasionally the world that a police chief occupies is a cold and unforgiving one. Do not dwell on that fact but do recognize its existence.

More often, there will be signs that someone in authority may be planning to get rid of you. The warning flags could include:

- Your boss is evasive and appears to be avoiding you. He or she is not as accessible to you as previously.
- People are not returning your calls or messages. Those who usually contact you have stopped.
- Your employees and even members of your command staff are treating you differently, perhaps distantly.
- You encounter overt hostility from individuals who have not acted that way towards you previously. Your people do not appear to fear the consequences of openly disrespecting you.
- Friends, colleagues, or members of the community call to ask if you are "alright."

- You get an actual warning from someone you trust that trouble for you is pending.
- Your employees actually take a "no confidence" vote in your leadership. Regardless of the outcome of the vote, that is probably the ultimate notification that rough waters lie ahead.

The presence of one or even several of these danger signs does not necessarily mean that you are doomed, but the existence of multiple trouble indicators should certainly be a matter for serious concern. But it is not helpful simply to wonder about what all this really means. It is time to ask your boss, clearly and directly, exactly how you stand. Hopefully your supervisor will be honest and ethical enough to tell you the truth. Then, you have a tough decision to make, assuming one has not already been made for you. Do you *want* to try and save your job, and what are you willing to do in an effort to save it?

Once again, assuming that the final termination decision has not already been made, you need to find out from your boss what you would have to do to continue your employment. Is it being more receptive to his or her direction? Is it to establish a better working relationship with your officers or the community? Is it to get rid of the cop who has been getting too many complaints? Is it to obey a directive to give the mayor's son Elmer a cushy job? What is it? Then, you must decide if what you are being asked to do is something you *can* do and still maintain allegiance to your personal morals and ethics, not to mention obedience to the law. In other words, is staying employed, at least for the moment, worth what you would have to do?

You know not to make key life decisions when you are emotionally upset. This would certainly qualify as one of those emotional moments. Don't spout off and say something you will later regret. Don't in a moment of theatrical fervor throw down your badge. (Your boss may be very quick to retrieve it!) Take your decision-making home and discuss it with close others. If you have connected with a mentor, get his or her opinion on your dilemma. Sleep on it, perhaps for more than one night. Do not rush to a resignation decision and then end up trying to undo it. Be certain about the course of action you have chosen.

Now, assume that the decision to go has been made, or has been made for you. You are leaving, the remaining question is exactly how. Naturally, if possible, you want to leave gracefully with your pride and reputation intact. If you are departing of your own volition after a successful career your leaving should be a bittersweet affair in which a lot of people will be sorry to see you go. If that is not the case, just how much leverage you will have to influence the conditions of your departure will depend upon why you are being let go. If you have been responsible for serious misconduct your room to maneuver will be small or nonexistent.

Simply put, you want to get as much as you can at your time of departure, regardless of whether you are leaving in sunshine or stormy weather. What do you need in order to continue your life? Even if you did not have a contract (and very many chiefs do not), you may be able to negotiate a severance package that includes some continued salary and benefits for a specified time, or perhaps a lump sum at departure. Most city and town managers do not want to see a lot of drama at termination time and may be willing to agree to some kind of accommodation. Ask. If you have made some influential friends in the community, as you should have, they may be willing to help you by putting a bug in your boss's ear.

If your manager has already decided that you have to go, you may at the very least be able to convince him or her to permit you to resign, instead. That obviously will look better on your employment record. Do not resign, of course, if you feel you have solid grounds for a civil suit against your employer. Permit him or her to go ahead and fire you. You will need an attorney well-versed in employment law to advise you in that situation.

Obtain what concessions you can, settle where you must. But don't be shy, as your future and that of your loved ones is at stake here. You are walking a fine line. If you come across as arrogant or threatening, it is probable that any negotiations are at an end. Stay firm but remain respectful and courteous, as well. It's likely that you *and* your boss want to get an unpleasant scene behind you as quickly and smoothly as possible.

But much of the preceding describes an unhappy, probably forced departure. As an ethical, competent leader, that is less likely to be your fate. It is more likely that you are the one electing to hang it up, either to pursue other opportunities or enjoy retirement. Knowing when to go will be up to you. You will decide on the time after giving the whole thing careful thought. There can be a myriad of reasons why you have decided that this is the time. You don't like the look of the direction the town or city is headed and you see trouble ahead.

You have a new boss and after your best efforts it just does not seem that the two of you can work amicably together. You have a great new job opportunity. Your closest other wants or needs you to re-locate, for whatever cause. Or simply this one: For whatever reason or reasons, *it just isn't fun anymore.*

There can be a world of reasons why it is not enjoyable any longer, but clearly it is not. Every job has its good days and bad, but when the bad ones outnumber the good it may be time to take action. Life is too brief for anyone to be chronically unhappy. Being a judicious and responsible person, hopefully you have maintained enough financial security to talk away from the job when you are good and ready. Being that judicious person, you also have kept your resume current and maintained contacts away from your current position who may be able to help you find another one, if that is your desire. It is even better if a position you are looking at will help you become more financially secure than previously. Weigh your options and try your best to shunt emotions aside, at least to the extent humanly possible.

One more piece of advice to consider when planning your voluntary departure: Try to avoid the role of being a lame duck chief for an extended time period. Once it is known that you are going, people, including many of your own employees, will begin to treat you differently. Some will be seeking to position themselves for the regime change. A very few passive-aggressive types may be openly disrespectful now. To some, you will start to seem irrelevant. In short, an extended period of serving as a lame duck chief whom everyone knows is leaving can result in discomfort for everyone, especially you. If you already know that your boss wants six months' notice, fine. But ask him or her to keep it strictly confidential for quite some time. How much time? Two weeks' public notice would be great, but six weeks is certainly better than six months. Your aim is to wear the label of departing chief for as short a time as feasible.

Nevertheless, you must leave yourself time for your good-byes. Most likely you have enjoyed your time as chief. It is truly something special. Very, very few people will ever have the privilege of wearing the chief's badge. Bask modestly in the acclamations and honors you will receive when word gets out that you are leaving. A lot of people are going to be sad to see it happen, and that in itself is a major tribute to you. Appreciate those sincere feelings. You have earned them. It is perfectly alright to shed a few tears with your well-wishers.

Knowing when it is time to go is a big part of taking care of yourself. It is a decision that just about everyone has to make sooner or later. Through work well-done and a life well-lived, you have earned the right to make the call when the time and feelings are right for you and those closest to you. That's a pretty good way to go on to the next stage of your life.

THERE'S LIFE AFTER YOUR JOB

OK, you have made the big decision. The work life that you have known, perhaps for a long time, is disappearing in the rearview mirror. What now?

What you choose to do next depends a lot upon the stage of your life that you feel you are in, and what you *want* to do. If you are ready to go fishing, cruising, mountain climbing, or whatever other retirement activity suits you, go for it. You have earned it many times over. But for other law enforcement leaders, those things are still in the future. Right now, they want to use all of that accumulated education, training, and experience to do something else. They are not quite ready to go sit on the porch and watch the grandkids, although that may occupy some of their time, too. Indeed, if your life as chief has kept you running at 70 miles per hour for quite some time now, many psychologists will tell you that going from 70 to zero in a sudden stop is not good for your mental health. Your personality may be better suited to tapering off as opposed to going cold turkey.

If you are truly done with the police chief thing, you still may have access to a lot of other opportunities. Many of your peers have gone on to teaching, consulting, and security management positions. There is no doubt that you still have much to offer, so one of these areas may be a route you want to explore. Your experience as a law enforcement officer and a chief has certainly prepared you for most of the challenges that a new job might present. If you have done the same as some of your colleagues, you may have made and nurtured some contacts during your chief's career that might result in a job offer once you have left the police CEO role. It would be a good idea for you to make those outside contacts now, assuming you are still employed, even if you don't ultimately use them. That's what networking is all about.

Other former police chiefs have gone on to new careers that have nothing to do with law enforcement or security work. One ex-chief bought and operated a dude ranch. Another entered the ministry, something he had long thought about doing. There are plenty of great endeavors out there that do not call for carrying a badge and gun. Maybe you have long harbored the desire to try your hand at something entirely new. Now could be the time to do it.

Your chief's job is both important and interesting, but one day it must end. If you have taken good care of yourself, you should have a lot of life yet to live. The very good news is that there are some terrific times still ahead when you are not the police chief anymore. You probably will worry less and sleep better. You will still have friends, associates, and loved ones who care about you. Enjoy them and your new life, whether it is police-related or not. Great things are still to be discovered and celebrated!

SUMMARY

You do a lot to take care of your department and your community. You serve as leader, role model, decision-maker, community partner, and the face and voice of your agency. You also serve your department as safety officer, media relations specialist, performance evaluator, counselor, and disciplinarian. You do a great many things and take care of many people. But the question arises: Are you taking care of *yourself* so that you can maintain your own physical and mental health needs while caring for others?

If you are anything like many other police chiefs, you have spent many days and nights taking care of others. At times, you may have done it while neglecting your own needs. That is noble, but it probably isn't the best thing for your own health and happiness. You must take care of *you,* too. Fortunately, there are reasonable steps you can take to do just that.

In order to take care of yourself, you first will need to be aware of the things that you must avoid doing in order to prosper and remain healthy. This chapter identified many of them. You also will want to take care of your loved ones and consider the real value of having a confidant or mentor, or more than one of each. You will make the decision to be a life-long learner, realizing that you can never know enough. You will realize that there will be reversals and disappointments along the way, and you will learn how to recover from them. Finally, you will be able to recognize when it is time to go and know how to go about it on your own terms. As a part of leaving, you will know that there is plenty of life left after hanging it up. You will be prepared to take full advantage of that fact.

You have spent a significant part of your life taking care of others. You have served a noble profession fearlessly and ethically. Whether you choose to remain where you are, try out another job, or go sit by the fire, you have earned the right to take care of yourself and those closest to you. You remain a leader.

Take care of yourself. Always.

INDEX

D

E